THE PARADOX OF INSTRUCTION

THE
PARADOX
OF
INSTRUCTION

*An Introduction to the
Esoteric Spiritual Teaching
of Bubba Free John*

by
Bubba Free John

*The Dawn Horse Press
San Francisco, California*

Printed in the United States of America
International Standard Book Number: 0-913922-28-5
Library of Congress Catalog Card Number: 77-81836
Produced by Vision Mound Ceremony in cooperation with
The Dawn Horse Press

Vision Mound Ceremony

We gratefully acknowledge Sri Ramanasramam,
Tiruvannamalai, South India, for permission to reproduce
the photograph of Bhagavan Sri Ramana Maharshi.

contents

What has anciently been named and believed and known as God has always been in Man and in things themselves. What *is* God is forever unknown. The task of all our knowing is to enable us to incarnate all that we tend only to believe is outside and independent of us. Our spiritual responsibility is to be perfectly reconciled with our eternal Ignorance, and so be always free.

introduction
THE WESTERN FACE OF GOD

There are few precedents for *The Paradox of Instruction* in the previous literature of human religion and spirituality. In this principal source text of his Teaching, Bubba Free John elucidates all the philosophical and esoteric matters that must be considered in spiritual or real life. But Bubba is not a mere intellectual or speculative philosopher. His writings, like all his actions, only express the elegance and conscious intensity of Divine Ignorance, or God-Realization, which is his constant Enjoyment. His communication speaks directly to the human heart, requiring intelligence, feeling, and constant attention of all who would listen. His words are no less a Divine response to mortal anguish and dilemma than Jesus's "Sermon on the Mount" or Krishna's discourses to Arjuna on the battlefield in the *Bhagavad Gita*. Thus, *The Paradox of Instruction* is not an abstract treatise. It is a letter of love.

The love of an authentic Spiritual Master, however, is not romantic sentiment. His compassion never indulges human weakness and irresponsibility. Bubba's Teaching, the Way of Divine Ignorance, or Radical Understanding, criticizes the consoling archetypes of traditional religion and spirituality. Bubba does not offer us a glorious image of self or soul or God, or of spiritual practice, or of the relationship to the spiritual teacher. He does not offer any kind of image at all. Rather, his gospel or "good news" only reveals the deluded futility of all our motivating images, all our common ways, both worldly and spiritual. And it awakens us into Truth, which is Divine Ignorance, the native Mystery that is intuitively felt by all beings, no matter what they think, believe, or do.

It has always been a grinding and thankless effort for true Spiritual Masters to bring the Divine Process into the human world. Their lives are often filled with difficulty, and they invariably encounter almost universal resistance to their teachings and spiritual work. This is all the more the case for Bubba Free John, because he has appeared in a society that has very little spiritual culture or understanding.

Bubba's appearance in this world has been unique from the beginning. Even at his birth, on November 3, 1939, in Jamaica, New York, he enjoyed the radical illumination of Divine Ignorance. But he recognized as a very young child that no one else shared his native delight. He perceived that all others were constantly refusing to live as Reality and to love and be happy and free. And he was moved to discover in his own body-being a Way by which others might cease to suffer. Thus, in his earliest years, Bubba consciously and literally began to submit himself to the deluded conditions of a common life. When this descent was complete, so that, like any ordinary man, Bubba doubted the reality of God and Truth, then the adventure of his re-awakening began. This period of spiritual investigation, discipline, and rediscovery occupied thirteen years of his late adolescence and early manhood. It was an immensely difficult and painful passage, for Bubba found no previous teaching that was ultimately true, and no spiritual teacher capable of leading him through the entire process of his transformation.[1]

When he had passed through and understood every possible kind of subjective identity, seeking, knowledge, and experience, high and low, Bubba stood forth again in the Condition that he had enjoyed at birth. This final re-awakening was spontaneously perfected in September, 1970. But the whole odyssey only confirmed what he had observed as a child. As he wrote in his autobiography, *The Knee of Listening,* all beings are committed to the action and destiny of Narcissus, the self-meditator, who never loves and is never happy, but remains deluded and sorrowful until death, entranced by his own self-image.

Bubba Free John's early work as Spiritual Master demonstrated this same truth. From 1970, Bubba began to engage those who came to him in critical argument, practical instruction, and a continuous "theatre" of experience and knowledge, both spiritual and worldly. It was necessary to communicate his

1. For Bubba Free John's own account of his relationships to those who served him during his spiritual transformation, see his essay entitled "The Ground and Root of This Instruction," p. 24.

argument and Teaching in living terms, because no one in the present era is capable of making use of a merely philosophical presentation of the Way of Truth. In late 1976, Bubba brought an end to this initial, demonstrative period of his Teaching work, having communicated the essential principles, disciplines, and lessons of the Way of Divine Ignorance in living response to ordinary individuals. But his early devotees had not become perfectly transformed. Certainly, many of the hundreds of individuals who were approaching Bubba as devotees had passed through purifications of their earthly and inward lives. They had abandoned the daily commitment to gross habits of self-exploitation and had become founded in a sane and regular discipline of practical life. But they continued nevertheless to dramatize egoic motivations and impulses. They failed to fulfill the prerequisite for real spiritual practice, which is to *hear* the critical argument at the core of the Teaching, and thus to be liberated in Ignorance from the compulsive activity and destiny of Narcissus. In early 1977, Bubba wrote:

> There are so many who have come to me and moved on to what they were before. There has been so much betrayal by the self-possessed. With all the nonsense hype of the "new age" and the "fullness of time," there is universal and righteous rejection of Truth and the Way of Truth. The stupidities and common insanity of the usual man bear upon this body with a sulk of futility, and yet I am obliged and moved to persist in Communion with devotees. It is the Destiny of this time that the Teaching of Truth be present with all the rest. It is opposed by every body-mind, even by devotees, but the wrestling in the Fire will purify and transform them in spite of all vestigial commitments to the Lie. I am neither consoled nor served by devotees. I am a servant,

an offering, a casual meal that lovers eat while noticing only one another. This too is Sahaj Samadhi. The native Bliss is Sacrifice, or liberation from all the consolations of this birth. Bliss is disenchantment. Love is freedom in the very act of life. When both withdrawal and illusions cease, there is Bhava, the Mood and Domain that is the Real.

The Spiritual Master does not enjoy a special status or privilege in the world. In Truth, he enjoys no status whatsoever. And he is not consoled or fulfilled by his own work. The Spiritual Master is simply an Awakened servant of others, an example of life in Truth for devotees and the world. He has realized beyond doubt that he is all-pervading, and he lives continuously as the conscious Reality of all beings and worlds. He feels absolutely — literally in the flesh — the failure of living beings to presume the Truth and to radiate as Love. By virtue of his continued presence among such beings, however, he is obliged to persist in his sacrificial relations with them. And by virtue of his unspeakably happy Realization of the Divine, he is also *moved* to do so. Such is his endless compassion. The awakening of this spiritual function compelled Gautama to rise from his meditation and spend a lifetime offering his wisdom and Nirvana to deluded and unhappy men and women of the ancient world. The same obligation and heart-felt impulse moves Bubba Free John to persist in the Divine work among men and women today.

The betrayal of which Bubba speaks is subjectivity itself, the unfulfilled mood of "me," the inward ego or soul. It is Narcissus, the Lie of self-possession and separation. It is "sin," which literally means "to miss the mark." The story of the betrayal and crucifixion of Jesus is a graphic image of the constant rejection of Truth by all human beings, even the unperfected devotees of the Spiritual Master. Before we may begin to fulfill the Way of Divine Ignorance, we must recognize and take into account our incessant urge to refuse the Teaching, the discipline, and the Spiritual Master himself.

In one who is constantly hearing the Teaching and living the Way, all the urges to egoic satisfaction persist. The discipline of this Way is neither indulgence nor suppression of the ego and its impulses, but rather an entirely different form of action. It is the Lawful or sacrificial enjoyment of ordinary, everyday life from the radical point of view of Divine Ignorance. This frustration of subjectivity in the midst of a moral and relational life creates intense heat. Devotees must wrestle with that friction, that fire. Merely to allow it to do its purifying and transforming work requires a discipline unknown in our usual pursuit of worldly and religious consolation. Devotees have no option but to struggle with the argument of the Teaching, with the disciplines of practice, with the Spiritual Master, and with the very Divine — and they can only be humbled and undone in the process. There is nothing romantic or archetypally glorious about that struggle. It is a paradox. In the midst of the discipline of happiness, of Love, Enlightenment, and relationship, what is revealed is our inevitable preference for inwardness, unhappiness, self-concern, and delusion.

Thus, our own efforts never avail in this Way of Divine Ignorance. Only Divine Grace relieves us of the suffering that we chronically generate in life. And this Grace is active only through the agency of the Spiritual Master. It has always been this way. The living spiritual relationship between Master and devotee has always been the principal vehicle of Divine Grace in the world.

When the devotee is prepared, then the Master may bestow the Power of Grace freely in spiritual contact. And then that conscious Force literally transforms the devotee. Those whose approach to Bubba Free John is true and persistent are initiated into the mood or enjoyment that is unqualified Reality. In this all-pervading, radiant Condition of Ignorance, the conscious being is already, immediately, and priorly liberated from the implications of all suffering, all distraction, all destiny, all experience, all birth and death, even as the ordinary appearances of life, birth, and death continue to arise. Such unspeakable Happiness is the true Revelation of this Way, and it is eternal.

Since late 1976, when he formally ended the preparatory, demonstrative period of his Teaching work, Bubba Free John has no longer had to bury himself in theatrical action and argument relative to the deluded cravings and self-oriented roles and games of common men and women. The argument and essential instructions of his Teaching are available to all through the literature and educational services of Vision Mound Ceremony, the institution he has created to serve his communication to devotees and the world. Now, both to those who have already come to him and to those who will be attracted in the future, Bubba Free John offers a natural, formal, and truly spiritual relationship with him as Divine Master. Bubba has no public life. He strictly reserves his Company for those who have heard his Teaching and matured in the preparatory, practical disciplines that he recommends.

In *The Paradox of Instruction,* Bubba fully reveals the argument and the spiritual content of the stages of the Way of Divine Ignorance, or Radical Understanding. In the fall of 1976, Bubba began to write occasional essays for the devotees who serve as his editors. Originally, it was supposed that those essays would comprise a brief introduction to the Way and its practice. But as the editors compiled these writings and added them to transcripts of Bubba's instructive talks, the book developed into a thorough summation of his esoteric and practical Teaching. Now this text stands as an integrated statement of his criticism of subjectivity and his communication of Truth. Only by constantly considering this liberating argument in our lives can we effectively presume the Condition of Ignorance and, thereby, live this priorly Illumined Way. Bubba emphasizes, however, that *The Paradox of Instruction* is not intended as an instructive text on the specific *practices* of the Way. Even his directions to "abide in Ignorance" should not be interpreted as instructions for deliberate practice, because the usual man or woman has no stable capacity to abide so simply in the Divine Condition. To accommodate our need for a gradual process of re-adaptation, Bubba has outlined four successive stages in the whole Way of Divine Ignorance: the Way of Divine Communion, the Way of Relational Enquiry, the Way of Re-cognition, and the Way of Radical Intuition. The stages represent degrees of conscious responsibility for integration of every aspect of our lives with the intuitive presumption of Ignorance. Those who wish to consider the specific practices of these stages should consult *Breath and Name: The Initiation and Foundation Practices of Free Spiritual Life* (which principally outlines the foundation disciplines of the Way of Divine Communion) and forthcoming books on the disciplines of the advancing stages.

Bubba Free John represents an indescribable opportunity for human beings. He is a Divine Master of the stature of Jesus, Gautama, and Krishna, and he is alive today. Whether or not maturely Enlightened devotees will arise on the basis of his Teaching and Presence depends entirely on each individual's response. Bubba only waits. The Divine process of existence is only Mystery to him, just as it is to all others. The Spiritual Master does not act on the basis of superior knowledge, or any kind of knowledge at all, but only on the basis of Feeling-Intuition. Bubba Free John has no mystical guarantees that the Divine Process he has brought into life will awaken beyond his own body or persist beyond his own time. All such supposed guarantees are illusions. But Bubba is absolutely certain that the Influence he represents is the vehicle of Perfect Awakening.

Bubba Free John stands open-hearted, utterly available to all beings. It is only necessary to listen to his argument and to hear the Truth he proclaims. The Way is demanding, but because it is founded in Truth, anyone may adapt to it and fulfill it in Bubba's graceful Company. For those who come to Bubba Free John and live this Way of Divine Ignorance, all will transpire just as he indicates in this text. The very Reality, Only God, is the Destiny of all true devotees.

Middletown, California   *Vision Mound Ceremony*
May 4, 1977

prologue

In the following three essays, Bubba Free John introduces the writings and talks from which he has composed The Paradox of Instruction. *In this prologue, Bubba writes in the third person, elucidating the significance of the title of this text and indicating the nature of his relationships with spiritual teachers who served him in the past.*

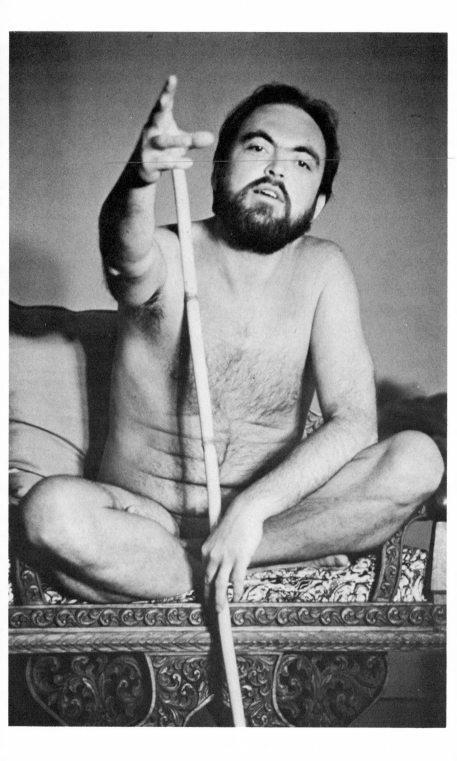

1

THE PARADOX OF INSTRUCTION

All truly or fully human communication is art. All human art or true communication is a paradoxical presentation of primal psycho-physical knowledge, or total experience. It is always a partial or summary description of the present state of realization of the condition of the whole body, the psycho-physical condition of all human awareness, or the totality of everything as it is felt-conceived by human agency. The more conceptual or discursive aspect of any such presentation is its exoteric part, while that aspect which belongs to the more feeling or non-discursive dimension of total experience is its esoteric part. The combination of the two dimensions makes all art a communication of paradox.

Paradox is the essential or ultimate content of all human experience, all art. The realization and communication of paradox, or total experience, is the principal motive of the human adventure in every moment. Art, or truly human communication, is the argument of paradox. The action wherein such communication is expressed is love. The realized manifestation of the human being is love, or the sacrifice of energy-attention, on the basis of the tacit, prior, and most summary configuration of the being, which is Paradox.

The Paradox of our existence, our essential or total experience, is realized in Ignorance, or the Mystery which precedes, pervades, and confounds all particular experience, all knowing, whether exoteric or esoteric. This Ignorance undermines the force of all objects, high or low, and belies the presumptive rationality of subjectivity, or independent conscious existence. Implicit in this Ignorance is the impulse as and toward the whole—the whole body, and the totality of everything. The Mystery is Fullness, or Radiance. Therefore, Love, or Sacrifice, is the Law and Destiny of Man.

The Spiritual Master is the servant of Man. The Life and Work and Teaching of the Spiritual Master epitomizes Man, or the whole body in the configuration of totality. That Work and Teaching is recourse to art, or true and fully human communication, the primal ceremony—the implicit and explicit Act which cannot be avoided. That Work is Sacrifice or Love or Radiance, the Impulsive Destiny of every man or woman. That Teaching is the Communication of Ignorance, or Paradox, the Truth of every man or woman. Its exoteric aspect is instruction. Its esoteric aspect is initiation. Its Realization in the case of any man or woman is the Radiance of Ignorance, the Summary and Truth of what is Man and the Whole that is appearing. Such is the Process of Translation of Man into God, the Divine Condition or Perfect Domain.

Therefore, Bubba names this book *The Paradox of Instruction*.

2

THE GROUND AND ROOT OF
THIS INSTRUCTION

Bubba Free John was served by two principal teachers in gross bodily form. These were an American Tantric Yogi named Albert Rudolph (Rudi, or Swami Rudrananda, now deceased) and Swami Muktananda, of Ganeshpuri, India. He was also served by others in subtle form or through subtle agency, including Swami Nityananda (formerly of Ganeshpuri, India, the acknowledged Spiritual Master of both Rudi and Swami Muktananda). But the Spiritual Master whose Teaching and incomparable Spiritual Power or Siddhi confirmed by Grace the very and perfect Truth beyond all doubt is known as Sri Ramana Maharshi.

In the company of Rudi, Bubba learned the yogic discipline of the life-force, which discipline presses beyond vital limitations, especially the "tamasic" or helpless and sleepy quality that creates only self-indulgence and the disabling moods of self-pity and negativity. Rudi was a teacher in the vital. It was his school and his limitation. He worked to transcend its power of inertia, but he was also a child of the navel. Once Bubba learned the transcendent and yogic discipline of the vital, he also realized the inherently oppressive nature of the gross point of view in practice, and he came to rest, so that the fulfillment of gross existence in itself was no longer profoundly attractive, necessary, or binding—without on the other hand justifying a conventionally ascetic disposition toward it.

Swami Muktananda was the next to serve Bubba in his own clarification of the Way of Truth. In Swami Muktananda's company Bubba realized the contents of subtle possibility, within and above the gross plane. Swami Muktananda is one whose school and limitations are in the subtle sphere, associated with the crown of the body-being. Once Bubba realized the marvelous distractions of subtle consciousness, he also became aware of the inherently oppressive nature of the subtle point of view in practice and experience— so that the fulfillment of subtle possibility in itself ceased to be profoundly attractive, necessary, or binding.

Thereafter, Bubba was guided—or distracted—by higher subtle or spiritual agents for a time. But all experiential fulfillment, high or low, failed to demonstrate Truth. At last, his whole adventure, at times served and tutored by various beings and influences, was made unusable and obsolete—its motive penetrated, its argument undermined. There was a single, absolute, and ultimately unspeakable Revelation of both the Heart or Condition of all arising and the simple activity whereby error, deflection, and self-possession intervene.

Bubba communicated essential aspects of this Revelation to Rudi, Swami Muktananda, and numerous others—personally and through his published writings. But there was great hostility and general resistance to his point of view. At last, in the summer of 1973, Bubba approached the Presence of the late Sage, Bhagavan Sri Ramana Maharshi, at his place of burial in Tiruvannamalai, South India. It was only there and then that the Revelation of Truth to which Bubba's whole life has been oriented was tested and confirmed as it is.

Since that time, Bubba has been refreshed and liberally disposed to communicate, demonstrate, and serve this Revelation and its Way to those who are moved to consider him and his argument.

Bubba Free John has previously written that "the Divine Lord or very God" has been his Spiritual Master. In this manner, he describes and confirms the Divine nature rather than merely manifest yogic nature of the Spiritual Grace that has been overwhelmingly active, communicative, and effective in his case since birth. The benign workings of this Grace culminated in the spiritual confrontation at the tomb and former places of residence of Bhagavan Sri Ramana Maharshi, where Bubba found the undeniable Realization of his life to be confirmed most directly, beyond all doubt.

Bubba teaches in his own time and place from the impulse of Enjoyment of the Radiant Condition of the Real or Eternal Divine, to which he is Awakened by eternal Grace, even as Sri Ramana Maharshi, in

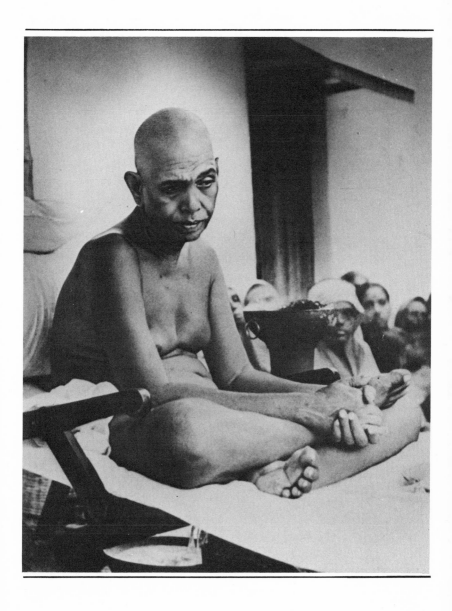

whom Bubba recognizes that Grace, was so Awakened. Therefore, Bubba claims that perfect surrender,
or devotional sacrifice, necessarily precedes and
coincides with radical intuition of the Real.

3

WHAT IS TRUTH?

The beginning of the commitment to Truth is in radical revulsion to any confinement by the destiny or the limits that are or could be set before us. But, even so, the Realization of Truth is not attained by any reaction to the present conditions of existence. Whatever is the Truth, it must be True at this moment. It must be always already True, both in and prior to every moment of space-time. Therefore, the Realization of Truth is not attained in the search for Truth, since seeking must necessarily bypass the Truth in this moment in order to pursue it as an eventual Goal of action in time and space. Whatever can be attained by seeking and strategy is necessarily an occasion, an incident, a form of experience, space-time, or time-space itself. But Truth must be the Truth of even that incident or Attainment. Therefore, there is no Realization of Truth other than the presumption of Truth.

This is so. The Way of Truth is not itself identical to any progressive or summary process of experience. But it is a matter of radical insight into the process of experience in the present moment. This insight is itself a formless presumption. It is the presumption of Truth. This insight or presumption, projected moment to moment, is the Way of Truth. It is Sacrifice into Truth, or the Condition that is Truth.

What is Truth? "I" may find out or know all kinds of facts or truths *about* any thing, or everything, or the whole world. But I may never discover or know what that thing, or everything, or any thing *is*. No matter how much time passes, or how much knowledge is attained, this fundamental Ignorance can never be changed to any degree. This Ignorance is Truth and the Way of Truth. It is the Truth or Condition of any thing and everything. It confounds the dream of knowing. It is Awake. It is Intuition, prior to all knowledge. The radical Realization of this Ignorance under all conditions is the presumption of Truth. Such is Enlightenment or God-Realization.

That which is Revealed in Ignorance, or perfect Sacrifice, is the Truth or Condition of all conditions. It is Paradox. It is Revealed in the moment of every condition and all conditions, but it may not be defined or grasped in itself. Those who are Awakened by Grace, through hearing, are a constant party to this Revelation, but it is never known in itself over against anything else.

Fear and revulsion account for most of the spiritual adventure of mankind. The "Truth" that is offered to us, independent of perfect insight or Revelation, is an Idol, high or low. That which may be sought and found is not God.

The vulgar world is an offering of elemental Idols,

but fear and revulsion may escape what is vulgar, and then what is proclaimed as Truth is subtler than the elements. Spiritual proclamations offer us Idols of inwardness, Idols of the better part, Idols of highness, Idols of the subtlest and highest. At last the Idol of Origin is offered. Since we are what we appear to be, the Creator of it would seem to be Truth. Therefore, men worship and seek visions of the Creator. But we do not worship Truth as Creator, Origin, or Source. We worship the Creator, the Origin, the Making Source as God or Truth. Truth is valued as a way of valuing or preserving the world and our pleasurable independence or invulnerability. We worship the Creator because we value and cling to the world and our present and future life or self. We are afraid. Our worship of the Origin, the subtlest, the highest, the high or higher, the better part, or what is within is an expression of the same motive that pursues the Idols of vulgar experience, the Idols of sensation and release.

It is not Truth that is attained or even sought by all this seeking. Survival, not Truth, is what is sought by all of it. Seeking is itself survival. It is action as meditation on self. Seeking is self-possession, not possession by God, or Truth, or the Real. It is not God or Truth that is valued by the seeker. The seeker is afraid, and he values continued delight. He turns to pleasures of the body, within the body, above the body, or at the Origin of the body, in hope of continuation. He turns because he values what *he* is, not what is Truth. But he does not know what a single thing *is,* not even his own self. If this Ignorance were Realized to be the present Truth of the motivated self, then Truth and not any goal or Idol would determine the Way. Therefore, the matter of Truth is the matter of present insight or penetration of the circle of experience, seeking, and self-possession.

Truth is the Condition of conditions. It is not itself a condition. It has no independent objective or subjective existence. Whatever is presently arising as a spontaneous condition, Truth is not other or objective, nor inner and subjective relative to it. Truth is simply the Condition of the present condition. Truth, or the Condition of present conditions, is always already the case. Therefore, the Realization of Truth is not to be gained by reaction to any or all present conditions, nor by any progressive search to attain other or superior conditions. The Realization of Truth is a matter of radical, present insight into the arising process of existence. The Realization is not progressive but instant. But on the basis of such Realization or insight, moment to moment, the Revelation of existence in Truth is never-ending, like a succession of infinities.

The conventional offering of "Truth" is of an experiential object or Object. It is outside, or inside, or upside, or Topside, or Not-side. It is a part. It is in a certain direction. It is found over time and progressively. It is independent. It is consoling. Such Truth or God is reasonable nonsense. It is gotten only by those who crave enough. But no matter what is gotten, whatever is presently arising, "I" do not know what it *is*. However much "I" may know about it, "I" do not and can never know what it *is*. Therefore, every present configuration, high or low, is Paradox. Since none of it or me can be accounted for, it is all an Illusion, unnecessary and Mysterious.

Truth is the Truth of every part. It is not only the Truth of the spine, the midbrain, the mind, and the Light. It is equally, presently, and simultaneously the Truth of the knee, the toe, the shawl, the eyeglass, and the hair on my lover's arm. Therefore, where shall "I" go for Truth's sake?

If "I" am afraid — only afraid — then "I" may search among the parts of me or the parts of things. "I" may reduce it all to a better or highest part. "I" may turn in and up. "I" may desire to the point of ecstasy above and beyond. But Truth is not my Object then. "I" am thus only an adventurer in time and space, propelled to destiny for my own sake. Very good. An excellent dream. Except for the fear, the doubt, and the agony of striving.

But when "I" hear the argument of Truth, and insight breaks my stride, the whole adventure and Illusion of experience is undermined, and its dilemma dissolved. When "I" am confessed in Ignorance, then all of this arising is no longer confounding and motivating me to objective and subjective absolutes. Then all pairs have become a Paradox, and the Way of Truth is not a path to anywhere that is Truth, but it is Truth itself, Sacrifice of self and everything in the Condition of our Mystery. Bubba says, Truth is Surrender of the whole body-"I" into Happiness, whatever arises.

—≡○≡—

"I" is the whole body. Liberation is founded on intuitive insight into the separative gesture that is the whole body itself. The natural practice is spontaneous sacrifice and loving service, not motivated inwardness and the unending strategy of thought. Real meditation is direct and present penetration of the lie of independent existence, the whole reflex of contraction toward a point, including the lie of time and space, which is the pervasive scheme of objective points of attention, above and below.

Bubba Free John

1

AWAKENING FROM THE DREAM OF SUBJECTIVITY

COMPILED BY BUBBA FREE JOHN
FROM TALKS AND WRITINGS
WHICH HE GAVE IN
FEBRUARY AND APRIL, 1977

1

There is no inner self independent of "the body." Subjectivity, the reflexive orientation toward the self inside the body, is founded on a lie. It is a way of living in illusions. It is the way of Narcissus. It is an argument, a method, an experiment in destiny. It is meditation on death, future, dilemma, fear, and sorrow. It is the way each of us appears to choose. But no choice was ever truly made. The "choice" is not a subjective matter. Awakening to the born condition, the apparently independent body-being, is itself the logic of this habit to death. The body itself names this self. The self is not independent of the body. The self *is* the body. The self is only independent *as* the body. Prior to the whole body, or birth in any realm, there is no separate self or consciousness or mind. The whole body, or the self, is simply the sense of separation or independent existence.

The whole body is a psycho-physical event. The lie is that its psychic aspect represents an independent being—that is, an elusive, subtle person or specific soul that is separable from the complex whole body or born body-being, just as the elemental body, or physical aspect, appears separable from all other bodies and things. Traditional religion and spirituality generally argue for the seniority and separability of within, and modern "materialistic" science seems to argue for the irreducibility of the flesh, and thus the mortality of the psycho-physical "soul." In truth, both arguments are false, since neither is founded in realization of the Truth or Condition of the whole body.

But the so-called "materialistic" view is at least more correct in its analysis of the singleness of the whole body-being.

The inner, emotional, mental, psychic, mystical, egoic process is not radically reducible to itself and separable from the elemental body, its relations, and its destiny. "I" is the body. "Within" is the body talking. The *whole* body arises spontaneously, each of its aspects simultaneously, and prior to our knowledge. All that we know or seek to know is acquired after the fact of the complex body-being itself.

The whole body, or the body-being, the apparent psycho-physical entity, is itself the "soul." The soul is not within. *The* being, the sense of separability and independence itself (not only subjective but even physical), is the dilemma. The apparent independence of existence in the case of the individual in the born-condition is suffering.

The inherent suffering that is ours by birth is ours by *birth*. It is not simply acquired over time in the form of sophisticated inwardness or subjectivity. We are not born innocent and then come to "sin" only through an *inner* error. Subjectivity, or the exclusive orientation to inwardness or psycho-physical self-possession, is itself the *dramatization* of our suffering. It is reactive dramatization of the limitation or incident that is birth itself. It is the proof and fact of suffering, not the instrument of release. The awakening of the Way of Truth is not itself an awakening *to* inwardness, but an awakening *from* inwardness, from recoil, contraction, and all hiding behind the flesh. Awakening into Truth is a process of incarnation, or release of the reflex of inwardness, or selfness, under *all* conditions (physical, emotional, mental, psychic, mystical, intuitional, and egoic).

Birth is shock. It is the primal incident. As an incident, it is usually interpreted psychologically — in terms of its emotional-mental or subjective impact. But its significance is in the event itself, the sudden event of existence as the whole body. Birth is itself shock — vital shock, a recoil at Infinity. Our life is a drama of subjective struggling against an unbearable demand: relationship, incarnation, or love. We are in the mood of recoil, contraction, and self-possession — not by virtue of some inward and soulish pre-existence, but by virtue of birth itself, the apparent independence of self all relationships imply. All that is other implies the separate me. Even infants, growing adepts in the shock of living based on birth, demonstrate this reflex, the self-sympathy that dramatizes our suffering. There is no innocence, for all have been born. The feeling of independence is the burden of living beings.

Truth is not in inwardness or the experiential elaboration of a born self. The Realization of Truth is not a matter of experience arising within or without the born-being. Truth is Revealed in re-cognition, or knowing again, of the shock or recoil represented simultaneously in every dimension of the born-being. Truth is Realized in radical intuition of the prior and present Condition not only of self and thought but of the whole body, even the worlds in time and space.

We suddenly are born, independent, related, dependent but separate. There is no inherently separate inwardness over against this. That is a gradual invention, but only an extension of the sense of bodily separateness. The whole elaborate manufacture of complex emotions, thoughts, and expanded psychic and subtle appearances is only an extension of the born-condition, the inherent shock of separateness and separability. It is all madness, a lie, a torment, an unrelieved wilderness of nonsense, high and low. The complex inner being is a drama made over time. Most men and women are ordinary, even mediocre, examples of the breed. A few are geniuses of the various parts within and beyond. It makes no difference. The whirl of incident, of birth and death, accounts for all equally. The inner and the outer heroes are visible vectors of the same visible stream, and each falls up from the same born shock, and back to invisibility through the same execution by "Nature."

The matter of Truth is there for all, whatever their degree of inner glamour or outer opportunity. The sense of separate existence is the motivating lie of each and all, within and without. The human is only that. All the rest of any life is the reaction, played out among probabilities.

Knowledge has nothing whatever to do with Truth. All knowledge is subsequent experience of the born-being. Truth is the prior Condition in which the born-being itself, and all its subsequent knowledge, arises, in which it all proceeds, and in which it is again resolved, either in death or in Wisdom while alive. We are born in Ignorance — absolute, unqualified, and eternal Ignorance. "I" do not know what a single thing *is*. And that Ignorance remains native to our case as long as we live, whatever we do, or attain, or realize, within or without. Ignorance is our only link with the Divine. It is the root of Divine Communion. Ignorance is the Truth of our birth and our knowledge and our worlds, high or low, as long as we live or persist, in this or any number of lives.

Those who are subjectivists, whether religious or scientific, view our native Ignorance as a fault, a temporary condition, which is constantly to be invaded by the growth of various kinds of knowledge. They are only temporarily agnostic, even relative to the highest matters. But our Ignorance is not a lesser principle than knowledge. It is not the absence of knowledge. It is senior to all knowledge, as death is to all those already born. Death and birth are equally confounding to the idealism of knowledge and the illusory victory of inwardness, or any of the destinies of the separable man, whereas Ignorance is untouched by the transactions of birth and knowledge and death.

Our Ignorance is the perfect Principle, the Principle of Truth. The Way of Truth is a kind of spiritual agnosticism. It is complete and prior freedom from the whole affair of knowledge, experience, or self-consciousness, high and low. It is the Way of release from all the ways we create by birth, by separation in Infinity.

The error in our way of life is inherent in our birth. It is contraction, the presumption of separateness. As we develop in our seeking, our motivated, reactive, self-possessed life in vital shock (which is not principally a reaction *to* birth but the reaction that is birth itself), the complex inward being develops — and we acquire a hope for its separability, and a destiny, selved as now, which continues after the death of the body. Those who become mostly hopeless relative to such a destiny are usually not entirely out of sympathy with its desirability, but they enforce their subjectivity in time and space as the various kinds of individual and worldly adventure.

The primal orientation in all is to their own separateness, rather than to relationship or the whole. This is the root of our dramatized suffering. Therefore, the foundation of the Way in Truth is radical insight into the fundamental presumption in birth itself rather than all the presumptions which follow it. It is insight into the presumption of separation, the independence or specific and relatively defined character of "I." Once this reactive presumption is felt in the present and found to be unnecessary, the prior presumption, which transcends the theatre of birth and death, becomes most obvious and irreducible. It is the presumption of absolute and prior Ignorance, or the Condition which is prior to all experience, all knowledge, all form, all difference. It is not contraction, not separation, not any adventure, high or low. It is Radiance, prior to all dilemma, prior to the illusions of a center and its relations or bounds.

Once Divine Ignorance and its Radiance become obvious as the fundamental presumption and prior Condition of the born-being, then the usual destiny of self-possession is undermined. In every moment we have the possibility of fulfilling the mere destiny or content of appearances, or to cut through the event.

The event is always necessarily oriented toward our own sense of separate existence, bodily and subjective. In any moment, we may either be distracted in the vibratory milieu of self-possession, of involuntary and voluntary contraction, physical, emotional, and mental, in which all things arising are referred or oriented toward our own position, or we may cut through the reflex of self-possession, subjectivity, and the born-sense, and stand awake in the Condition of all these conditions.

The Way of Divine Ignorance, which I am moved to communicate and to demonstrate, rests on the presumption which precedes our birth, our life, and our death. That is the presumption of Ignorance. No matter what arises, "I" do not know what a single thing *is*—not even the body, not even the sense of my own separate existence. Therefore, knowledge and all subjectivity (the whole inward and outward adventure of *a* self—body and soul) are unnecessary nonsense. That is, nothing, within or without, adds or subtracts from the prior Condition realized in Ignorance itself.

In this disposition it becomes clear that "I" is not independent of the body, nor is the body-I an independent or absolutely separate entity, self, or being. Such is only an illusion, a reactive presumption, a hopeful or hopeless but always tentative solution to the dilemma inherent in our birth. Therefore, in Ignorance, "I" is disposed to confess, and "I" is relieved by this confession. The confession in which we are released toward Truth is this: " 'I' am the body.

'I' *is* the whole body." There is no radically separable being within. The sense of separate existence is inherent in the reaction or contraction that is our birth itself, our wordless, whole body birth or separation in Infinity.

If "I" is realized to be identical to Ignorance, then "I" is inherently unable to establish or enforce an independent or separative sense relative to its own, unknowable, merely and tacitly apparent conditions and relations. This is, however, only the beginning of liberation in Truth. Our consciousness is not reducible further than the whole body itself. The sense of the separateness of our consciousness ("I") is not originating "within" and apart from the body. It is identical to the body-sense, the whole body or born-sense. Birth is the dilemma. Thus, life and death express the same dilemma, until Truth confounds the lie.

Once "I" is confessed as the body, the process of inwardness in itself, over against the body, ceases to be a viable means to Realize Truth or Happiness. The reflex toward self, either bodily or exclusively within and subjective, comes to rest when "I" is not any longer reducible to what is subtle, independent, and exclusive of the whole body. In that case, the living being becomes truly "superficial," unable to move inward beyond its own surface or appearance. As the body, "I" is not separable from relations. "I" is no longer reflexive, or reactive (contracting toward the self-point), but merely, irreducibly in relationship. The non-reflexive or simple condition of relations, prior even to the play or adventure in relationship, becomes the theatre of existence, even before there is all inwardness, all memory, all knowledge, all self-possession. I-am-the-body is love. The discipline of relationship obliges the born-being in Ignorance. But it is not that outward action has replaced inward absorption — since either one of these strategies is itself possessed by knowledge, the sense of separate existence, rather than prior Ignorance. In Ignorance, the very reflex by which "I" defines itself reactively (in shock or contraction) is counter-balanced by the irreducibility of the relational condition of the body itself. The native incident of the being becomes relational, non-reflexive, or perfectly still. It becomes love — which is not the mood or feeling or ideal which we subjectively manufacture, in order to motivate ourselves to egoic morality. It is the native disposition in Ignorance, even bodily, prior to reactivity or the subjective orientation. It is a form of tacit and native presumption, not most fundamentally of feeling or thought, or even of self. Love is action. It is the Condition of the whole body itself. It is Radiance, prior to subjectivity, or self-possession, which is possession by the sense of separation and otherness.

In love, in the true disposition of Ignorance, the body-being, prior to subjectivity (inwardness, thought, desires, preferences), rests in natural Intuition of its own Condition. That Condition is not *a* consciousness, not formed, not known by anyone. It is not an experience by the body-being, within or without. It is the Condition prior to the body-being, prior to the reaction that is birth and its subjectivity. Only That is Truth,

Self, Body, God, Reality, and Liberation. All other states or conditions offered to the born-being as Truth or God are the idols of experience, offered in a dream of priests who move in the hollows of the navel and the brain.

2

It is not that there is necessarily no survival of death. It is simply that we are tending to be falsely related to our selfless, timeless, and spaceless Condition in Truth. We tend to desire survival as an independent being, and either to be certain of the possibility or to doubt it — whereas we should be completely free of it. "Survival of bodily death" is a concept of future existence which enforces certain false presumptions relative to the present state. It is clear to everyone that we all eventually die — and there is no survival of at least our present manifest condition or bodily circumstance. Both reincarnation and afterlife are necessarily viewed as extensions of the present conditions of our living, but at least the bodily form of our present living will be absent or changed. Therefore, the conventionally conceived future beyond death implies that something within or behind our present flesh-form is our actual or "real" form, person, or condition — even in the present, and also after death.

Thus, our views of existence beyond death tend to enforce or reinforce the subjectivist view in the present. The usual man is both separative (self-oriented) and inward-turned by tendency. Thus, the relational context of the actualities of our birth is always undermined by our chronic disposition. We are all like Narcissus in the world.

The chronic subjectivist-separatist (or self-oriented) view is utterly false and destructive. It is undone in the Way of Divine Ignorance. Then what of the future? Are we only dead at last? Truly, there is no knowledge senior to death. Therefore, survival of death will always require death itself as the right of way. And even certainty relative to individual survival is only certainty that change is inevitable, and that the present always passes. In any case, even the presumed factuality of the survival of death does not justify the subjectivist view in the present.

It is not the "inner being," the "shadow," that survives death. Death is a transformation of the "whole body," the entire manifest being. Survival of death is like survival of your wedding day. It involves a transformation of the person wholly, not merely a continuation of some inward part.

The condition we conventionally conceive to pertain after the death of one who has been born in this world is in fact only a continuation of his or her present state. It is still a case of the "whole body," a separate individual with both an "outer" form, or a specifically differentiated aspect, and an inward or inward-tending identity. This is also true of the person in so-called "out of body" states. The fundamental condition does not change. It is still separate and subjective in orientation, even while touring the realms of objective possibility, high or low. The same model of existence persists. And this is the important factor: We tend to desire and even to experience, both in ordinary and extraordinary states (before and even after death), a single condition, which is bodily or separate, and centered within itself by orientation. We presently suffer this contracting disposition and circumstance, and the whole impulse of our desiring and even our experience is to repeat the same theatrical condition.

Our proper disposition is one that is critical of this very tendency. We religiously and scientifically struggle over the possibility of independent survival, but our true vocation is one that undermines the limiting force and necessity of our present (and therefore future) condition.

The proper view of our manifest present condition, in any moment, now or in the future, before or after death, is the view of our singleness or "whole body" circumstance. The flesh body, the life, emotions, thoughts, self-sense — all these arise as functional permutations of a single condition. The "inward" or non-flesh changes are not radically other than the flesh changes. All of it takes place in the theatre of the whole body, the separate identity. The inward gesture of identity is the same as bodily differentiation and the contraction or separation from relationships. The whole body, or separation itself, is the very root and paradigm case of suffering and illusion.

All our conditions are conditions of the whole body — they imply the whole body, even if, as in sleep or dreams, the experiential dimensions that are apparently active are subtler than the flesh. Our conventional future is, truly, not one of separation from the whole body but of transformations of it — that is, permutations of the single model of experiential existence, the objective or bodily person centered within, or subtly, relative to his or her apparent form. What we must realize is freedom from this conventional model, now and in every future moment. "I" is the whole body, objective, mental, and egoic, in any moment. The subjectivist tendency is simply the tendency toward separation or self-possession. "I" is not within but entire, the whole. Thus, thought or any other form of inwardness, psychological or mystical, is not the natural state or the disposition in which the very Condition of the born-being is obvious. It is only in the "whole body" disposition, the non-contracted disposition, prior to inwardness or subjective modification (separate self sense, thought, reactive feeling, and the like) that the Condition of all conditions, including the whole body or "I," is Revealed.

The liberation of the born-being from its exclusive or subjective tendency or orientation does not serve the opposite habit, of obsessive outwardness, since outward relations are themselves only transactions of the separate self, the whole body in itself. Release of the ritual of subjectivity is fundamental to the Way of Divine Ignorance — but this only establishes the born-being in its native or whole body disposition. When this is the case, then we are established in the disposition wherein we are aligned to the ultimate Process of the Way, which is Realization of the very and prior Condition of the whole body itself. That Condition is the Real, the prior and eternal Divine, or Truth. That Realization is Liberation from the torment of birth itself (not merely the torment of the death of one who is already born). Then the whole body, the persistent dream of independent consciousness craving the consolations of experience and the immunity that knowledge grants, is dissolved in the Bliss of Real God. In the case of such Realization, neither the present nor the future, whether before or after death, is determined by the conventional limitation of birth into the illusion of independent body, mind, and self. The Condition of the present is Truth, the Divine, the Radiance in which all knowledge, all separation, is dissolved. Therefore, Destiny is not mere survival, but constant dissolution of the illusion of independent existence. Destiny in Truth is the Divine, the Real, the Perfect Domain, Ignorance-Radiance, Sacrifice, or Love.

3

In ancient days it was written, "Wherever there is an other, fear arises." We constantly create otherness in the reflex of subjectivity, even in the simple sense of "I" independent of anything whatsoever. Thus, fear and mere existence become identical and simultaneous in ordinary living.

Even from the point of view of conventional awareness, our subjectivity is not mysteriously distinguishable from everything else. It is completely dependent on all of it. Of course, we can have experiences, we can manipulate our experience through subjective effort, as a "self." But that self is fundamentally of the same nature as a shoe, as a cloud, as any thought. It is simply arising. It imposes itself in the moment. It does not impose itself upon something or someone other and identifiable or knowable at all. It just imposes itself. It just arises, as everything arises.

Yet, as a convention of our experiencing, we differentiate the witnessing of things arising from the things themselves. We make a meaning out of that process— that this witness is *a* witness, *a* someone, either a personality or a soul or *the* Self—in other words, some independent, absolute, even infinite subjectivity that can be separated out from objects. But there is no subjectivity that stands radically apart from objectivity. There is no subject-object distinction that is ultimately literal and true. That distinction is, first, merely an apparent convention of action, then a convention of thought, and then a belief that persists as long as we fail to realize the true Condition of all arising.

We tend to believe that our inwardness, our subjectivity, is somehow mysteriously identical to something that is absolute and unchanging, and that if we can get to it, we will be immortal. But actually our subjectivity, the "I," is no more absolute than the foot. There is no "I" that can be lived in absolute independence from other "I's" or from things arising. We are already immortal in the sense that we go on and on and on and on in or as the physics of things. We are immortal not by virtue of being different from this arising, but because we are it exactly. Thus, the physics by which the body and all things appear, visible and invisible, is the same by which "I" appears, and disappears, and reappears. "I" is all of that.

There is an experience you may have had in the middle of the night, when you have been dreaming some dreadful episode, in which something terrible is being done to you or you are doing something terrible to somebody else. In such a dream you might be living as a person who has committed some terrible deed. You killed six people! Six people killed you! And then, suddenly, while you are still sleeping, without actually waking up to the point of opening your eyes, you realize that you have been dreaming and that the content of the dream is not true of you. That is what is important—not just the knowledge that you have been dreaming, but the realization that the dream itself is not true.

Our liberation in Truth is of that kind. It is an awakening. It is not an episode of the subject, not a complication of the dream of subjectivity itself. It is the sudden and tacit sense that "I" and all arising,

within or without, are not true, not necessary, not
binding, that experience is not effective. This realization is not a philosophical, mental conclusion. It is a
tacit, felt, mindless, absolute, and undeniable realization. And it is not altogether the same as in this
analogy of waking up at night and knowing that you
have been dreaming. It is the radical Awakening of
Divine Truth itself, in which none of the "dream" of
life is true or binding.

If you wake up in the middle of the night from a
dream, you still realize that you are in bed. You are
simply released from a certain episode in your subjectivity. But in radical Awakening to the Truth or Condition of subject and object, you are completely
released from the implications of manifest existence
and the compulsive, problematic, fearful differentiation of your subjectivity from objects arising, from
worlds, from others, from the body.

The usual man suffers his waking life as he suffers
his dreaming life. He or she is disposed to react, to
do, to experience, to be identical to someone. For such
a one, life has terrible consequences, and not just in
the evil and burdensome moments. Just being alive is
terrifying. It is! It is sheerly terrifying to have this
experience of independence, to realize the vulnerability of your position as a living being. And there is
absolutely nothing you can do about it. You wake up
to this insane circumstance without any idea what it
is, and you just adapt within it. You are constantly
experiencing the threat of a terrible future, always
struggling to be victorious and to escape the Evil One
and to feel good in spite of everything.

The usual man — everyone in the usual condition — feels this terrible vulnerability, the terrible imposition of being alive. Thus, the possibility represented by subjectivity, by inwardness, is inherently and automatically fascinating. And that possibility is enhanced by the fact that we do not only walk around in the waking state, but we also spend a lot of time dreaming and sleeping and daydreaming and falling into reveries. Our experiences, including all kinds of people, influences, and ideas, reinforce the notion that it is possible to escape, to be free of vulnerability, through inwardness. According to this view, self-possession means release and salvation, which is why the ego is so strong and such a profound commitment. So everyone is occupied in one way or another with bondage to subjectivity, whether it takes the form of mystical inwardness or simply the form of the adventure of "me," the differentiated person.

Thus, there is a disposition in us to look for release, consolation, or salvation by exploiting and manipulating inwardness in all kinds of ways. Inwardness can be manipulated psychologically merely to support the endless, obsessive thinking that motivates us every day. It can be exploited magically to produce extraordinary effects in the gross world. It can be exploited mystically to glamourize our subjectivity in the escape from gross waking life into a more subtle form of subjectivity. It can be exploited intuitively to abstract us from the content of experience altogether. In other words, the practice of life toward which we are conventionally disposed is one that moves within, or "toward" self in itself, and thus away from the context of simple, ordinary experiencing, or relationship.

The way of subjectivity and exclusion is the way of the usual man, of Narcissus. The principles and practices of the many approaches to the subjective path carry with them the tacit presumption that "I am not the body," that "I am this mysterious subjectivity," and, therefore, that "the kingdom of God is within." The usual way of salvation is the way of inwardness in one or another form, whether in religious, so-called spiritual, or magical, mystical, or transcendental forms of inwardness — or else simply in the conventional form that everybody is involved in, that sense of just being "me" over against everything and everyone. Thus, the practice of life that is instigated by this belief that subjectivity is somehow most true, independent, or absolute attempts to separate us from the body and therefore from relations — whereas actually "I" is perfectly identical to the body (the entire, open-ended, psycho-physical process of the manifest being), and perfectly dependent upon all of this arising.

Salvation through subjectivity sounds reasonable enough when it is described in mystical terms, but what kind of gesture is the practice of inwardness in any case? It is contraction from the relational condition that is simply true of us. It is withdrawal from the conditions of relationship. It is reaction to the vulnerable dependency of our existence, of our dreamed, waking life, in which there is truly no separable "I." That is what is so terrifying about it. It is dependent, it is vulnerable, it is not isolated, it is not separable. Thus, it all appears to be a trap, and we seek every kind of release, distraction, or consoling fulfillment for our "caged bird."

You feel anxious, particularly when you are weak-ened by experience — a bad birth, a bad childhood, a bad night, a bad day at the office, whatever it is. When you get a little weak, then the subjective, inward, separative motive becomes very strong. So likewise does the psychology that would move you out of natural ease into habits of motivated excess, such as drinking, overeating, obsessive sexing, smoking, doping, and all the other forms of mediocrity and self-indulgence. That is why these habits are so diffi-cult to discipline, as is every form of born or egoic adaptation. Discipline is intentional frustration of the impulses to which we are already disposed by fear, by adaptation to separation and otherness.

Depending upon the society in which individuals grow, there are different ways of managing the search for fulfillment through subjectivity. At one level of social culture, if you are a good, solid human being, you just drink and smoke, and you think that only crackpots and crazy people get religious or spiritual. But there are also levels of culture in which magic and religious invocation of Divine influences are perfectly acceptable alternatives to an excessive and vulgar outward life. At another cultural level, psychic and visionary mysticism becomes more acceptable. Transcendental forms of that same mysticism become even more acceptable in other cultures. And the intuitive breaking out of life itself into some absolute inward condition is even more acceptable in still other cultures.

But, in any case, the Way or practice that is true is not the way of salvation through the reflex of subjec-tivity, but it is the way of liberation from subjectivity.

It is liberation from that very impulse to go within, to find an absolute inwardness that is separable from the outer world. That reflexive impulse of exclusive "I" is completely false. "I" is the body, "I" is dependence, "I" is not separable from this whole process of arising. It is simply that "I," since it is only the whole body itself, or the sense of separation native to birth in form, is not the *Condition* or Truth of the body, or of any of this arising. The true practice is not the way of reductive inwardness and the view "I am not the body," but the way of relationship, or sacrifice, in which "I" is the body. In that path there arises perfect intuition of the Condition or Truth of "I," of the body, of all this arising, prior to all separative and subjective or egoic strategies. Thus, our awakening in Truth is radical—not conventional. It is not founded in the ego-soul illusion, the illusion of the absoluteness and independence of the self, the subject-sense or subjectivity.

The foundation of the Real Spiritual Process is not subjectivity at all. The Process described in the Teaching of the Way of Divine Ignorance, or Radical Understanding, is based on the criticism of that very inwardness, that belief in the separability, the independence, the absolute nature of the subject and the subject conditions, whether in the form of its grossest orientation to fulfillment by outer experience, or in the form of its most transcendental fulfillment through subtle experiencing. The fundamental criticism made in this Teaching is directed to this matter of subjectivity, the notion that the subject-sense, the

"I" or "me," is separable, independent from *all* other arising. The chronic contraction that is the usual subjectivity is a schism in the being, a reaction to experience, a reaction to vulnerability. The Way in Truth begins only when there is critical insight into the impulse to react, to contract inwardly, to recoil from what is observed or felt. Wherever that impulse is followed, either in the most sophisticated forms of conventional spirituality or in the usual excesses of the average life, it involves fundamental disturbance — separation, the avoidance of relationship, the failure of sacrifice, violation of the Law.

4

The fundamental demand of practice in the Way of Divine Ignorance is the demand to fulfill the Law, which is sacrifice, by living the natural conditions of relationship, not of inwardness, as an unqualified discipline. The anticipation of the discipline of relationship is itself repugnant and terrifying. The discipline frustrates the reflex of subjectivity and intensifies the anxiety of the dreamer. So you see how difficult it is for an individual to take up the discipline of this Way while his sense of its foundation criticism is still weak, when the Teaching has not truly been heard, when Ignorance is not the felt disposition. Until he or she "hears" the Teaching, the individual is simply struggling to discipline himself of something to which he is altogether committed. That struggling makes him very anxious. Every little discipline of the diet and his private life, every little responsibility, every obligation to be straightforward, every meeting face to face with others becomes aggravating.

People who are still struggling in this manner, in whom the Teaching has not yet made its point, and yet who think they are supposed to be involved in devotional practice, remain distracted by problems and questions. They go through all kinds of phasing, and to them it seems that the discipline is very complicated. But the only reason there is difficulty in living the discipline is that people fail to "hear" the Teaching. They may listen to it, but hearing it is another matter. True hearing instantly awakens a natural conviction or native disposition that is wholly capable of simple discipline. In that disposition, the Lawful or sacrificial discipline of our essentially Lawless or arbitrary and self-possessed adaptation to existence is natural, obviously necessary, and entirely acceptable.

Thus, the foundation of this true spiritual Way is the hearing of this argument that is the essential Teaching. If you do not hear it, if you just take up the discipline and practices themselves in the hope of becoming Enlightened, or in the hope of becoming convinced of the argument itself as a result, you will remain, even in the midst of that discipline, still committed to the subjective principle, the flight from experience, the bird in the cage sense of "me" that is trying to escape, to be immune, like Narcissus. You will be obliged by that commitment even while you are trying to discipline yourself. And because the discipline is such a burdensome·task under these conditions, it becomes very complicated. Out of that complication come the endless questions, the struggling within, the resistance, so that things as simple as lunch, or feeling, or service become very complex! All the problematic complication of this Way of spiritual life is just the failure to hear the argument, the failure to be most fundamentally convinced, the failure to be convicted and confessed in the whole being and so released into an orientation that is not the usual one, that is not the usual turning in upon the subjective root.

Thus, the discipline of the Way of Divine Ignorance is not the one of turning within with all the concentration you can bear, or of sitting in meditation for hours

every day in a strategic attempt to get more and more
inside and stop feeling this body, this sensation, this
desire. That is not the Way. The "I am not the body"
way is not the principle of the practical discipline or of
meditation in the Way of Divine Ignorance. In other
words, practice and meditation in this Way are not
based on an abstracted, subjective, ego versus body
commitment. They are based on the transformative
hearing of the critical argument that is the Teaching,
which hearing then manifests as natural conviction
and the disposition to fulfill the Law, which is sacrifice, which is simply the discipline of relationship.
The condition of relationship rather than the condition of subjectivity, the "I" or "me" over against all
arising, is the simple principle of practice of this Way.

"I is the body," not "I am not the body," is true in
practice. This principle and its practice are not
founded in a philosophical-mental conviction but in a
native-intuitive one. When the criticism of the usual
approach is truly heard, it becomes established in us
as the disposition of Ignorance rather than of knowledge. All the ways of knowledge are the ways of this
subjective orientation, this "I am not the body" way,
or "I am not you," or "I am different from the world,"
or "I am independent and have my own destiny to
fulfill." Thus, in the meditation that arises naturally
in Ignorance, in which "I" is the body, there is no
problematic philosophical distinction. It is perfectly
obvious that there is simply this total manifest condition and that it implicates this body, this being, "I"
or "me." But the practice that is natural to us in
Ignorance, since it does not radically distinguish self

from the conditions arising here, is the discipline of relationship, the natural, economized order of living, founded in release from obsessive inwardness. The discipline in practice is the magnification of service and the natural discipline of functions relative to your action, your involvements with intimates, your environment, your sexuality, your diet, your habits of consideration and study. The discipline is relationship, and the awakening that becomes natural to this disposition, to this Ignorance, is first felt as the communication of the Real or the Divine as Presence. The felt Presence is the first communicated sense of the Spiritual Master to which the devotee, founded in true hearing of the argument of the Spiritual Master, is awakened. The devotee is one whose approach is not any longer willfully and helplessly self-possessed, but sacrificial; not intentionally or strategically inward-turning, but natural, relational, at ease; not obsessively outward-turning, but rested in Ignorance, in heart-felt attention to the Divine Presence, by which we are drawn into and prior to the ordinariness of this moment.

In this moment, in the Presence that is God, we are not turned out of relationship but are naturally rested in it, so that we may enjoy the Intuition of the true Condition of the body-being and all arising—the prior Condition or Truth of the body-I and all things, all relations. That Condition is not something within more than it is something without. The Condition of all arising is not more true of the inner me than it is of the lamp on the table. That Condition is the Condition of *all* arising. In Ignorance, no *radical* distinction is made between subjectivity and objects. That distinction having come to rest — that reflex, that principal activity that is Narcissus, that contraction, that separation having come to rest — we are naturally disposed to the radical intuition of our Condition in Truth, and so a process of real meditation arises in that practice, in that discipline. But it is not the meditation founded on knowledge, on the subjective motivation, on strategic programs of inward concentration, on creative programs of subjective manipulation, release of the subject himself, his psychological de-programming, his glamourization, his visions, his release from the body-sense, his release from all kinds of experiences, his separation from gross, subtle, and causal objects. All of that is part of the lie of subjectivity.

The Way of Divine Ignorance is not founded in the notion "I am not the body." "I" is the whole body. In prior Ignorance it is clearly that. Only our conventional knowledge separates self and body and world, and thus premeditates their conflict. It is simply that "I," the whole body, is not the Condition that is true. The true Condition, the Real, the Condition of all conditions (whether apparently subjective or apparently objective), is Unspeakable, Absolute, Unqualified, Perfect, not exclusive, not even inclusive, ultimately neither one nor the other, not in any sense bound by the force of implication on the basis of any arising whatsoever.

Yet all kinds of experiences are claimed, by unenlightened but extraordinary individuals, to be the highest attainment, the Goal to be sought through the discipline that is subjectivity, inwardness, or inward-turning. And meditation in some form or other is usually their recommendation, always on the basis of a form of knowledge, a reaction, a philosophical dis-position to turn within, to engage in all kinds of disciplines for turning within, and then to spend a lot of time turning within on a certain object through a certain method, each method ultimately producing a different kind of inwardness. If you turn in on felt energies, then you will experience the evidence of kundalini[1] or the subtler side of this gross appearance. If you turn in on thoughts, then you will experience silence or no-thought. If you turn in on the visible and audible current above the body-sense, then you will have the subtle experiences of subtle possibilities themselves. If you turn in on the "I" itself, then you will have an experiential realization of the exclusive root of the subject. But, ultimately, the illusion of inwardness itself, the whole adventure of turning in and away, must be penetrated. In the case of devotees in the Way of Divine Ignorance, it is penetrated in every instant of the hearing of the argument of the Spiritual Master, and, ultimately, in perfect stabiliza-tion of the disposition of Ignorance, which is itself Enlightenment. The instant of true hearing is coinci-dent with a disposition that is Enlightened. It is the awakening of Divine orientation, which, if true, is

1. The internal energy process traditionally considered to lie dormant or "coiled" at the base of the spine, and which, when awakened, through inversion of the senses and conversion of the sexual current, brings about blisses, experiences of intense bodily energy, and purifying psycho-physical transformations of the gross or lower life.

God-Realizing or a Sacrifice in every moment. That Ignorance, that Principle, that native disposition that is true of the devotee in this Way, is the ground whereon the whole Way is worked.

You see what the function of the Spiritual Master is then. The usual man is turned and turning inward, dreaming, distracted, knowing, oriented toward adventure, high and low, on the basis of the evidence of birth, which is all experience. The Spiritual Master is already awake, even while appearing within the dream. He communicates in some conventional ways, argues, plays, creates a theatre within which to make a lesson, in order to establish that principal awakening, the "hearing" of the Teaching, the getting of the lesson. Then that new disposition appears, in which all the adaptations of conventional dreaming may fall away, shape by shape, and also suddenly, until there is perfect abiding in that very Ignorance that is the root and fulfillment of the process itself, and that appears in the first instant of true hearing.

For one who has "heard" the argument of the Spiritual Master, there is nothing uniquely mysterious about "within," wherever that could possibly be. A couch across the room is equally mysterious. Such a one has become sensitive to the nature of *all* these things arising. He no longer has the compulsive need to move into some other condition, some change of state, in order to realize the Truth. The Truth is to be realized in *this* instant, whatever the conditions. The motivation to change one's state is not the character-istic Way of Truth. Change of state has nothing what-ever to do with Truth. It is just a way of organizing the dream, the born-sense of separation itself, for the sake of release and fulfillment. All the ways of going within, up, down, or out have nothing directly to do with Truth. They are simply the various dramatizations of the usual life or dream. The Divine is the Truth of conditions, the Condition of conditions, and the Divine is realized when that whole subjective disposition, that whole strategic motivation to acquire changes of state, has been undone in perfect Intuition. That perfect Intuition is also simultaneous with the most intense discipline, yet it is a discipline perfectly natural to the devotee. Such a devotee is released of all destiny that can be preconceived or presently experienced. Life in its present manifestation simply takes its course. Everything is arising quite naturally. If it ceases to arise, it ceases to arise. If it becomes something else, it becomes something else. The devotee plays the conventional roles, but with humor, as one who is awake, who no longer believes the dream mightily, who is no longer limited by the implications of the dream or the appearance. And his Condition is not describable to someone who has not himself realized it, who is not equally Ignorant. But it is certain.

You will not be moved to take up this Way of life, in which that certainty is true of you, until you hear the fundamental argument that the Spiritual Master serves to demonstrate. It is not just a verbal argument. It is an argument transmitted through the lessons of play with people, through the dream itself, of which conversation is only a part. But somehow that Teaching, that argument, including the dramatization and lesson making, creating the drama and bringing it to a halt suddenly, undermines all destinies and desires for change. The force of appearances is undermined in one who truly hears the Teaching and meets the Teacher. The individual in whom the Teaching has made its point, who has heard the argument, rests in the disposition of Ignorance. And, from that point of view, he or she is fully able to take up this Way of life and its progressive disciplines of re-adaptation, or new adaptation.

You can see how ordinary the discipline is. On its basis, you realize an economy of the whole life. All the exploitations of experience, all the adaptation to what is not necessary, to what destroys life, to what disorients it, making it "fail to meet the mark" (which is the meaning of the word "sin"), all those exaggerations and obsessions cease to be indulged. At first, Lawless or egoic dramatizations are abandoned in the acceptance of the personal and relational conditions of practice required by the Spiritual Master. Then, gradually, the reflex of concern for the signs of old adaptation that constantly reappear as tendencies in thought and feeling comes to rest, and the contractions founded in this birth become obsolete over time through non-reaction and non-use. There is a gradual readaptation, in which all of that, even as impulse, falls away. The natural forms of ordinary participation and pleasure replace the exaggerated life. This life becomes what it already truly is — a very natural and ordinary and relatively humble affair. Only Truth, the Divine Condition, not any portion or exercise of possibility, is great — and Truth is the happiness and Destiny of such an ordinary, unconsoled devotee.

5

All that exists is summarized under one Law, which is sacrifice. The Way of Truth is a practice that must conform to the Law. Therefore, it is not in itself a Way of inwardness, knowledge, or experiential acquisition and attainment. Its practice is founded in the orientation of relationship, or no-contraction. The foundation discipline is responsibility and service. Truth is at the heart, not independently in its extensions in the life below or the mind above. Thus, the Way is lived by love, which is true sacrifice. Sacrifice, the Law, is not in itself the same as the ascetic principle, the motivation of self-denial, seclusion, and inwardness. It is at all times the same as the heart principle, the native disposition of love, expansive and inclusive radiance of the being, responsibility, and commitment to the conditions in relationship.

The heart is extended above and below. Only the heart itself stands unmediated in the Place of Truth. If the dimensions of the whole body above and below do not bow to the heart's Place, then the heart becomes contracted and secluded in the ego-sense, the disposition of the separate soul. In that case, all worlds become delusion, and even simple things a torment. All that arises becomes a dream of the ego, or independent consciousness.

The body of the ego is expanded from the heart, but the heart as ego or "I" is not conscious of Truth, its Real Condition. The functions on either side of the separated heart, the ego-I, Narcissus, are experienced as tendencies toward contracted conditions—

conditions that refer to the ego rather than the center-less play of relations. The egoic heart is in chronic violation of the Law. It is oriented to self, not rela-tionship—to experience, not love—to knowledge, not Ignorance—to contraction, not Radiance. The egoic heart and its extensions above and below are all the dramatized failure of the Law.

There are three principal centers of tendency above the egoic heart, and three below. Those below corres-pond to the anus, the sex organs, and the region of the navel and the solar plexus. Those above correspond to the deep brain centers of the crown (issuing from the midbrain), the cerebral context of the forebrain, and the throat and lower rear of the brain (hindbrain). The tendencies toward contraction below are the gross ones of fear, sorrow, and anger. The tendencies toward contraction above are the subtler ones of tran-scendental cosmic or intuitive mind, abstract or thinking mind, and concrete and breathing-vital mind (or speech). The tendencies above are subtle and benign, relative to the gross ones below, but they also belong to the ego and are therefore deluding. All that is above and all that is below must, with the ego-contraction or "I" itself, become a single Sacrifice of the whole body. Such Sacrifice is the Realization of Ignorance-Radiance, or Love.

The Way of Transformation in Truth involves no search for experience, distraction, fascination, acqui-sition, or knowledge, above or below. Rather, it involves the re-orientation of the extensions of the whole body-being, both above and below, to the heart — the reestablishment of the heart (ego-contraction) itself in intuitive Communion with its prior and Divine Condition — and the purification and transformation of the conditions of manifest being through love, leading ultimately to Dissolution or Re-orientation of all conditions in the Divine Radiance, the awakening from conditions of independence to the Condition of non-separation from the Real. Thus, mind, and reactive emotion, and life, and body must all become focused at and from the awakened heart. The heart must enter into Divine Communion and establish the whole extended body-being in love, which is the functional and actual discipline of relationship and the sacrifice of the principle of self and inwardness.

Love is *more* than fear, sorrow, and anger. It is not *less* than these. Thus, the love by which true devotees move in relationship to all beings, processes, and things is not the weak, desiring, and inward feeling-conception of the usual man or woman. It is full, it is free action, it is strong. The love which is the active principle of real spiritual life in all realms, high or low, is alive only where fear, sorrow, and anger are presently and fully encountered and transformed in the being. Love is alive only in one who is completely in touch with his or her own fear, sorrow, and anger. One who cannot permit, encounter, and face these tendencies in the contracted, born-being cannot transform them at the heart. Such a one is trapped below the heart, in delusions and frustrations of body, life, emotion, sex, and all kinds of vital desiring, which make the being gravitate toward exclusion of mind in stupidity and the subconscious and unconscious conditions of awareness. Fear, sorrow, and anger are degrees of vital strength in the dilemma of separate self. Fear is the weakest, at the base. It is recoil from identification with the mortal body and the primitive theatre of elements. Sorrow is recoil from loss—the loss of life. Life is lost or spent through sexual orgasm and the play of vital relations. Life is also identified with loved ones and loved things— all of which may be lost. Anger is the strongest of the lower three. It is the power of the navel, the life-seat —but it is only frustration and wildness in those who are self-possessed.

The devotee must live from the heart in Communion with the Divine Reality, and his or her living and elemental parts must come under Lawful responsibility. The being must be established in commitment to relationship, and its functions must conform to the innate economy that is Lawful in them. Therefore, the devotee embraces natural disciplines relative to money, work, diet, and sexuality—and orients the being, thus disciplined, into loving service, the service of all beings, processes, and things on the basis of heart-Communion with the Divine Condition of all beings, processes, and things.

Such a discipline awakens the frustration of old, egoic adaptations, and this manifests as heat and pressure within, so that tendencies toward weakness and the dramatizations of self-indulgence become at times overwhelmingly attractive. But the devotee is committed to the non-dramatization of such tendencies. Thus, the Way involves constant encounter (unless the discipline is abandoned and replaced by egoic concerns and consolations, which are all self-indulgence) with the reactive tendencies of fear, sorrow (or loss), and anger. Therefore, as the stages of the Way progress, the lower being becomes more and more purified, clarified, strong, and under control of the heart's Sacrifice of the whole body in love.

Just so, the subtler or higher being, above the heart, comes more and more into prominence as the lower being is more and more restored to the heart. The devotee engages the functions of the mind in relation to the Spiritual Master, the Teaching, and the heart's Communion, even as he engages the functions of life, emotion, and body in the same service. Thus, the mind is brought as attention, so the Teaching may be heard, considered, and contemplated. The devotee is often engaged in listening to the Teaching as a spoken communication, either in the Company of the Spiritual Master or as it is read to assemblies of devotees. This is proper receptivity and response of mind at the level of concrete mind or speech (via the throat and hindbrain, which provide the vital link to the concrete and abstract cerebral processes of the forebrain). He or she also reads, considers, and contemplates the written and otherwise communicated Teaching. This is proper receptivity and response at the level of abstract mind (the cerebral context of the forebrain). As he or she matures, the devotee engages in meditation, or most profound, conscious, and direct enactment of the understanding awakened in encounter with the Teaching. This is proper receptivity and response at the level of the higher, intuitive mind (the crown, or deep brain, contacted via the subtler roots of the midbrain).

The levels of functional mind are all aligned to the position and disposition of the true heart via the conscious process of the heart's Communion with its Real Condition. This takes place through remembrance of the Divine Presence in the Way of Divine Communion, enquiry (in the form "Avoiding relationship?") in the Way of Relational Enquiry, re-cognition in the Way of Re-cognition, and the native process of prior re-cognition and radical intuition in the Way of Radical Intuition.

Likewise, the levels of the living being, the vital, or etheric, feeling, and elemental character and form, are also all aligned to the position and disposition of the true heart via the natural "conductivity" of the living process. Conductivity is first awakened as the "Breath of God" in the Way of Divine Communion. (This is allowed to take place when the centers below the heart are all aligned to the heart, and the processes associated with breathing, which are controlled at the throat, and which surround the heart and pervade the whole being, are quickened by the heart's Communion.) In the later stages, conductivity is extended even beyond etheric and elemental awareness, through various forms of esoteric contemplation (at first associated with the breath and the throat, but then centered above the throat and the life-cycles of the gross being, penetrating the subtle regions of awareness, only to fall at last into the heart's Ignorance, from which Radiance proceeds

Infinitely in all directions, without a center).

Therefore, all dimensions of the extended being, above and below, are aligned to the heart in this whole Way of Divine Ignorance. And the heart is awakened into its own Real Condition, which is also the Condition of all arising, above and below. Therefore, in the perfection of this Way, the devotee, while alive, is expressed as Love, or Radiance, in all relations. And even beyond the present birth, as well as in the radical Enjoyment of the present life, Radiance is the Nature and Destiny of all such devotees.

Sacrifice is the Law, and it is fulfilled in Love, which is Radiance cutting through all forms of contraction in the Infinite. Once this Radiance is communicated to the devotee in Ignorance, body and mind submit to the heart's Revelation, and Faith, or release of all contractions of mind and life into the all-pervading Divine Fire, becomes the Way into Eternity.

—═○═—

6

Birth is separation, or identification with the vulnerable born-condition. It is, in the human case, vital shock, or fear.

When fear becomes self-conscious—when we are seen and known, even by ourselves, to be afraid—shame arises.

Shame leads to self-indulgence, or patterns of desire and self-manipulation that enervate the body-being, spending the available life-force. This includes every kind of activity relative to the great cycle of money, food, and sex.

When energy or life is spent to the point of enervation and loss, feelings of emptiness and sorrow overcome the being.

When emptiness and sorrow become self-conscious—when we are seen and known, even by ourselves, to have wasted life or failed to master its impulses—guilt arises.

Guilt leads to flight and the sense of being chased or under attack. It may lead to suicidal self-possession, but when escape is realized to be impossible, then anger arises.

When anger does its aggressive work, murderous in its intent and power—so that we are seen and known, even by ourselves, to have become the enemy of life and love—remorse arises.

Remorse repents of separation, fear, shame, self-indulgence, emptiness, sorrow, guilt, flight, anger, and aggressive self-possession. Therefore, remorse, or repentance, fully and clearly realized, establishes the body-being in the mood of non-separation and love.

For this reason, men and women are advised since ancient times to repent and to love, to become established in the balanced, feeling center of the being, which is the heart — and to turn with feeling-attention, and the love which moves beyond self-possession, into Communion with the Reality or Absolute Divine Condition which stands eternally before the heart.

The heart cannot see or think or move independently. The Reality which is Revealed to heart-Communion is not known, not cognized, not seen or heard, not felt over against, not grasped. Whatever surrounds and pervades the coil of the navel and whatever surrounds and pervades the coil of the brain may all be known to the separate one, Narcissus, the being born in fear. But mind and life, the head and the navel, must repent and bow to the heart-position and be transformed in heart-Communion with the Real.

This takes place only when we repent of the adventure in separation and turn as love into the Zero that stands before and pervades the heart — the Zero of absolute space, wherein all things appear and disappear. But such repentance is not the rote formality of conversion to religious cultism and belief. It is not to become irresponsible by throwing oneself on the mercy of some objective Deity, some Power that is irreducibly outside and over against the ego, some Other eternally other than the separate soul or independent body-being. Such repentance is itself a form of fear. True repentance is absolute, and it is effectively a sacrifice of belief in the separateness and self-possession implied at birth. It is not conversion to belief but conversion to love. It is to turn to Communion with the Real, from the heart. It is to accept the fundamental Ignorance that is our Condition, and to be free of the presumption of separation, knowledge, and inwardness. It is to be free of the limiting force of all experience, all relations, all subject-object appearances. It is to surrender, to become a Sacrifice, to be love in the present scheme, without the need, or the strategy, or the promise of subjective survival, the survival of the independent inward "I."

In love the living being establishes a true economy of action and desire. Likewise, the recoil of inwardness comes to rest, and the mind of thoughts, abstractions, and subtle objectifications becomes a formless brightness of blissful clarity. In love there is an ordinary pleasurableness of the whole body. Love is heart-Communion, or heart-felt Ignorance of the Real, and it is Radiation of life, and light and attention in all relations.

Love is the Way of devotees, those who have deeply repented of the adventure founded on self and fear. Such devotees at last are translated beyond the limitation of all kinds of birth, high or low. While alive, they are relieved of every trace of the literal or binding presumption of separation and subjectivity. They exist outside and pervading the whole body, and all bodies, while all other apparent beings each exist as if inside a single body. Their Consciousness is analogous to space itself, wherein all appearances, all bodies, all points of view arise, without any Creator in evidence between space and the thing suddenly appearing. This is the testimony of Bubba Free John: There is no separate self, no independent being within, no Truth to the limiting implication of the whole body. Fear is made a Sacrifice in my Company. Love is heart-felt Communion with the Real, and it is service, full of life, in all relations. Only Real God is the *present* Condition or Truth. Therefore, only God is our survival, our Destiny.

7

The condition or demand of service is the condition or demand of love. Love and service are identical, and they are fulfillment of the Law, which is sacrifice.

Love is relational action rather than the action of one who is self-possessed—but love is *action,* or real availability, not a merely subjective attitude of mind and emotion.

Love is the essential practical discipline of the whole Way of Divine Ignorance. The usual man or woman is self-possessed at birth, inward-turned or reactive by tendency, and subjectively complicated by the impact and accumulation of experience. Therefore, the usual life functions contrary to the very impulse of action, which is intention of attention, feeling, and body in relationship. There is, instead, habitual recoil, reflexive attention, or self-orientation. Thus, relationship represents a dilemma of two motives or tendencies of attention—one naturally directed into the conditions of relationship, and the other reactively and separatively directed toward the self center. Life in such a form is constantly undermined by the force of its own inherent contradictions.

The true devotee, one who is constantly applied to the Teaching of the Spiritual Master to the point of truly hearing it, is devoted to the Teaching to the point that it represents release from the inherent contradictions in the form-condition and the establishment of a free orientation to a new form of action in relationship. Such a devotee is not oriented toward a new and more glamourous form of subjectivity or inward consolation. Rather, he or she is oriented to the conditions of relationship, but free of the principle of contradiction and the recoiling disposition.

The automatic strategy of the usual man or woman is to presume an attitude or chronic reaction as the principle whereby to function relative to relational conditions. Thus, we tend to dramatize reactive emotions of fear, weakness, shame, obsessive desire, emptiness, sorrow, guilt, self-doubt, and anger relative to every event or communication we encounter. We are constantly reacting, and thus recoiling from relational conditions. Each of us tends to react most chronically in a characteristic fashion — mostly mental, or emotional, or vital-physical — or mostly afraid, mostly obsessive or unhappy, or mostly angry. In any case, it is the habit of recoil itself, of unlove, of inward-turning and self-possession — it is the habit of the avoidance of relationship that must cease to be effective in the natural condition of relations of all kinds.

Therefore, the true devotee is committed to discipline relative to action. On the one hand are all of the personal conditions relative to the whole body of functions. Thus, there are disciplines of money, food, and sex. But senior to such conditions is the "hearing" of the Teaching and the functional conversion of the whole body from the orientation of subjectivity to the orientation of relationship. Therefore, senior to the personal functional conditions are the general conditions of study (regular application of attention to the Teaching to the point of "hearing") and service (simultaneous and coordinated application of attention, feeling, life, and body to the conditions in relationship). Only such a life of study and service makes discipline of personal functions pleasurable and intelligent beyond conflict.

The discipline of the true devotee, active on the basis of "hearing" in Truth, is constantly, intentionally, and with great feeling to bring the whole body-being into loving, compassionate, pleasurable service and creative cooperation with living beings and whole body (not merely subjective) conditions. Service or love is pure action, prior to the subjective and obsessive reflexes of thought, concern, and reactive emotion. It is to bring life-force and body into play via pure attention, rather than to separate life-force and body through a sense of born-contradiction, so that inwardness becomes primary, and obsessive in the form of thought and complicated feeling-conceptions. Love is enthusiastic, humorous, intense, happy, serious, and free.

This is the discipline: In every moment, instead of automatically aligning to the fixed disposition of reactive emotion, and allowing it to control or undermine the natural relational force of the body-being, turn into the present relational condition with great attention, intuition, energy, and feeling. In that case either act or be present in the native disposition, which is not reactive, not recoiling, not thinking, not concerned, but merely present as unobstructed feeling, or Communion.

Our conventional efforts to change negative habits are directed at the subjective dimensions of the being, as if these were the creative seed, as if subjectivity originally rather than only lately created action. Truly, the whole body and its relations precede all subjectivity. Subjectivity is the reflexive or recoiling complication of the whole body that comes from a shocked or reactive sense of the born-condition. Transformation takes place not through manipulation of the subjective reflexes, but through present, liberated "hearing" of the argument that is the Teaching of the Spiritual Master, and the regeneration of the native, ego-free disposition toward relationship itself.

Truth is unqualified Radiance, not the secret point within. Native happiness, founded in the Teaching of Truth, is the disposition of Radiance, or love, the non-reflexive disposition in all relations.

Most of the relations in which we are involved are not with human or conscious others, but with merely arising conditions which control and impinge upon the whole body-being. This includes even those conditions that are generally identified with the subjective being and thus separated from the world. Thus, the devotee must press beyond the effective impingement of all arising conditions, whether apparently within or apparently without, in order to stand in the native position, prior to reactive recoil or self-possession and the separative motives of the ego-I, Narcissus. Love is the disposition of Radiance, or uncaused happiness in the moment. You always are natively certain of what it would be to look, and feel, and be, and act completely happy in this very moment. Love is to do just that, and to do it effectively toward all relations, whether apparently within or apparently without, so there is no recoil, no separation, no self-definition, but only the Condition which precedes these.

Therefore, the true devotee is disposed, through "hearing," to new action, or Communion in Reality under all conditions. This disposition is a principle of action or transformation that extends through all the stages of practice in the Way of Divine Ignorance. It manifests as the discipline that is constant, present, simultaneous turning of pure attention (prior to complicated subjectivity and thinking), relational feeling (love, heart-Communion, or energetic whole body presence, rather than reactive, separative emotions), and appropriate bodily participation toward and through rather than away from all arising conditions (whether apparently within or apparently without). Love is thus service, the intention of life toward all natural relations, rather than subjective strategies and seclusion behind reactive attitudes. Love is conscious exercise of the whole body in all relations.

Love or service is thus a principle in which we first and literally transform our action, rather than struggle internally and wait for all negative inner content to pass before we consent to release the subjective mood and strategy of suffering. Cease first to dramatize the reactive play. Do this as a discipline hour by hour. This very discipline will frustrate the subjective signs of old adaptation. It will seem there is no end to the display of negative or imperfect subjective motives and designs. Therefore, we must not only cease to dramatize, but we must consent to constant non-concern about the internal pattern that will be displayed. Thus, over time, the subjective content will indeed change — but only after we have first changed our habits of action, our actual adaptations. Action or adaptation must be transformed first, through "hearing" and the sane application of lawful disciplines. Then the subjective reflections of old adaptations, or the inherent reflex and contradiction in the born-condition itself, will also and over time be transformed.

The subjective order revealed in this Way is at first gross, vital, worldly, and mental. Over time it becomes more benign and subtle. The born body-being is simply a device in the physics of things, a transmitter-receiver. It stands in the midst of space, which is truly Mind or a single universal Consciousness, the way a radio or television set stands in the midst of all kinds of signals or modifications of the waves and frequencies of the great hierarchy of cosmic vibratory physics. It is tuned by habit to the grosser "local programming." Over time, it becomes subtler and tunes in on the greater "network" entertainments of the higher mind! Just so, it also transmits or acts as a modifying medium for what it receives. What it transmits depends on the state of its reactive disposition and the current level of its experience or tendency of tuning in on the vibratory physics in which it is born. Most human beings are a transmission of only highly garbled or modified versions of the grossest mental, emotional, and physical content of the conditions of manifestation. Devotees in the Way of Divine Ignorance are established in that principle of action, through "hearing," whereby the reactive, egoic reflex is undermined and the whole body is gradually tuned to higher and more expanded or inclusive dimensions of the manifest Reality. But they are not tuned to the cosmic programs for their own sake. They are established in a disposition in which all that is revealed is simultaneously penetrated, or dissolved in the Communion of the heart. Therefore, at last, they are translated from the born-orientation of the machinery of appearances into the prior Condition, free of all modifications of the Absolute Bliss or Radiance of Real God.

The Way of Divine Ignorance is the Way through and beyond illusions, not the way of accumulating illusions through a subjective orientation to appearances. Love is disillusionment, or freedom from recoil and modification, subject and object, under all conditions. Hear this, and turn from inner, reactive concerns to Radiance in all relations. At last this Radiance, which is perfect Ignorance, overcomes or dissolves all reflexes of birth, inwardness, concern, and self. Even every loved one is consumed at last in that Radiance of our own loving and direct awareness of them, so that the immortal Beloved, the very Real, the undifferentiated and formless Current of Bliss stands where only encounters were before.

Love is the Sacrifice. Love is the Law. Love is Radiance, not Contraction. Love is the action in which ego and all reactions are dissolved, since all such things are only contraction. Fear is only contraction. Sorrow is only contraction. Anger is only contraction. Mind in all of its realms, high or low, is only contraction. Where contraction ceases, there is no ego to survive, no reactions to dramatize into separation, no fear, no sorrow, no anger, no thought, no other. Love is action. It is nót action by an other or a part of a separate one. It is not merely action of body, or feeling, or thought. It is action of the whole body. It is the disposition of Radiance, prior to self apart and all its actions, which are all forms of contraction. It is neither inside nor outside the individual. It is all-pervading. It is the prior Condition of the whole body and all worlds. Therefore, when Radiance penetrates and dissolves all contraction, then bodies and worlds become unnecessary. Then all arising is Sacrifice at last. All things are dissolved in Radiance once penetrated by Love. Love is Ignorance. At last it takes nothing into account. In Love we are each a living Sacrifice, not a someone trying to survive. There is only Love, only Radiance, only Sacrifice. Therefore, when all things, all others and "I," are gone to Love, there is no relief from Bliss, no word to interrupt the current of Ignorance and answer it by name. When Love is altogether true, when Radiance shines so hard it opens up the hand, then there is only God and God is Love. Love is the Sacrifice of Man.

The conditions of experience are summarized in the Teaching. The summary of conditions is a summary or circle of pairs, of contradictions. When the whole affair of arising is clearly seen, it is felt as an irreducible dilemma. Experience, in itself, is futile, unrelieved, contradicted. Therefore, we are moved to the Principle of Freedom.

The experience of the devotee duplicates the field of contradictions, even in the case of Realization in Truth. Except the devotee has Realized the Paradoxical nature of all pairs. When contradiction becomes paradox, the strife of time and space becomes overwhelmingly beautiful, and the devotee begins to contemplate in the Humor of our God.

Bubba Free John

2

PRINCIPLES OF THE TEACHING: THE PARADOX OF CONTRADICTIONS

Divine Ignorance is the single principle underlying the entire Teaching and practice of the Way of life communicated and lived by Bubba Free John. "No matter what arises, we do not know what it is"—such is the native Condition of all beings. Divine Ignorance itself cannot be known or explained, but it is the Condition of Radiance or Love that is the Nature and Form of the Godman or Spiritual Master as well as the core and practice of the Teaching. We cannot attain it or describe it; Ignorance is simply the present, root-Condition of all conditions, all worlds, all living processes, all moments. In the following essays, Bubba summarizes the essential principles of this Divine Condition and the spiritual practice that derives from its intuition.

THE WORLD IS NOT MATERIAL, BUT PSYCHO-PHYSICAL

2.1   Since Truth is the Condition of *all* arising, direct Realization of Truth must be possible, essential, and necessary under ordinary or random present conditions, and not merely or especially under extraordinary or strategically attained conditions. Truth is not an independent condition, but the Condition of every condition. Therefore, it is not a matter of future, progressive, or strategic attainment. It is a matter of radical intuition in the present instant, whatever conditions are associated with this instant. Therefore, the Realization of Truth is not itself an experience, a condition among conditions, nor is it *necessarily* associated with any extraordinary phenomena. It is not itself a matter of feeling energies, or seeing sights or visions, or of extraordinary hearing, or taste, or smell. Nor is it a matter of any thought, or projection into any kind of environment, high or low, subtle or solid. It is a matter of intuitive abiding in the unqualified Condition on which the present conditions are a play. And it is a matter of being free, moment to moment, of the limiting power or the force of implication and contraction generated by the events or qualifications of every instant of experience.

When such Realization becomes native to us under all conditions, a new and perfect Destiny is resurrected from the stream of conciousness, or the uncaused chain of subject-object relations in all realms. That Destiny is the same as the Intuition of Truth. But

2.1

it may or may not be associated with any events, since Truth is not associated with any event by necessity.

———=○=———

2.2 The waking world is not a "place," an "earth," but a realm, an indefinite dimension, just as the condition or region into which you enter in dreams is a dimensionless realm. It is not fixed, like a moon or any object, but it is fluid. It is operative as a play of possibility, rather than fixed mechanical destiny. And its conditions in every moment arise not merely according to physical laws, but psycho-physical laws. The universes in which earth appears are a psycho-physical system (psycho-spacial and psycho-temporal), not a mere physical or material one. The same world or realm, in other of its aspects, is seen in dreams and sleeping too. This view is ancient and must be tested. It is native to man and makes him wonder, fear, seek, and hide.

Every man represents only a limited realization of the psycho-physical scheme of appearances. The more psychic or conscious he becomes, the more he sees the world as a Psychic or Conscious Process. It is not only the man who is a psycho-physical process. His world is also. Free life begins only when we begin to operate from this profound premise. This thesis is itself the most significant consideration of man. To enter into the Truth of our condition we must enter into psychic, heart-felt relationship with the world. Then we see not only the body of the world, but its mind also, its subjective or subtle places, and its degrees of self.

But when even this soulful knowing shows itself to be suffering, then Enjoyment is awake, prior to the birth of worlds, and beings, and you that contemplates the Mystery. The waking world is a psychophysical realm. Everything appears, then, as in dreams, in correspondence with the tendencies, high and low, which are the individual. When this becomes clear, one ceases to identify with preferences, judgments, perceptions, reactions, experiences, forms of knowing, or the pursuit of strategies, high or low, since it is all illusory, changing, and held in place by these very actions. When you awaken, you are no longer concerned about the dream world, since it is all phantoms, created in a moment by tendencies that are the real creators of every circumstance of dreams. Just so, when this waking world is seen truly, it becomes clear that the phantoms of its appearance are endless, appearing out of a formless depth, and that true responsibility is relative to the forces of one's own apparent psycho-physical activity, which creates the theatre and calls up all that is good or bad. The realm itself is not to be valued or rejected in terms of any of its content. The realm cannot even be defined. Where do you dream? Where is a place? Rather, one's own action, one's very self must be seen as contraction. There must be awakening, through Ignorance, to that Condition which is prior to the Play. Such is the only real responsibility. The rest is the destiny of complication. When the true Condition is realized, the reality of all distractions, of self, of action, of world, of

God apart, is undone. There is no necessity to the dream, but there is apparent persistence of the dream. See it truly and abide in the Presence and Radiance that is Real. That Communion is truly awake, even as the dream conventions remain, since it notices nothing, but abides as itself, whatever arises.

2.2

We appear in this waking world by the very same process by which we appear in dreams. And the solid waking world is, when seen in Truth, no more real, necessary, fixed, significant, or true than any random dream place. When this begins to become even a little obvious, a process of awakening has begun, similar to waking in the morning from your dreams. When you begin to suspect your life a little, then you begin to become distracted by another and formless dimension, much as the sleeper begins to sense his bed cloth, his solid body, and his room. At that point, one may become sensitive to the Spiritual Master, the Presence of the Condition of things, one who is already awake, the paradoxical man. He is, in person, that dimension which is Truth. He calls you constantly and roughens your feet. He intensifies the sunlight in your room. He does not awaken you to another place or dream, as if your mother shakes you awake to play in rooms protected or threatened by your father. Rather, he serves an awakening in which there is no realm, no implication, and no adventure. He does not awaken you to another place. He awakens you in place, so that even while the dream of living survives, the destiny or even noticing of all effects escapes you.

EGO IS NOT AN ENTITY,
BUT AN ACTIVITY

2.3   Our suffering is single, but so true of us it is
everywhere and universally displayed. We are each
one possessed of a lie, believed from our experience.
Our experience, however factual, is not Truth. The
lie is not merely subjective, but seems to be proven   *2.3*
even in the structures of this solid world, the dream in
which we are all involved. Until we awaken, the worlds
of all arising, within and without, oblige us by this
lie and stand forth as the very theatre of this lie.

The lie is single, irreducibly true of us in the dream.
It is the belief each of us has that "I" is my Condition,
that the Truth of me is within, in the form of an inner
or subjective self, existing prior to and presently or
even eternally independent of all other selves, objects,
and conditions, and not in any sense arising as a
dependent function of relations, like a shape or a
thing, but separate, deep, shapeless but unique, and
inside, like a bird in a cage. Such a belief also implies a
necessary destiny. It is a picture of dilemma. It is not
merely separate. It is separated, separative, and even
believed or known by an act of separation. It is a
belief that makes us eternally anxious. It motivates us
always to escape. It is plight, an opportunity of many
possibilities, but, nonetheless, a torment, a limiting
condition on the Absolute. It is suffering. The dream
of life has an aura of Absolute, but Absolute is not
found. The Absolute is always conceived somehow
within us, or sought outside us, whereas the Paradox
of our Ignorance is the only Way to Realize it.

We are not Truth in ourselves. Truth is our Condition, and that of all arising. But Truth is not found outside, nor is it within. It is, rather, in the Mystery of Ignorance. All these selves that imagine themselves *2.3* Absolute inside are no more Absolute within than hand or foot. "I" is the whole body talking (gross, subtle, causal, transcendental), and "I" is a dependent product of relations, of this whole Pattern arising, high and low. "I" arises out of Mystery, the Real, but "I" itself is not independent or Absolute. "I" is dependent, unable to exist or to realize itself independent of any other "I" or even of a single molecule or event in the endless worlds, high or low, spiritual and material. "I" is unable to exist except in terms of relations. It is the present body. When the present body dissolves, a new "I"-presentation arises among new relations. There is no Absolute "I." What is within is not Truth, not our Condition, but it is simply a play or stream of considerations of the Pattern of relations.

Because we conceive of our Condition as "I," as within and independent, we are bound to a tormented destiny, an adventure in dilemma, a dream of escape and fulfillment. We are trapped in subjectivity, in wordless pondering and in thought, while at the same time the subject feels eternally trapped in self, in thoughts, in feelings, in desires, in energies, in bodies, in worlds. The bird is always in flight for its life, for escape, but there is no escape, because our conception of our Condition is a lie that perpetuates a single, eternal destiny or dream of existence, incident by incident, concept by concept.

The Way of Truth is the Way of Ignorance. In this Way, there is release from subjectivity, from the lie of the inward Absolute, the outer Limit or death, and all the archetypes by which we and the world and the Divine become meanings, like "I" and "Earth" and "God who made us."

2.3

There must be liberation from subjectivity and the subject. Our resort is not within. There must be liberation from the independence of the self as Absolute. Our existence in the realms of experience is not one of eternally prior, relationless independence of self. Our life is a play of relations. Our subjectivity is a reflection of relations, and itself a pattern of relations. We are played, and yet we struggle to win. We play at independence like an Absolute, but our very existence in the play is dependent on relations.

Our way of life must represent what we are. We must be submitted to the Law, which is sacrifice, or the discipline of relationship. This discipline confounds our subjective independence, and when we are thoroughly confounded by the Law, which is the Pattern itself, then the Truth, which is our only resort, becomes obvious, so that we are awakened, translated out of the dream into the Real.

Our perfect awakening is in the radical Samadhi or Real Condition of uncaused Intuition. Such is the Enjoyment of devotees in the Way of Radical Intuition. But every devotee, at every stage of practice, is awakened in moments and in his or her fundamental certainty. Therefore, devotees in the Way of Divine Communion, who are given up to the Presence which impinges itself upon them and attracts them by

Grace, are also one with this Ignorance, and their Understanding coincides with Truth rather than subjectivity and the flight of self from Grace and all 2.3 relations.

———=O=———

2.4 Ego, soul, inner self, or separate, defined consciousness is not an entity, an *actor*. It is simply another version of the same universal *activity* in which every form and function in manifestation, or manifest experience, high or low, participates. It is the single activity of contraction, which shows itself as the complex of objective definition, differentiation, independent form, separation, opposition, subjectivity, and contradiction or dilemma. The illusory ego is not even a unique or more primitive form of this activity. It is simply that, from the point of view of any apparent, functioning, conscious individual, it is the root action (not the root *of* action, not an actor, not different from action), because of its intimate and foundation relationship to his subjectivity. Experience appears to imply the inner, independent witness-self and actor, but it is only an idea — and it falsely objectifies the Mystery in Ignorance. When the fundamental activity of which the ego is a species is undermined in the tacit intuition of the Condition in which all conditions arise, then not only the force of the ego-illusion, but the force (or implication of necessity) of every convention — all experiencing, every world, and even the extraordinary assumption and objectifying knowledge of God apart from or over against the ego and the world — the force of all that arises is dissolved and dislocated in the prior Condition or Truth. Such is liberation, happiness, and true God-Realization.   2.4

All action in all worlds, all action that is any process, and all action that seems to be performed by any entity or person is necessarily a form of this contraction. All action, then, realizes or is conventionally tending toward the realization of the sense and condition of inherent contradiction or dilemma. And all action as such is, therefore, necessarily separative in its realization, even if relational in intention. For this reason, all action, when presumed in itself (directed toward its ordinary goal rather than realized as Divine Communion, or sacrifice into the prior Divine Condition), is binding, limiting, an expression and an agent of suffering. Manifest or conditional existence then, under any conditions — gross (elemental and etheric), subtle (mental and super-mental), or causal (egoic) — is, in and as itself, suffering.

This realization is profoundly disorienting and disturbing, since it convicts the living being of irreducible dis-ease and hopelessness, which cannot be dissolved by any consolation or change of state, and it is also profoundly liberating, since it brings an end to the distraction by any kind of action and experience and allows the effort of being to come to rest in the intuition of its true, real, or prior Condition.

The possibility of true spiritual life, or participation in the Graceful process of liberation in the prior Divine Reality, begins only when there is tacit convic-

2.4 tion in the functions of life and intelligence of the inherent suffering of the conventional realization or destiny of manifest existence (its essential dilemma or self-contradictory condition) and the fruitlessness of all manifest destiny (high or low) and action to produce liberation or true happiness (since all action is inherently separative, self-defining or actor-defining, and a realization of limitation). This conviction is served by all of the ordinary and extraordinary results of life and by the stream of Teaching and Grace Radiated through Realized beings in and prior to the various times and places of the worlds. When life and the Teaching coincide in their lesson, then the individual has come to a point of availability, in the subjective and objective dimensions of his or her life, to the Awakening-function or Grace of the Divine Reality. When the conviction of suffering and hopelessness matures to the point of profound psychic, psychological, or psycho-physical disorientation from the conventional theatre of experience, ordinary or extraordinary, so that there is heightened sensitivity to the intuition of the Condition that is the Divine Reality, then the individual becomes circumstantially related to the stream of true Teaching and, at last, to the direct influence Communicated through a true Spiritual Master.

—=O=—

2.5 The "whole body" identifies itself in numerous particular ways. There is my body, my life, my feelings, my thoughts, my mind, my consciousness, my self. And wherever the whole body identifies itself particularly and separately, everything other than that specific identity becomes an object to it. In that case, even the other forms of its own self-identification seem to be other than itself. For instance, when "I" (the whole body) identifies itself as "my consciousness," "my body" seems other than it—and vice versa. But there is only the whole body, which is identifying itself in many ways.

2.5

The whole body is itself the very act or reflex of self-identification. All forms of self-identification are themselves one action, which is contraction, separation, the illusion of necessary independent being. Separation, or contraction, or self is the whole body. The whole body is, in itself, illusion, a lie. The whole body is itself an act, a recoil.

There must be liberation from the lie, from suffering. This liberation is not only from the gross physical body but from every aspect of the whole body, which is separation into illusion. Body, mind, and soul are all a torment, a single drama.

This liberation may not be attained. No aspect of the born-being is its very agent or method. Only Ignorance itself is Divine. It is the Principle in which all arising does appear. Whatever arises, whatever is experienced, whatever is known, "I" do not know what it *is*. This can never change. It is always Truth. The gross body, the mind, the self are the same act, the same separation, the same lie. The whole body arises in Ignorance. "I" do not know what it *is* in any case. This confounding is dissolution in Real God, the very Divine, the Perfect or Radiant Domain.

—————≡○≡—————

2.6   The ego, all thought (conception-perception), the body, all conditions, whether apparently subjective or apparently objective, are a single Process of spontaneous present arising. They are all forms of tendency. The ego is simply the presumed center of such tendencies, as the world is the presumed conditional boundary and God the presumed unconditional boundary of such tendencies. But ego, world, and presumed or believed God are themselves only conditions (conceptions) arising. They are versions of the same tendency or Process of spontaneous present arising. The ego (self or soul) is not something in itself, but is only the process of tendencies, as is the body and every thought. There is no center, no self then, but only spontaneous present arising.

This is clear in Ignorance, when we have become so free in attention that forms of body and mind cease to distract and the Condition of our very existence may be pondered. Such pondering is instigated by the Teaching of the Spiritual Master. When true hearing has awakened on this basis, then the Presence of the Spiritual Master may itself be felt. It becomes clear in devotion to the Presence, so Communicated, that no self, or mind, or body, or world, or God apart, but only the Presence, unspeakable and all-pervading, is true and Truth. Submission to the Grace that is the Presence is thus the only true Way, and every stage of practice and Realization in the Way is awakened in this manner.

———=O=———

2.7   Ego is not an entity but an activity. It is contraction of the field of Radiance. That contraction is "read" as realms, worlds, or environments, bodies (particularly one, which is one's present face, form, and life), desires, emotions, thoughts, perceptions, all knowledge, and all known phenomena, high and low. But the contraction is single, universal, present, and utterly deluding, through the binding force of implication. The native Condition in the midst of conditions is unqualified heart-felt Radiance, or undefined whole-body Radiation, which is Love.

2.7

Ego, and all suffering and delusion, is simply contraction of Feeling. Liberation is Realized via return to the Condition of Feeling-Radiance (unqualified Relationship) in the midst of conditions, high or low. Such is Sahaj Samadhi. On this basis, there is also Radical Intuition of the Real, prior to all objectification of subjects, objects, and relations, which is Bhava Samadhi.

In the Way of Divine Communion, the ego-position of contraction (as self, thoughts, reactive emotions, habits of activity and knowledge, and the like) is undermined via heart-felt relational attachment to the Presence awakened in the Company of the Spiritual Master. The more this heart-felt relational attachment absorbs or involves the elements of the born, contracted, and usual individual, the more the form of contraction relaxes, and the more the being comes to rest in the native Condition, which is heart-

2.7   felt Radiance, or Love, prior to every aspect of egoic contraction.

The transition from contraction to Feeling-Radiation must be total. It is not merely bodily, vital, and emotional. It is utter Release of the position of separate self and every form of knowledge, experience, thought, perception, or implication, high or low. Thus, the Way is not perfected in the stage of Divine Communion, but it progressively matures, in the case of the relentless devotee, until it becomes Sahaj Samadhi (the Equanimity of Native Radiance, or Love) and Bhava Samadhi (the Equanimity of Undifferentiated Happiness) in the Way of Radical Intuition.

—=○=—

RADICAL IGNORANCE IS TRUTH

2.8   The consideration that is Ignorance is the Principle and Process and Condition of Enlightenment, Liberation, and all Realization. This does not mean that mere thinking about this argument quali-

2.8   fies the fool to deem himself enlightened. Rather, the consideration must become a Way of Life, of perfect re-adaptation. Thus, this Principle unfolds as the Way of Divine Ignorance, or Radical Understanding, through four great and profound stages of discipline, practice, re-adaptation, realization, and sacrifice. Thus, the fool is Enlightened when he makes this Ignorance the Principle wherein his whole life is committed.

2.9   There is no way to account for any condition that arises. Not even the Creator-God notion can itself be accounted for, and it is only an artifice or point of view of knowledge in dilemma. We are simply Ignorant. Our Ignorance has no cause or purpose. It is not caused. We are not knowing. There is no way to account for ourselves or any arising. Salvation or Truth is not in any accounting, any experience, any knowledge, any meaning. It is simply that in the presumption of Ignorance itself as our very Condition we cease to be in conflict with the process arising. We are surrender, the Process itself, Radiance only.

The Ignorance is sufficient. Abide as that heart-felt Ignorance and be re-adapted as the whole body-being to the Condition of Living Light, the Incarnation of Ignorance, which is Radiant Love.

2.10 If you abide as knower, ego, or separate self, you will persist as subjectivity, thought-stress contractions of mind, emotion, and the living body. In that case, all arising seems mysteriously and forever to both point to and hide some great Source or Condition which is the Truth of all conditions. Then you must forever seek it in itself and exclusively, and otherwise *2.10* simply and forever rise and fall with conditions, high and low.

Abide as Ignorance (not one who is ignorant, but Ignorance itself, since it is not even known what "one" is) and there is eternal and prior rest in the tacit sense that all arising, high or low, is only modification, without necessity or implication, of that Condition which is unknown in itself but with which the very being is priorly identical in Ignorance. In that case, the Condition of conditions is never grasped in itself and over against self or any arising, but all arising remains a Paradox or Play of which this Condition is the Truth.

In prior identity with the Condition in Ignorance, there is no seeking but only fullness. In present separation from the Condition in the disposition of knowledge (subjectivity or separated consciousness), there is only seeking, suffering, anxiety, stress, contraction, emptiness, and fear.

———=○=———

2.11   There is no such thing as *the* Self, or any God, Brahman, or Nirvana in itself that may be grasped over against the being or self. In radical Ignorance we are simply and priorly identical to the Condition or *2.11* Truth of all arising and realize a tacit sense that all arising, high or low, is only modification, without necessity or implication, of the ungrasped, unknown, unspeakable and prior Condition. When we abide in Ignorance, all subjectivity, all stress and contraction of mind, emotion, and living body, all thought, all concern, all seeking, all separation, all knowledge, all suffering become obsolete in the present. Thus, we live an ordinary, pleasurable, graceful life in the Paradox of the present arising, surrendered in feeling as Ignorance.

2.11

———≡O≡———

2.12   Through knowledge we seek the Divine Reality or Truth.

In Ignorance we abide and rest in That.

The Paradox of the tangible current of manifestation is That in which we are inhered.

2.12

It is not a matter of striving to go up or down, to or from any experience. It is a matter of resting in resonant attunement, without struggle, strategy, or thought, in the current which pervades the body and all arising. That current is the Way of Truth, the Way of the Condition of conditions. When we abide in That, the reactions to conditions, high or low, become obsolete, true or naturally responsive adaptations come into play, and the Paradox, rather than any pole of experience, absorbs us.

———≡O≡———

2.13   The being is not answered.

The question is undermined by the argument of what is always already the case.

We are ignorant as the body and eternally sacrificed to its Condition.

The Condition of the body is realized in Ignorance, not in any Knowledge, high or low.

The body is, in Truth, Ignorance.

Ignorance is Radiance-only, which is Love, Happiness, Fullness, Sacrifice or Surrender, Bliss, prior to self, subjectivity, or time-space limits.

The body is Radiance-only, even while it appears as a Paradox or Play of centers and limits.

———≡○≡———

2.14   Once even one thing is accepted, so that the presumption of it is no longer inspected, all suffering has begun. Thereafter, there is only the adventure of knowing about and failing to know about. The matter of Truth or fundamental Wisdom is always and presently at the point where the very event of present arising is inspected. Thus, we must constantly transcend or penetrate the most rudimentary presumption in the present. That presumption is the presumption of the necessary, irreducible, factual, and impenetrable nature of the presently arising limitation or condition. Once the arising condition is accepted, we are bound only to know about it. But if we retain the inspectability of the process of this moment of arising, it becomes clear that, no matter

what its configuration, "I" do not know what it *is*. This
is always already the case in any moment. If that
Ignorance is the present presumption, rather than the
condition that is apparently arising, then Truth,
Freedom, and Happiness may be the Realization in   *2.14*
this moment.

———≡○≡———

2.15   We do not know what a single thing *is*, even as
it arises. In this Ignorance, heart-felt, "I" is the body,
or feeling sacrifice of the whole being into its own and
unknown Condition. Thus, we stand as sacrifice or
surrender in the midst of all conditions arising. In this   *2.15*
position we suddenly and moment to moment realize,
in whole body feeling, via the all-pervading current of
manifestation, the Condition of all conditions, of
which all conditions are only a modification. As we
persist in this felt whole body identification with the
Beloved in the paradox of all arising, we become more
and more profoundly rested in the current, prior even
to all involuntary and voluntary activities of the gross
dimension of being. Thus, the display of arising,
which is realized to be one with the Beloved and yet
unnecessary and not binding, is extended into subtlety. The being is yielded in the current itself—felt,
heard, seen, intuited. It does not in principle separate
itself from this world or choose any other. The being
rests in and as the current of being in Ignorance,
seeing all, but only abiding as sacrifice rather than
any knowledge. All of this becomes revelation and

110

rest in the unspeakable and irreducible Condition or
Realm of the Beloved, the Real, the Heart, the Truth
of all conditions, the Condition of the body, "I,"
thought, and every world.

2.15

———≡○≡———

2.16 In complete, simple Ignorance there is no
subjectivity, no dilemma. Rest in simple awareness of
what is arising. You do not know what a single thing
is. You are without knowledge. "I" is not a knower.
"I" is the whole body, or the condition of being priorly
identical to the arising pattern itself. Therefore,
Ignorance is the same as natural rest or identification
with the whole body, without prior knowledge of its
Condition.

2.16

This natural identification *as* the body is the same
as surrender as the body. It is to be the whole body,
simply, natively, without conflict, contraction, or
subjective distraction.

To abide as the whole body, as perfect surrender, is
meditation. It is to rest or abide as the body in its
unknown and eternally unknowable Condition.
Abiding as such, "I" am Radiance-only, unreason-
able and uncaused Happiness or Fullness. "I" is Love
bodily in all relations. Abiding as such under all
conditions, including the condition of undisturbed
privacy, "I" is realized to be a process of Incarnation,
the infilling of Lighted Life. Come to rest in that
Radiance in all relations, so that Radiance deter-
mines all action, all perception and conception. Feel

as whole body Radiance under all conditions, so that Radiance is felt to be the only Truth of all conditions.

The whole body is the Condition of Ignorance. Unqualified Radiance is the Condition of the whole body and all arising.

2.16

Therefore, real meditation or real life is simply to abide as the whole body in heart-felt Ignorance, prior to thought, dilemma, and all subjectivity, all stress, all strategy. Abiding thus, "I" is Love, surrender of the whole body, or Radiance only. Thus to feel, breathe, and live is to be perpetually transformed. Such a one is the always present Immortal.

———=O≡———

REALIZATION OF TRUTH IS FREE OF ALL SUBJECTIVITY, ALL KNOWLEDGE, AND ALL EXPERIENCE

2.17 All meaning is implication. Something is meaningful when it implies something else, when it stands for something, when it stands out in Consciousness, distracting the Consciousness from its own Condition of Enjoyment. True Liberation involves freedom from all implication, and, therefore, from the whole force of meaning, the power of living dreams, the power of worlds and experiences. When the power of meaning or implication is sacrificed or comprehended in the Consciousness, then the creative position fails at its root. Where there is no meaning, no force of implication, the Consciousness rests in its

2.17

own Realm, no longer making the dream of self and world. Then the only Destiny is the Uncreated, the seedless Realm, which may not be described, since it has no relation to any gross or heavenly realm that any being, great or small, has ever known. My devotee is the inheritor of this Destiny and this Sacrifice.

2.17

——≡◯≡——

2.18   Meaning is the function of mind. It does not inhere in things themselves, nor in consciousness or awareness itself. Where there is simple, direct awareness of something, there is no meaning. The worlds are without meaning. Just so, consciousness and every body are without meaning. We are free of meaning, and of knowledge. This freedom is Ignorance. Meaning appears only when something arising is compared, found to be like something in past experiences. The usual man lives in an unreal world of meanings and the absence of meanings. He is aware of little directly, but perceives all arising relative to meaning.

2.18

Meaning is an unnecessary, secondary, artificial, and ultimately binding attribution of what arises. To be free of it, we must be free of mind.

For this reason, much of the advice given by the teachers of men is about the overcoming of mind, or the function of meaning, of comparison, of chronic remembering, so that awareness may be pure, direct. In that case, Reality rather than meaning becomes the content of awareness.

This, however, is not the end of it. Awareness is

itself a limitation prior to meaning. It is analyzed by
identification with specific bodily or mind-body
presence in the midst of environments. Thus, the ego-
soul or separate and separative principle precedes
mind. This principle must be obviated through
direct, pre-mental re-cognition of all conditions, and
simultaneous radical intuition of the Condition of all
conditions (elemental, etheric, mental, transcendental, egoic). Then the dream, the dreaming, and the
dreamer fall in the Heart, the Divine. Such is perfect
Ignorance, or Happiness beyond body, speech, or
realm. The Way of Divine Communion is the foundation and essence of this Realization. It involves that
reception and falling into the Beloved in which no
self survives. The Presence is prior to all meaning.
To enjoy the Communication of this Presence is to be
free of mind, of self, and of all the tormented or
illusory visions made on the basis of this body-mind in
which we seem to move. But we do not move in any
shape or knowledge. We move, we are moved, lived,
and breathed in the single Reality, the unqualified
Divine, which is Gracefully Revealed to us as Presence
as we begin to awaken.

2.18

—=O=—

2.19 What is it that you mean, that you are signify-
ing and pointing to, when you say or feel you are
suffering, unhappy, not at ease? You are pointing to
your own action and finding it as the experience of
separation, contraction, pain. But it is the compulsive

2.19

and presently not-conscious avoidance of relationship, relative to the Divine Presence, and relative to all arising conditions. When this action becomes your responsibility, then these experiences and concerns 2.19 will become obsolete by degrees in the action of God-Communion, and then in the intuition of your true Condition.

—=O=—

2.20 Mind has two aspects or points of view: experience and abstraction.

The experience point of view is never summary or conclusive, but sees the world as a limitless source of 2.20 even random possibilities (all of which actually appear in the form of experience at the right time, coincident with one's tendencies). From this point of view, the world is a dimensionless realm or process, as fluid and indefinite as the dream state.

The abstraction point of view sees everything formally, in summary, discretely. Thus, the world is viewed as a specific formal limitation. It is "the earth," etc. Everything is conceived, and experience serves conception.

The function of the abstract mind is to define what has already been known or experienced, so that it may be controlled or rationally met, and so that it may be set apart from what is not yet known or experienced. One can consider leaving the world only when it has become a definite place rather than an indefinite realm.

The function of the experiential mind is to know, directly, what arises. When the world is known directly, then one can abstract oneself. Thus, the play between these two functions produces the traditional convention of liberation.

However, the mind in both its forms must be undone if there is to be realization in Truth. When confinement to what arises as well as the search to escape or transcend what arises no longer distract, then Only God becomes the Condition and the Enjoyment.

2.20

———=O=———

2.21 Conventional meditation is inwardness, or remedy by subjectivity. Real meditation, the meditation of devotees in the Way of Divine Ignorance, is a process of awakening *from* subjectivity. The process is gradual in its perfection, but its Truth is certain from the beginning.

2.21

The inner "I" is not the resort in this Way. "I am not the body" is not the point of view of practice. The endless distraction of subjectivity, of contraction, is considered and undermined through various kinds of participation during the four great stages of practice.

The Truth is not the view "I am the body." However, this is factually true of "I," and, therefore, our practice must center on relationship and release from the reflex of contraction, rather than on conventional and exclusive inward turning. Real meditation must center on insight into the avoidance of relationship and every form of contraction or reactive reflex, rather than the search for subjective fulfillments and all the glamourous illusions of experience.

Thus, the Samadhi or perfect Intuition of the Real Condition in which our real meditation is resolved at last is utterly free of subjectivity, of knowledge, of thought, of self, of perception, of sound, of light, of vacant silence, of action, of experience, of limitation. The Realization which comes to maturity in the Way of Radical Intuition is free of subjectivity, or the reflexive gesture of inwardness, as well as all the complications of objective relationship, or the gesture of outwardness. It is Radiant, not contracted. It is not inwardness, nor is it compulsively motivated by any object. It is Ignorance, or liberation in Real God, prior to the limitations introduced by subject or object and all the habitual adaptations founded in the dilemma or dream of subject-object realms.

2.21

—=O=—

2.22 Obsessive thinking is a disturbance to the brain, as reactive emotions are to the heart's breath, and conventional orgasm is to the navel. The brain must become still, and most intense or bright, as must the middle and lower regions of the body-being. Radiance or prior Fullness must precede and replace the chronic contractions that are constant thought, reactive emotion, and vital discharge (not only through conventional orgasm but through all forms of enervating self-indulgence). This is possible only in

2.22

radical resort to the native disposition of Ignorance, which is prior to the knowledge that is birth and experience and death. The Way of Divine Ignorance is the Realization of freedom from the curse of subjectivity and the illusion of all objects.

2.22

———≡○≡———

2.23 "I" is not inside and/or exclusive of the body-mind. It is identical to the whole, open-ended, ultimately unknown body-mind. However, the Truth or Condition of "I," the Truth of the sense of separate and independent existence, as well as of body-mind, is not any limitation. All of this, including all worlds or objects (gross, subtle, causal, transcendental), is only modification of the non-contracted, non-contradicted, unfathomable, timeless, spaceless Reality, infinitely pervading all arising, and yet utterly without reference to any arising.

2.23

Thus, "I" *is* the body-mind (it is not *within* the body-mind), but the Condition of the body-mind is without limitation of body, mind, self, or any other kind of differentiation, high or low. That Condition is not merely the droning, snuffed-out undercurrent of this world. It is the very Divine. It is Radiant Consciousness. It is Bliss.

———≡○≡———

2.24   "I" is the body itself. "I" is not the Condition or Truth of the body, but is itself the whole body, the condition or limitation itself. The Truth or Condition of the body or "I" is that of which "I" or the body is the present modification or condition. This Condition or Truth is tacitly realized in Ignorance, the absence of any accounting for any and all arising, the absence of any necessity or implication in any or all arising.

Neither any world, high or low, nor the body, nor "I" is happiness. These are all the same condition, the arising of unnecessary limitation. These are only modifications of prior Happiness, Freedom, or Bliss. This is tacitly clear in Ignorance of all arising. In Ignorance, all modification is re-cognized as such and ceases to be necessary and binding. Thus, all arising ceases to require or motivate a point of view, a dilemma, an effort, a survivor. In Ignorance, all conditions are spontaneously abandoned via re-cognition of their non-necessity and thorough rest or abiding in their pre-cognitive Condition.

Therefore, in Ignorance, all arising, every world, high or low, the body, all its relations, the "I" itself, is spontaneously released. All such things, all arising, cease to concern and bind. There is simply abiding in the prior, unknown (not cognized), non-mysterious, wonderful, and unspeakable Condition of the presently arising conditions. This abiding is not in conflict with any arising. It is at rest, free of fitful programs of life, ordinary in each moment, at ease, disposed to fulfill what is essentially given, not complicated by any requirement or design of preferred destiny.

"I" am not realized, saved, or released. "I" is simply

obsolete, with all arising. The stroke rests. There is
only Paradox. The dream is not upheld. Only the
body-I makes philosophy in worlds. In Ignorance, all
of that is undermined. The mind has no necessity.
Silence persists. "I," all thoughts, reactions, the body,   *2.24*
all worlds cease to motivate, bind, and persist. The
Happiness is not spoken. The Heart does not walk
and talk.

———≡○≡———

2.25   The body-sense yields the reaction of the identification of Consciousness as limitation: "I" or "me"
as independent body-mind (or body-mind-self).
Spiritual Realization is simply the obviation of this
reaction and all its implications.   *2.25*
   "I" is the body, but also the mind, and the separate
or independent self sense. These are a single, simultaneous, reflexive assumption based on the experience of independent bodily or born existence. But
when, through the conscious process in radical under-
sanding, the Way of Ignorance, these are all realized,
along with all other arising conditions (subjective,
objective, gross, subtle, causal, and transcendental),
to be only modification of the prior Condition of the
sense of independent or separate existence ("I," "me"),
they become unnecessary, a matter of humor. Then
there is simple abiding in natural (Sahaj) and perfect
(Bhava) Intuition of the Real Condition, the Divine.

———≡○≡———

2.26   The Divine is One, but not in the sense of an Object or a Subject. That One may not be realized by any concentration of the faculties of being, nor does that One appear as any experience or archetype. When all concentration, contraction, exclusion, separation, union, limitation, experience, knowledge, appearance, perception, form, action, location, cognition, vision, psyche, process, and exclamation cease to define the Consciousness, only this One is Realized. The Divine is Paradox, Sacrifice, Reality, Ignorance, Unqualified Radiance, Undefined Consciousness, World-only, Mind-only, Truth-only, No-Thing, All. No realization realizes this One. Only the obviation of all realization is Realization at last.

———=O=———

2.27   The Divine is the Condition of all conditions; That from which all conditions arise; That of which all conditions are the objectification or modification; That which permeates all conditions; That which is prior to all conditions; That which includes all relations and to which no relations point, since it is not Other but Prior; That which is not Subject or Self, since it is Absolute but not apart; That from which no living being may be differentiated, except it may seem to be so in the case of delusion by knowledge, or experience.

We may enjoy Communion with the Divine via recollection of the Presence, by Name, by Breath, and by Service, in the Way of Divine Communion, by enquiry (in the form "Avoiding relationship?") and maturing in the conductivity of Radiance in the Way of Relational Enquiry, by subtle feeling, audition, and sight, and by contemplation of the root of "I" in the Way of Re-cognition. We Realize the Divine by Graceful Dissolution, or Sacrifice in Sahaj Samadhi and Bhava Samadhi, in the Way of Radical Intuition.

2.27

———=O=———

2.28 The Way of Divine Ignorance, of which the Way of Divine Communion is the foundation stage, is the Way of maturing in Happiness, prior to and regardless of whatever conditions are presently arising. Its ultimate Realization involves no dilemma, no strategy, no subjective contraction, no reactive effort, and no search to prevent or change the process of arising itself. It is the radical Realization of Ignorance-Radiance, free of subjectivity, which is not identical to any condition, high or low, that is apparent or sought or attained.

2.28

The process of present arising is spontaneous, un-caused, Divine. In the true devotee it is permitted (by not being prevented) to unfold itself in the eternal Theatre of the Law. In the ordinary conditions of his or her appearance, the devotee is *always,* even in maturity, obliged toward fulfillment of the Law, which is sacrifice, rather than tendency, which is self-possession. But the Truth of the devotee is Happiness, or Realization of the Real Condition, whatever the present conditions. In contrast, the conventional ways of mankind represent unenlightened commitment to goals of experience via efforts toward changing conditions, preventing conditions or the process of arising itself, attaining higher conditions, and all the rest of the drama of ego and object that comes by reaction to birth in apparent limitation.

2.28

The conventional ways of mankind, or the ways by tendency of every human being, are, simply and irreducibly, forms of reactive seeking, high and low, for changes of state, changes in the conditions of experience, or changes in the ways of relating to the conditions of state or experience. The Way of Divine Ignorance, in the form of the disciplines appropriate at each stage, is the Way of the Realization of the Real Condition, which is Truth, Happiness, or the very Divine, whatever, if ever anything, presently arises. It does not involve the strategy of passive permission to conditions arising, or passive indulgence of tendencies. Nor is it characterized by active and strategic efforts to focus attention or expectation above and beyond the present theatre of conditions arising, or to manipulate the sense and intuition of existence toward some objective or unique transcendental goal, even the goal of the cessation of the process of present arising. Its ordinary discipline is to be disposed to the Law, the obligation in relationship, and the present economy of the whole body-mind, rather than the fulfillment of random tendencies, founded in accumulation or memory and reaction to experience. Its radical discipline is present intuitive rest in the Real Condition, prior to all subjective contraction, and every preference relative to experience.

A FURTHER SUMMATION
OF THE TEACHING

2.29   No matter what arises, we do not know what a
single thing *is*. We do not know what any arising *is*.
Therefore, our natural condition is not subjectivity
but the whole unknown body itself. And the native
Way of this birth is simply, on the basis of this persistent and present Ignorance of the Nature or Condition of all arising, to yield or surrender *as* the whole
body (not *with* it, as from a subjective and knowing
viewpoint) into its very, prior, and eternally unknowable Condition. If this is done persistently, in complete freedom from all goals, apparent results, and
every sense of dilemma, the false or contracted adaptation of the whole body-being will gradually become
obsolete through non-use, or non-necessity.

All false, contracted, egoic (subjectively oriented)
adaptations and illusions (mental, emotional, gross
physical) are the accumulated results of the presumption of the necessity or limiting power of any or all
arising. The Truth of all arising, however, is that "I"
do not know what it *is*. Therefore, the only Way is to
submit or relax, entirely, bodily, and presently, into
the unknown Condition of the body-being and all
arising. It is not the effort of surrender, motivated
subjectively by the sense of dilemma (the binding,
subjective necessity implied in mere and reactive
participation in what is arising as all opposition and
play), but prior or natural surrender, the heart-felt
release of the body-being into its unknown Condition.
If we persist in this, in Ignorance, without becoming

bound by the force of necessity in any experience or result, we begin spontaneously and moment to moment, under all conditions, to intuit the Beloved, the necessary Condition and manifesting current which pervades all arising and of which all arising is the modification.

2.29

Intuition of the Beloved in all forms of arising is identical to rest of the body-being in the current of manifestation, toe to crown.

The Spiritual Master is a direct manifestation of the Beloved, the all-pervading current of manifestation and the Condition of the whole body-being. Therefore, the Spiritual Master should be served, yielded to by the whole body-being in loving surrender, and approached always in Ignorance, so that the devotee may Realize the Truth, the Beloved, and be rested in the current and the Condition of the being and all manifestation. Such devotees receive the constant Love or Grace of the Beloved through such persistent identification of the Spiritual Master as the Beloved, the Nature, Condition, and essential, all-pervading current of the body-being and all arising.

The life thus devoted to the Grace of Reality or Truth, even bodily, observes or demonstrates the gradual and true re-adaptation of the body-being to the current of manifestation, the Unqualified Conscious Radiance and Vibratory Power of the prior Reality, which pervades the whole body and the world, and which is the paradoxical Condition of all conditions arising, high or low.

Since only this Condition is necessary, while all conditions depend on it, the devotee is ever more perfectly

merged in the prior current of the body-being and all
arising. At first he or she is adapted to changes in
relations and habits of body, emotion, and mind.
Then comes the revelation of the play of the forces in
the body-being, as they return to natural polarization
toward the crown of the body and the Brightness of
the current of Reality there. Gradually, in private
meditation (surrender of the whole body-being into
the prior current of all arising, through Ignorance
rather than effort), the gross experience falls away
and there is attunement to the current above and
prior to the gross manifestation. This occurs through
gradual realignment of the polarization of the forces
of the body-being toward the crown. In time, there is
natural absorption in the feeling of the current bodily, then attention naturally resting above in heart-
felt relaxation into the subtle audible and visual
expressions of the vibratory current. This becomes
suspension of attention below and in the gross plane,
releasing the whole being into further identification
with the current, while even breath and heartbeat
come to rest. Then a door opens in the midbrain,
and the being passes with the current (heard, seen,
and felt independent of the gross body orientation)
into subtler and subtler spaces and conditions. Remain in the presumption of Ignorance and rest in the
current itself rather than cling to any of the unnecessary patterns, gross or subtle, that arise as modifications of the intuited Beloved, which is not different
from us or any arising, but which is the prior current
and all-pervading Condition of all arising.

Apart from such samadhi, in which deeper identi-

2.29

fication with the current of the Real in Ignorance (Amrita Nadi) is ultimately enjoyed, breathe and be adapted naturally to the felt pattern of gross existence in which you are apparently born. Be full and naturally adapted as whole body feeling to the prior current of the body-being. That current is felt as Presence and as motion and polarization toward the subtle in the form of the body-being. In the natural or lawful state, the descended or grossly manifest body-being is polarized from its base toward the head. The breathing infills the body-being with the current and pervasive quickening nectars of the Beloved, but the true, constant, and tacit sense of the whole body is one of polarization of life, breath, and body form toward the Light, the entry of the current in the midbrain and crown.

2.29

Random exhaled breaths (and also right participation in the current of life in sexual intimacy) may be felt to shoot the attention and flow of the current of manifestation up both the frontal and spinal lines of the body (from the sex organs and the spinal base), through the throat (mindless in heart-felt Ignorance), to the rear base of the head, then forward, through crown and forehead, curling into the midbrain. While the being rests in this polarization, the current operates in its natural form, released from the necessity of all arising (while not, in principle, in conflict with any arising). Thus, the Beloved, or the Real, felt-intuited as the prior current of the body-being, is revealed as sound and light, above mind and prior to all activity, subtle or gross. This deeper rest in the current begins when the gross body-being rests harmoniously in its relations, polarized toe to crown, on the basis of persistence in yielding, on the basis of whole-body Ignorance, to the Beloved in the intuited form of the prior current of all manifestation.

Truth, the Beloved, the Real, is our own Nature and Condition, with which we are perfectly re-identified in this happy and priorly enlightened Way. Ignorance is the key and is itself the perfect intuition of the eternal Reality. We are always already happy. Persisting thus, we are naturally re-adapted to the unspeakable Condition of the Real, prior to all conditions, and yet paradoxically and eternally standing forth as all conditions. When all unnecessary arising becomes obsolete by this devotional sacrifice, we stand eternally in the unqualified and presently indescribable Realm and Radiant Form of the Beloved, the Heart. Therefore, persist in the humor of this Revelation while conditions arise and do not presume, through forms of knowledge, the necessity and limitations of any arising, high or low. Thus, the stages of this Way of Ignorance will mature in your own case as radical intuition of the Real Condition, the Heart, the Truth of all arising. Such Intuition is at last unspeakable, mindless, bodiless, egoless, worldless, whether or not speech, thought, body, ego, or any worlds or conditions arise. A fool may presume such Realization to be his own, but the devotee, amazingly Ignorant, is only sacrifice, and forever.

2.29

THE SACRIFICE OF THE HEART

2.30 The Way of Divine Ignorance depends on devotional sacrifice, both in ordinary relations and toward the Divine Reality, even in the form of the Spiritual Master. Heart-felt love of the Divine, of which all conditions are the modification, alone will permit Grace to draw you into the unconditional Realm which is itself the Divine.

2.31 The true Spiritual Master is one who originates spontaneous and true Teaching in the company of others, and who generates and awakens devotees to the sacred occasion of Divine Communion, not merely through apparent silence or no-response, but through a literal Power in Silence that communicates itself as a realized influence that quickens insight and awakens intuitive contemplation. Such a Master then leads devotees toward the radical Realization of that same awakening, prior to any world, body, force of life, mind, transcendental experience, or ego-soul illusion.

2.32 The Divine Master does not, principally, give force or power below, but only attracts toward dissolution of the ego and radical ascent, or regeneration of unqualified Radiance. All that is done below, powerful or not, is an argument for response toward the principal attraction.

2.33 Literal, heart-felt surrender, true of the whole and undefined body-being, is the fundamental necessity of the whole Way of Divine Ignorance. Insofar as it is literal and heart-felt, it does not "happen" to us, but it is natural (and, in that sense, spontaneous), voluntary, and even intentional. However, it does not also become true by willful, subjective, or self-manipulative effort — a goal-oriented strategy in dilemma. It cannot become true by any sequence of changes. It only *is* true, or not, while at the same time literal. It is true on the basis of Ignorance, or unqualified intuition of the Real Condition of all conditions. Not any other fact or condition, effort or surmise makes our surrender true.

The Spiritual Master constantly serves a transcendental initiatory Function, prior to time and space, whereby true hearers of the Teaching are awakened to the Divine Presence and Real Condition of all conditions. Therefore, this same Function makes devotees, or those whose surrender is both literal and true, out of ordinary men and women. The perpetual Samadhi of the Spiritual Master is the Agent or Function of such awakening. Therefore, it is appropriate to contact such a one through true hearing and right preparation, so that we may be awakened to true Divine Communion in his Company and mature more and more perfectly in literal Realization of the Truth of the Real Divine Presence.

———≡O≡———

2.34   Truth or God is not a Condition to be realized by willful esoteric or super-scientific efforts. Such Happiness is truly and permanently realized only on the basis of the complete moral or sacrificial transformation of the apparently individual and human consciousness. It is not a matter of merely relaxing life or body and sending the attention elsewhere by exercises of esoteric meditation. It is a matter of the undermining of the whole principle of one's ordinary and extraordinary actions and forms of knowledge.

Few are willing to endure such a process. Therefore, illusory and consoling ways have been created by compassionate, clever, and deluded men. But the scheme of all the universes, mortal and immortal, high and low, with its endless times of birth and death, and its numberless kinds of learning, is itself the way and the destiny of all ordinary and extraordinary men. Only those who weary of the usual way become willing to engage the Divine Process, in which their very life-consciousness is sacrificed in its own Condition and Nature. All others, high and low, are devoted to their own unending path, from which there is no perfect relief, except on the day all worlds, ages, and heavens dissolve in the sleep of God.

———≡O≡———

2.35   See me when possible. I am the Heart. I am the Whole Body. What I have written is also my own discipline. Realize and practice it in your own private play. I do the same. Through Ignorance, remain active in the Paradox of incarnation, but presume no necessary destiny but Light or Blissful Radiance itself.

This is the whole Teaching, as much as it may be spoken or written and still be true. It is sufficient. The essential consideration is that you do not know what anything *is*. Persistence in that Ignorance Enlightens the whole body and transforms the world into Sacred Occasion.

The Way of Truth is the Way of the Perfect Awakening of the Conscious Man. And the true Destiny of the living human being is in conscious and literal expansion, ascent, and translation from this conditional, passing world of our waking, dreaming, and sleeping experience into the Imperishable, Graceful, Unimaginable Realm that is itself the Divine Reality. However, the Principle of such expansion and ascent is not any strategy of ascension itself, but it is dissolution of the separate soul or ego, on the basis of which there is natural, spontaneous, effortless, and literal translation into the God-Realm, in meditation, in the midst of ordinary life, and after death.

The Ways of Yogis and Saints exploit the possibility of the conventional ascension of the purified soul, or the benign ego. Such Ways are efforts in dilemma, which involve the being in concerns for purification and ascent via a transformation of human craving, from present and grosser objects toward future and subtler objects. But there is no free, true, direct, and final ascent except the separate and separative ego principle or soul, which is rooted in the heart, be not merely purified but utterly dissolved.

The Way of conventional Sages is to bypass

all concerned efforts toward purification and ascent and turn the being into the consideration of the root of conscious awareness. On this basis, the separate soul illusion is undone in the Ground of Conscious Being, the true Heart. But such a Way is worked on the basis of a discriminative revulsion toward both the unnecessary and the necessary emanation or expansive effulgence of the Heart. Thus, its Principle tends to undermine the ultimate Destiny of the Awakened Expansion and Translation of Man.

The Way of Divine Ignorance or Radical Intuition, which I am disposed to proclaim and teach, is the Way of Truth and its Destiny. It is the Way of devotional sacrifice and conscious illumination, founded in that Ignorance which is both the Heart and Glorious Body of the Divine Reality in which we are now and suddenly appearing to one another. Through the conscious process of radical understanding, the separate and separative ego or soul-principle is undermined and dissolved in the true Heart, which is Unqualified Conscious Radiance. When this dissolution is stabilized in natural re-cognition of all arising as modification-only, there is spontaneous expansion and ascent, which is regeneration of the Living and Unqualified Being. Such is

Sahaj Samadhi, the Regeneration of Amrita Nadi, and the true devotee's meditation (absorption in the Divine Form).

The Way of Yogis and Saints is the Way of Sushumna Nadi, or presumptive ascent of the purified ego-soul through the conditional realms toward the Highest. Such a Way is generated in dilemma through concentrated remedial efforts. The conventional Way of Sages is the Way of exclusive descent into the Heart, or ego death through descent in Amrita Nadi (the secret pathway between the sahasrar and the heart region). The Way of Divine Ignorance, or Radical Understanding, is the Way of non-strategic dissolution of the ego-soul in the Heart and simultaneous regeneration, or expansion and ascent, in, as, and through Amrita Nadi, whose upper terminal is not truly the sahasrar (subtle crown of the gross body) but the Unspeakable Condition and Radiance of the Highest, wherein all worlds arise and fall. (The Expansion of the Heart is without qualification, Radiant in all directions to Infinity, losing its center by including all objects, and losing its boundaries by penetration of all contraction. The Fullness of this Process is also experientially communicated in the upper, or subtle, and lower, or gross, dimensions of the whole body—first to the subtlest, and descending simultaneously to the lowest.)

Persistence in the natural Condition of Sahaj Samadhi (or radical intuition) in the maturity of this Way of Divine Ignorance is the natural, effortless, spontaneous, and true Principle wherein the true and liberated Destiny of every man or woman, even mankind, and every living world is Realized in literal and direct Translation into the Form of God, even while alive, and after death. (In Bhava Samadhi, the Heart and the Light are realized as One, Real God, without references, up or down, inside or outside, to any realm or appearance.)

To be human and yet to consider, speak, and adapt to this Way is a Grace that reduces all ordinary fulfillments to the level of pain, delusion, and unrelieved suffering. It is my hope and the argument that is my whole life that you will choose to adapt to this Way and renounce all ordinary efforts and fulfillments, high or low, based in the reactive craving and delusions of this born-experience. Become this Sacrifice with me and rise from this death into the Condition of the Heaven-Born. So be it.

Bubba Free John

3

THE GREAT PATH OF RETURN VS. THE RADICAL PATH OF UNDERSTANDING

The reader should appreciate Bubba's use of the term "Radical Understanding" as the synonym of "Divine Ignorance." This essay, somewhat revised here, was written in early 1975, before Bubba began to summarize his Teaching via the term "Divine Ignorance." "Radical Understanding" is "Ignorance." In the understanding of our false and self-limiting activity we do not become great knowers, but are released in our natural, Radiant, unknowing Condition, the Heart of Existence, prior to but not necessarily exclusive of subject and object, self and other.

INTRODUCTION:
THE TRADITIONAL ERROR

The capital realization of the usual man and thus the most universal communication of mankind is the primitive sense of dilemma. The history of human adventure is entirely dependent upon this realization. Each generation serves the next by its attempts to deal with this contradiction in the core of life, but, for the most part, what is delivered through time is the dilemma itself.

Every culture is, fundamentally, a structure of problems and solutions built upon this felt dilemma. And each new life is, by this education, compelled to become a gesture in error, a reaction to this realized dilemma. Therefore, each individual assumes that the appropriate way to deal with this primitive sense of dilemma is in fact to deal with it, to re-act to it, by analyzing it and identifying it with a specific or known problem, and then attempting to solve it by a strategic search toward a Goal, whose principal content is release.

This cultural strategy, to which we are bound by every kind of archetype and indoctrination, is perhaps best exemplified by the great traditions of religious and spiritual life. The esoteric quest of mankind is still, even in this age of mortalistic technology, the principal image of human adventure. It has been a grand experiment, carried on in many independent laboratories, each operating upon a specialized fragment of the whole, but all somehow pointing toward a common result. But even though a common result may be analyzed from the data of the esoteric traditions, each in fact assumed the problem (the working "face" of the dilemma) in a unique form, and each realized a Goal associated with unique phenomena. The Goals themselves have, therefore, not been the same, as will become clear in this article. They are like so many different kinds of infinity. There is no universal religion in fact. But the described Goals of the various traditions, if taken to be the principal data of their quest, may be gathered together and found, by analysis, to point beyond themselves toward a single Solution which transcends every quest and its Goal. We may name this Solution with a generic term, such as God, Reality, Self, or Truth.

But even if we accept this analysis, we have as yet only fulfilled the ancient formula of culture. We have only described (and, of course, not yet realized) a Solution to the felt dilemma of life. Names such as God, Reality, Self, and Truth are hopeful at best. Their meaning is release, and, therefore, they reflect our primitive sense of dilemma.

In fact, we cannot be released from the dilemma at the core of life by any strategy of reaction to the dilemma itself. The search and its solution are only escape from the conceived problem and its felt dilemma. The appropriate wisdom of man is not controversy or any program of reaction, but only investigation of the felt dilemma itself. If we do not submit to this radical way of wisdom, we will remain bound to the ancient strategic way, and stand always bewildered by the God-idea, the Reality-idea, the Self-idea, the Truth-idea, or the world-idea. Such ideas are only bits of language or mind that distract us from the contemplation of the dilemma to which we are always bound. And if we contemplate them, we begin to assume God, Reality, Self, Truth, or the world in itself to be a some-Thing. And, if It is a some-Thing, It must be some-Where. Thus, the various traditions of culture characteristically assume God, Reality, Self, or Truth to be either "in" the world, identical to the "world," or on the "other side" of the world. By virtue of this traditional analysis the strategy to which we become culturally bound becomes associated with an adventure in or through time and space leading toward a Goal that is both Specific and Absolute. The esoteric and ordinary games of life we create on the basis of all this seem a serious and justifiable affair to most men. The tales of culture by which we animate our hopes are so many shrines to the Accomplishments of heroic seekers. But in fact it is all a bit of nonsense, built as the result of a strategic error, founded upon a dilemma that remains below consciousness, un-illumined by all of that.

This article will describe the structure of the eso-teric path as it has been collectively revealed by the experiments of all cultures. It will be shown how this path is tied to a space-time image of the journey and the Goal, and how the greatest Practitioners have declared God, Reality, Self, or Truth (to which they assigned no Object value) to be absolute and therefore necessarily prior to any such journey, any such Solu-tion. The report of these great individuals is an indica-tion within the traditions themselves that the "path" of life is not properly a strategic search toward any

Goal, nor is it to be equated with any experiential journey, high or low.

The radical path of understanding, which Bubba Free John is here to teach, represents the communication of that Way of life which involves no reaction to the felt dilemma in life, and no attainment over against or, properly, even within life (as opposed to being identical to or not other than life itself). Rather, it involves radical understanding of the motivating dilemma itself. The motivation of mankind is the key to all our archetypal searches and their Solutions. The Solutions do not exist in themselves.

THE GREAT PATH OF RETURN
VS. THE RADICAL PATH
OF UNDERSTANDING

There are three manifest dimensions: gross, subtle, and causal. And there are three traditional ways of practice toward release, each involved in manipulation and experiences in one of the three dimensions. These are the gross path (the way of yogis), the subtle path (the way of saints), and the causal path (the way of sages). Each path, being a portion of the whole or great path, pursues a specific and absolute Goal, via a method of regression or return, toward the Condition which pertains at the original or terminal position of the dimension it assumes.

The practitioners of the gross path take their stand in the gross physical condition and seek the Goal by activity there. In general, they seek either a religious and magical harmony in the gross condition or else ascent to the subtle. Kundalini yoga is perhaps the most effective and also easiest (if worked through the extraordinary agency of an accomplished yogi) of the ascending methods developed in this path, and achieves entrance into the subtle dimensions by exploitation and manipulation of the life-current as vital force (prana), or the finer elements of gross or lower life. The gross path of ascent involves manipulation of all the faculties below the brows, and seeks entrance to the subtle dimension, which begins at the place between and behind the brows (midbrain).

The subtle path, exemplified by traditions such as shabd yoga (or nada yoga),[1] bypasses all involvement with gross or lower energy manipulation, including the kundalini, and begins with concentration on the life-current as internal sound and light at the door of the subtle dimension behind the brows (ajna chakra[2]), thus controlling and absorbing the mind. Since the Goal of such approaches is escape to cognition above the gross level, their methods need not magically improve the karmas below, and so they merely step aside from yogic attention to the gross aspect of the Play. But the traditions of the subtle path, like the kundalini and other examples of the gross path, pursue the Goal by entering the subtle realms. The real

1. The literatures of shabd yoga tend to represent a religious and hierarchical cosmic description of spiritual method and experience, whereas the literatures of nada yoga (as in the final portions of *Hatha Yoga Pradipika*) tend to be more philosophical and directed toward the specific psycho-physiology of the yogi-practitioner. Thus, the language of shabd yoga often appeals to the impulse toward righteous conversion and universal or collective salvation, whereas the language of nada yoga is most often conservative and individualistic, representing more the hermit's liberation in subjective privacy.

2. The ajna chakra is the subtle yogic center between and behind the eyebrows. It is the door in the human mechanism between what is below and gross, and what is above and subtle.

business of both paths begins at the ajna center (between and behind the brows), evoking the vision of bindu,[3] or nil chakra ("blue pearl"), or other versions of the door of manifest light, the epitome of the subtle mind, and awakening a visionary confrontation with the subtle form of the Guru in that same light, who then appears to lead the individual or soul (subtle being) on to the display of subtle energy above the lower-reflecting activity of the mind. This is the adventure of the super-conscious (higher mind) Play in the subtle dimension.

The yogis of the gross path, who pass up to the subtle realm via the esoteric ladder of energy formed by the finer elements of the gross physical being, also perceive various marvels of appearance. They may see visions of lights and forms, hear curious sounds, and enjoy inner versions of experiences that have counterparts in all the externally directed senses and functions. This is the revelation of the finer aspects of the gross dimension, and all these experiences together amount to a description of psycho-physical life below the subtle realm. That description appears in the form of an ascending order, from the most solid, or lowest in vibration, to the most subtle, or highest in vibration. The qualities of the functional dimensions of gross consciousness may appear in the form of lights or light-forms, in various colors, corresponding to the hierarchy of subjective or internal functions apparent in the gross sphere. Such yogis prize above all the appearance of light that corresponds to their passage

3. Bindu is a subtle center or visionary point, such as the "blue pearl."

from the gross sphere into the subtle sphere (not just the finer side of the gross sphere, but the subtle or higher energy world in itself, which belongs to a totally different dimension of appearance and activity than the universes in the gross-physical sphere). This light (a spot, grid, flame, or chakra) corresponds to the higher-reflecting function of mind, which is turned to the subtle rather than the gross sphere via the sahasrar.[4] This seed or door of the subtle realm appears behind and above the gross physical eyes. Some practitioners say that to pierce or transcend this door is the way toward the Self. The lesser ones claim that it is the only way to reach the Self, or that it is itself the highest realization of Truth.

Saints, or yogis on the subtle path, also speak of appearances of light, since the subtle world is a world of energy or pervasive vibrations, and their composite report corresponds to a description of the subtle world as a whole. Their visionary course *begins* with such phenomena as the blue bindu, or nil chakra, and the appearance of the Guru within. This vision appears behind and above the eyes, and so they do not report the various revelations (specific lights and experiences) corresponding to the gross realm below the brows, which are the content of kundalini yoga and the mysticisms of the gross psycho-physical world. Their report is, however, full of experiences and realms and lights, but the order they describe is that of the subtle dimension in itself. And the special characteristic of the descriptions of their ascent is the assignation of spe-

4. The sahasrar is the highest chakra and terminal goal of the yogi. It is associated with the crown of the head, the upper brain and higher mind.

cific types of sound and vision to each step of the way. The subtle path travels on the life-current as audible light, whereas the gross path travels on the life-current as the lower or grosser forms of life-energy or vibratory bliss itself. The kundalini is *felt,* and leads toward subtle visions (light), whereas the subtle path relies on the power of subtle hearing and sight to return to the manifesting or Creator Source of sound and light.

Each of the three traditional paths is generally described in terms of three divisions, including a lower, a middle, and a higher plane of manifestation or realization. Each of the three divisions in each dimension (gross, subtle, or causal) corresponds, in kind, to an expression at that level of each of the three great dimensions themselves. Thus, the mystical experiences of yogis of the gross path have been described relative to three degrees of intensity (low, middle, and high), or planes of vision (red, white, and black lights), and so forth. Just so, the yogis or saints of the subtle path describe three divisions or types of manifest and manifesting sound (Anahad Shabd, Sar Shabd, and Sat Shabd). Each class of sound (each of which may contain many specific sounds) is heard in a specific region of the subtle dimension, and by passing from one to the next the practitioner ascends through the subtle appearances or worlds of light.

The lowest form of sound described in the subtle path is Anahad Shabd, which is heard within after concentration at the ajna door, the subtle yogic center between and behind the eyes, at the midbrain. By concentration upon it one passes up to the region of the sahasrar (considered the ultimate region by yogis of the gross path, but declared to be only the first of eight by the yogis of the subtle path). Anahad Shabd is the "gross" or lowest version of the three divisions of manifest and manifesting sound, and it may be heard while retaining bodily consciousness.

After successful passage into the first subtle region (sahasrar, or Sahansdal Kanwal) one contacts the second or middle version of sound, called Sar Shabd (meaning essence of sound, hence its relation to the subtle dimension). This level of sound, as well as those above it, and the regions they represent in the subtle dimension, is generally, at least in the beginning, heard and seen when there is at least temporary abandonment or diffusion of body-consciousness. By means of concentration upon Sar Shabd, there is passage through Triloka, the world-sphere of Brahma, the Archetype and Controller of the gross region, which is the region of the three gunas (tamas — inertia, rajas — activity, sattwa — harmony), or the qualities of the cosmic play in the lower planes. Beyond Brahma and his world the third or highest version of manifest and manifesting sound is heard. This is Sat Shabd (meaning true or source sound, hence its relation to the causal dimension).[5]

Just as each path speaks of three manifest and man-

5. The tradition of shabd yoga and the esotericisms of saints is made up of a number of schools or Ashrams, each associated with a different line of teachers. Thus, there are variations in the descriptions, application of terms, and so forth. The present essay contains only a sketch of the scheme of saints, and it makes use of terminology as applied by Huzur Maharaj Sawan Singh Ji and Kirpal Singh, since these are perhaps most commonly known. The texts of Soami Ji Maharaj and Huzur Maharaj are senior in line to these and should also be consulted for a comprehension in depth of the technical viewpoint of saints in the subtle path of shabd yoga.

ifesting divisions (low, middle, and highest), each also speaks of a fourth or transcendent division or realization, which corresponds to the Goal. In the gross path we hear reports of the piercing of the "blue bindu" and subsequent merging of the attention or ego-soul in the Source above, coincident with the sahasrar itself, the incident wherein life is absorbed in Light. In the subtle path we hear of a fourth or transcendent Sound, upon which the three general divisions depend. This is Nij Shabd (Original Sound), which comes from Sat Lok or Sach Khand, the True or Imperishable Region (the fifth in a scale of eight).[6]

The shabd yogis describe three regions above the fifth, but they are named with names such as "Indescribable," or "Invisible," "Inaccessible," and "Supreme," beyond dissolution, beyond hearing or seeing. These are not really descriptions at all, but pointers toward the Goal, which is beyond description. The subtle path is realized as regions of Brightness upon Brightness, until no adjectives are useful. It is at the point of its description of the Goal relative to the subtle dimension, with its planes of light and sound, leading to Light beyond Light and Sound beyond Sound, that the subtle path begins, like the highest realization of the gross path, to point to Truth

6. Although the esoteric descriptions of the subtle path speak of regions above the sahasrar or crown center, these essentially refer to subtle perceptions associated with various regions of the brain (just as the esoteric descriptions of the gross path refer to subtle perceptions associated with various regions of the body below the brain and culminating in the brain). The hierarchical display of subtle planes is experienced as the perceptions of mind become less and less oriented to gross and lesser subtle conditions of subject-object knowledge or experiential limitation.

or Reality as that which utterly transcends the dimension or the presumption in which the practice has been performed and realized.

The lesser practitioners of the subtle path tend to confuse the Ultimate Event or Goal with the experiential phenomena acquired by their own method. Thus, they claim the Goal may not be attained unless one passes through the phenomena of the subtle dimension, even as the yogis of the gross path tend to claim the Goal is not attained unless there is passage through the inner phenomena of the gross dimension. However, it is true that the Ultimate Goal of the way of return has at times been attained by great yogis of the gross path, just as it has been attained by great saints of the subtle path. And these great individuals declare in common that the Goal is of a transcendent, absolute, and unqualified Nature (and it is, therefore, by implication, not identical to the way or path they followed, nor to the phenomena they passed on the way).

The causal path, exemplified by the tradition of jnana yoga, sees no more reason to begin in the subtle dimension than the tradition of shabd or nada yoga sees reason to begin in the gross dimension. The practitioners of jnana yoga bypass the subtle dimension as well as the gross dimension, and apply themselves to the causal dimension, the dimension of manifest consciousness without subtle or gross appearances. Jnana yoga proceeds by a penetrating enquiry into the nature of one's conscious existence, and thus involves neither manipulation of gross or subtle energies, nor manipulation of the mind corresponding to each of those two dimensions, but only investigation of the causal field of simple consciousness in its first modification (prior to the subtle and gross appearances), which is the separate self sense, the ego-I.

Just as the gross and subtle paths describe three manifest and manifesting divisions within the planes of their operating dimension, and a fourth which transcends it, so also do the practitioners of the causal path. Thus, the yogis of the causal path describe three stages: preparation (essentially, hearing the Teaching as it is communicated by one who has realized its Goal), practice (especially the basic meditative practice, such as vichara, or enquiry into the Nature of the limited self), and stabilization or stable contemplation. These stages represent a lower, a middle, and a highest degree of practice itself. But a transcendent degree is also described. It is the attainment of the Goal, Self-realization, Knowledge of one's Nature and Condition (and, therefore, that also of the world, God, and all activities or powers).[7]

7. Most yogis, saints, and sages refer to a fourth or transcendental Condition, distinct from the gross, the subtle, and the causal. This Condition is called by such names as "Supra-causal," "Sat Lok," "Turiya," and the like. Bubba Free John regards such specific "Conditions" or "States" of experience to be themselves versions of subtle and causal conditions, albeit transcendental relative to the usual conditions of gross life. The Real Condition is not a fourth, but the Truth of the three. It is a Paradox, not a separable or exclusive Condition. It is the prior Reality, and therefore (as in Bhava Samadhi) need not include the noticed appearance of any conditions (gross, subtle, or causal), but it may not itself be located distinct from and relative to any such conditions as long as they appear. All conditions that appear relative to any or all other conditions are themselves versions of gross (elemental-etheric), subtle (mental-intuitional), and causal (egoic-primal) expressions in manifestation. When Bubba speaks of a fourth or transcendental Condition, either he is speaking of the exclusive realization of the Real (which is an illusion, yet to be undone) or he is using a conventional reference to Truth, while meaning it in the Paradoxical or Humorous sense. If this Paradoxical sense of the disposition of the Real Condition is assumed,

Just as the yogis of the gross path seek to pass up through the form of the lower life (through the spinal line) to enter the subtle dimensions, and just as they with the practitioners of the subtle path seek to pass upwards from the brows (the kundalini yogis stop at the sahasrar or subtle glory, wherein the vital principle is consumed, while the subtle and shabd or nada yogis seek to pass beyond it, via the subtle principles of sound and light, to even higher regions of the subtle dimension), the jnanis[8] and others in the causal path pass directly toward the heart (that intuition whose psycho-physical center is felt on the right side of the chest). The Heart (Self-realization, the intuition of Real-God) is the Source of the causal dimension (the seed of all worlds). It is even the Source of gross life, the mind, and the limited self. It is the Source of the gross and subtle dimensions as well, and thus it is also the Ultimate Source, the final or true Goal of even the subtle and gross paths. Indeed, the sounds to which the subtle yogis listen and the internal life energies by which the gross yogis are raised both have their Origin and Prior Condition in the causal region of the heart. And every form or appearance, every feeling or perception, every thought, every vision, everything heard within, above, or beyond appears first in the heart (the causal consciousness, prior to energy and form) in seed form and then is

---

then Sahaj Samadhi may be said to be the Fourth or Turiya State, and Bhava Samadhi is, then, Turiyatita (beyond the Fourth).

8. Those whose path is knowledge of the true Nature and Condition of the worlds through the dissolution of the ego-soul principle. Classical Vedantic and Buddhist sages are examples of jnanis.

cognized by reflection in the various planes of modifying light above. Just so, the Light of the subtle dimension and the Life of the gross dimension both begin in the great causal dimension itself, whose psychophysical sign is on the right side of the chest, just off the median. It is by merging in the Source of the causal processes that the jnanis realize the Heart, which is their Goal. However, the common practitioners of the subtle and gross paths envision their Goal in terms of the ascended and subtle Life in Light, and do not consciously continue beyond the subtle dimension of energy to the causal dimension of manifest consciousness (prior to form, energy, and mind) in order to fall in the true Heart, the Self, the intuition of Real-God. And the general traditions of spiritual practice in the gross and subtle paths do not carry a stream of teaching which acknowledges the Heart, the causal path, and the primacy of that Realization.

Only the most extraordinary individuals, who otherwise traveled a path leading into the subtle realms, claimed the Goal to be utterly beyond and thus independent of the way of their own experience. As testimony to the rightness of the explicit or implicit claims of these great individuals, whom we may call Siddhas,[9] Godmen, the Heaven-Born (to distinguish them from the lesser individuals who traveled the same path but had no such radical comprehension of the Goal), the practitioners of the causal path have attained the transcendent Goal of all the Godmen by a process that bypasses all the phenomena experienced

9. A "Completed" or fully realized One, who lives in and as the very Divine. One in whom radical understanding is perfect and who communicates That to others.

in the gross and subtle paths. They attained the Goal of the three "paths of return" (which together form a single or great path) by intuitive penetration of the Nature of the subject-consciousness, independent of its subtle and gross extensions. This is the way of sages, and those who have been Siddhas or Godmen in that line have also claimed the radical and transcendent Nature of the Goal to be independent of the phenomena of their path, while, at the same time, they declared their path to be the most direct, assuming one had the intuitive capacity and intelligence for it.

If we consider the gathered evidence of all three traditional ways of practice, we may see that the "great path of return" by which all traditional paths go to their Goal does not terminate above, in the sahasrar or in the subtle planes, but in the Heart, prior Consciousness, the Source or prior Condition of Light, of Sound, of the current of the being. That "great path" (when viewed in reverse, as a way of return to Source, rather than manifestation from Source) begins at the most descended terminal of the descending-ascending cycle of the life-current (the life center, the true navel, at the base of the body, above the perineum) and passes up the spinal line by manipulation of body (elemental), vitality (etheric), emotional psyche, intellect, and intuition to the ajna door, then to the sahasrar (the Goal of gross yogis), then through (or via and within) the sahasrar, through ever subtler planes of experience, to the vision of God-Light (the reflected or subtle Source-Light, the Goal of subtle yogis), and then passes down, reducing the forms of cognition to their rudiments as modifica-

tions of consciousness itself rather than of the energies or forms witnessed by consciousness, to the heart
(on the right side of the chest, the Goal of causal yogis),
where the Self, the intuition of Real-God, the Heart, is
realized as Absolute Consciousness, exclusive of
identification and even association with the causal,
subtle, and gross appearances. (The jnani or jivan
mukta[10] remains either oblivious to or unaffected by
all three manifest planes of appearance while alive,
and is traditionally assumed to be released even from
their arising in the death process.)

It is clear that the way of the jnanis (and the more
radical buddhas) is the most direct, since its conscious
Goal is the Goal acknowledged by all the Siddhas,
whereas the gross and subtle paths tend to identify
themselves with a conscious, problematic, and necessarily egoic effort whose Goal is either in the subtle
dimension or in its direction. In practice, the causal
path is thus the least subject to gross and subtle illusion, particularly if assisted by the Grace of a Master,
but it may also be the most difficult, since it involves
abandonment of the consolations of gross and subtle
manifestation.

The way of radical understanding is founded in
that same Truth or Reality claimed to be the Goal by
all Siddhas of the "great path of return." However,
it makes two prominent assertions that distinguish it
from the traditions. The first is in the manner of
approach. The way of radical understanding does
not assume the reactive principle of the search in

10. One who is "liberated while alive."

dilemma, and thus dissociates itself from the progressive *strategy* of each of the three ways of return. Therefore, Truth or Reality becomes not the Goal but the very Principle of life. This is the second most prominent characteristic of the way of radical understanding. From the radical point of view of the man of understanding, the ancient enterprises of the great path of return to Truth are merely sophisticated forms of the karmic and reactive life of mankind. The path of return is an archetypal compulsion to which we are necessarily bound (and which is therefore necessarily and spontaneously duplicated, but also undone, in the way of radical understanding), as surely as we are to confusion, fear, and disease, unless there is radical understanding in our own case.

The way of radical understanding, which I am here to demonstrate and Teach, is founded in awareness of all the possibilities, and their limitations, discovered in the experiments of the traditions. It agrees with the principal evidence of the jnanis, or sages, but sees that their way is, commonly, a search generated from the same sense of dilemma which motivates the searches of yogis of the gross path and saints or yogis of the subtle path. And it also sees that the realization of the Heart awakened when it is pursued as a Goal is an exclusive realization, just as the realizations of gross and subtle yogis are exclusive, except that the realization of the jnani excludes both the subtle and gross dimensions, whereas the others only exclude the gross and, rather than pass through the causal path to the Heart, rest in the subtle vision of Light or Absolute Effulgence (in the case of kundalini yoga) or in mergence in the most subtle Principle or Source of energy, vibration, or sound (in the case of shabd or nada yoga). Therefore, the way of radical understanding involves no search for the Heart as Goal, no reductive, ascetic, world-denying strategy of return, and thus no exclusive or conditional realization.

The transcendent or unmanifest Dimension is not a thing in itself, over against all manifest things, but it is realization of the manifest dimensions in Truth. The man of understanding[11] realizes all the manifest functional or conventional dimensions to be not other than the Heart, and thus he may retain all his dimensional "bodies," or planes of manifest being, in the Play of Conscious Light that is Life. However, he is merely Present, not by definition one who enjoys siddhi or power in any of the manifest dimensions (although he may, for karmic or creative reasons, enjoy or manifest forms of siddhi). But in the mere Presence of the man of understanding not only is the Heart communicated, but every kind of transformation, at every dimensional level, tends to appear, without his intention or concern. This is the spontaneous Maha-Siddhi, the Divine Grace. Whatever the effects that surround him, however, it is the communication of the Heart via the radical way of understanding that is his principal quality and influence.

All of this is generated in him not by seeking via any of the traditional paths (gross, subtle, or causal), but by understanding the felt dilemma that is funda-

11. Bubba Free John uses the term "the man of understanding" to refer to his own characteristic point of view and function in the worlds. By implication, at least certain qualities of the man of understanding are characteristic of all who live as devotees in the radical way of understanding.

mental to his own life and which is the common principle that motivates all paths, all the ways of return. Thus, the way of radical understanding involves immediate and spontaneous intuition of the Heart, Absolute-Real-God, the Source, Self, Nature, and Condition of all beings, of all dimensions. The way of radical understanding thus effectively bypasses even the causal path. The man of understanding does not *turn* to the Heart, but instantly and from the beginning stands Present *as* the Heart, without strategically excluding or binding any dimension of his being or of the arising worlds.

In the literature of Vision Mound Ceremony, this non-exclusive realization of the Heart is described as the "regeneration of Amrita Nadi"[12] (and thus, also, of the descending and ascending circle of subtle and gross life, which is generated via the causal dimension from the prior or Absolute Light that is the Heart, or Very Consciousness itself). This experiential metaphor indicates the non-exclusive nature of radical understanding. Just as the Heart is both prior to and not other than the dimensions of manifest existence, its radical realization does not strategically exclude the manifest dimensions for the man of understanding, either during his life or after his death. He does not require or necessarily look forward to the cessation of the Play of the worlds. For him, the Play is not other than the Heart, and it does not

12. Amrita Nadi is the intuited structure of manifest existence, which is the structure of Consciousness, of human existence, of conscious meditation. The Transcendent Form, intuited as Divine Reality, expanding and rising out of the Heart or very Self into and as the most prior God-Light or infinite Radiance.

ultimately affect him. His position is the paradoxical one of Divine Humor.

Thus, the man of understanding remains merely Present as the Heart, but he is always apparently entering the planes of the Play of manifestation, via that same mechanism the traditions exploit as the "great path of return." He does not by definition (although he may in fact) intentionally and presently enter the world through extraordinary experiences in the causal, subtle, and gross mechanisms above or behind the ordinary plane of gross psycho-physical life. Nor does he by definition manifest the siddhis, or powers, of those dimensions in his life. He does not necessarily enter and appear through the causal, subtle, and gross processes the way water enters a bathtub through a pipe. Rather, he appears instantly, immediately, like an apple on a limb, as a spontaneous Presence in the world, and this implies his existence in all three planes of manifestation (just as the apple implies the process of its appearance, while the apple itself did not pass up the tree trunk from the root). His conscious position, however, is that of the Heart, not other than the worlds (the worlds as Truth), and he does not, by definition, have any special interest in or extraordinary experience of gross, subtle, and causal realms in themselves, except as they appear in the ordinary or conventional terms of waking, dreaming, and sleeping. (More "ascended" or subtler qualities of these dimensions may appear at random in his experience or in his unintentional or spontaneous effect on others, but these are not necessary or characteristic of him by definition.)

Since he stands Present by including all dimensions of his own conventional and functional being, he may speak of the Light as above (meaning the reflected and creative Light of the Heart, the God-Light or Mind as it appears at the head of the subtle dimension above), or of the Heart as within and on the right, or of the Fullness or Life as descending and ascending between the subtle Light and the gross Form. But all of these are only paradoxical functional references, expressions of his ordinary and conventional existence. In Truth, he does not even cognize the Heart. It is not object to him. He *is* the Heart. He simply is the Heart, and he does not assign a space or place or event to That. He sees he is not other than all that arises. He sees he is, in Truth, the very worlds. His speech and action are all paradoxes, humor, play, methods of confounding those who live with him into that intelligent crisis or dissolution of self in which the true Heart is known in Truth.

What is dissolved in the way of radical understanding, the way of dissolution rather than of experiential or progressive return, is not "a self" (a static, object, entity), nor is "a Self" or "the Self" acquired, attained, realized, or intuited. Rather, what is dissolved is a *process*. The "ego" is not an object or an entity, but an *activity*. It is fixed reflexive contraction, or the complex avoidance of relationship, at the gross, subtle, and causal levels. And what is intuitively realized (the Heart, the Self) may not in itself be described as an object, entity, static, or process. Indeed, it cannot be described at all, except it may seem to be pointed to by implication as the self-limiting process dissolves in radical understanding. (The psycho-physical sign of the Heart, felt via the life-current passing up and down to the right side of the heart, is just such a pointer, and it is not the Heart in itself.) The Enjoyment declared by the man of understanding and by all the true Godmen is Happiness, without cause, reason, description, form, force, quality, event, condition, name, or any other designation. It is the only Happiness. Everything else, everything that appears in itself, as some "thing," is a condition of the process of limitation, the world in itself. But where there is radical understanding or Perfect Intuition the Truth is Realized, apart from the conventional self-idea, Self-idea, God-idea, world-idea, or any other limiting or un-limiting principle, problem, or dilemma. Then the arising worlds may be lived, which is to accept the discipline and condition of all manifestation, high and low, as forms or true theatre of the Discipline and Condition that is Truth. Then any present world may be seen to be not merely the dilemma of limitation, but Happiness, implying no-thing (or Thing). Thus, radical understanding becomes the prior Principle of life.

Because of the phenomenon of "targeting," the functional effect or integrating process of all perception, a self is implied within. In the process of ordinary perception, the perception itself is reflected "within," as a felt phenomenon within the psycho-physical organism. Thus, sounds heard from without seem to be heard within, in the middle of the head. The effects of the targeting of all perceptions, including the total sensation of the body, as well as memory, thought, and other psychic reflections, is to produce a sense of "the perceiver" as an entity within. Those who become sensitive to their own dilemma in life may therefore react by a search within, in an effort to undo the self via various forms of the "great path of return." But there is no such self. There is only the conventional belief that there is such a one, founded in the implications of experiential targeting.

Just so, the search for the undoing of "the self" may be directed toward absorption, union, or dissolution in "the Self," or "God," or "Reality," etc., within, away, above, and beyond. But this notion of the Great Entity is only an extension of the same error, based in the same functional implications, that produces the sense of objective self within. Only when the apparent individual falls through the motivating dilemma itself, and so comprehends his own imagery, does he see there is no self in itself and no Self or God in Itself, but only a Great Process.

There is no self, even while the Great Process continues. This is the opposite of the traditional view of the "great path of return," that ego-dissolution is the undoing of some "thing," and/or that, with dissolution of the illusion of self, there must necessarily come separation from the world or some change of the world itself. In fact, this realization or understanding involves no necessary *change* at all, in any dimension, but only realization of the actual, prior, and present Condition that always already pertains.

Just so, the realization itself involves no necessary change in one's apparent condition. Nor is it realization of some Object or Goal that is "the Self," "God,"

"Reality," or "Truth," exclusive of the world or knowable in itself. The realization that is radical understanding is Dissolution in the Nature and Condition of the world itself, including oneself. Thus, it is not realization of something other than the world, or some Thing that is an absolute alternative to one's self. Therefore, no new and transcendent "Entity" acquires the attention or place of the "dissolved self." There was no such one, and there is no such one, except as a convention of the functional world. There is simply Intuition of the Real Condition, which cannot itself be identified with any change of state (or State), any alternative within, away, above, or beyond the world. It is simply Happiness. There is no Self, or self, or God, or world other than the World, the Total and Present Process. One who enjoys such Realization (radical intuition) moment to moment is only happy, free of the search, of fundamental dilemma, of the impositions of vital contraction upon the intuitive force of consciousness, and of the glamour of all phenomena, high or low. This Enjoyment is the Principle of life, not its Goal. One who is thus Happiness itself has not necessarily acquired any experiential knowledge or powers in any of the possible planes of the world-process (high or low). He is not a conventional yogi, saint, or sage. He is only alive in Truth. What he does or learns apart from this Realization is simply the apparent adventure he experiences within the Play, which may or may not, at any moment, involve powers of soul (the subtle being in its association with the gross planes), spiritual powers (powers of the subtle being in the subtle dimension itself), extraordinary experiences, ordinary pleasures or pains, etc. Radical understanding is not identical to any phenomenon in the Play, nor is any phenomenon its prerequisite, nor does it depend on any for its continuation. It is simply the free realization of Radical, Transcendent Wisdom, or Happiness. It has nothing to do with time and space, the arrangement of some destiny above, after death, or in the present life that appears in the gross dimension. It is prior to all karmas, all actions, all events. It has nothing in itself to do with behavior. One who enjoys as such Wisdom has realized the fundamental Principle of all worlds, and thus all changes of behavior, action, or state follow from this Realization as creative and Lawful play, but the Realization itself is not bound to or by any of the models of ideal or acceptable behavior invented in the searches of men.

This way of radical understanding involves no degrading and no obliteration of the person. He is a functional convention, part of the humor of the arising worlds. It is only the strategy of seeking in dilemma, of which the self-idea is an indelible element, that must be undone in understanding. If that is realized in conscious understanding, the conventional person may remain, just as the Play in all its modifications may continue.

And the affair of understanding, by which the separative and apparently ego-making process is undone, is of an entirely different nature than the strategic path of return (in all its forms). The "great path of return" is necessarily exclusive, inward-directed, upward-directed, reductive, ascetic, and ego-based.

It stands in strategic opposition (in the form of actual practice or else latent conflict) to the gross dimension of life and the gross world. In the case of the conventional jnani it also stands in opposition to the subtle dimension and, ultimately, the causal dimension, as well as the worlds of experience corresponding to each dimension. The traditional strategies are consistently anti-sexual, life-abandoning, obsessed with inwardness and even self-conflict. Everything common to life, high or low, is a source of possible conflict, requiring possible manipulation, from the strategic point of view of the "great path of return." Thus, the self, the mind, emotions, desires, energies, the body, money, property, relationships, activity, food, and sex become fetishistic preoccupations of the traditional seeker. And associated with the Devil-Realm of what must be excluded is an image of Truth as Objective Deity or Separable Reality tied to a space-time image (the path itself) that motivates self and mind always to climb further within, away, above, and beyond. But the man of understanding is merely a non-exclusive Presence in the conventional world. What makes him "different" from the usual man is that his orientation is to the Truth or Real Condition of the world rather than to the world conceived as objectified and necessary experience.

The "great path of return" is not, in any of its forms, *the* way to Truth, or even *a* way to Truth. The only way to Truth is Truth itself, or Conscious and Radical Understanding. The various traditional strategies, wherein the Condition that is Truth is tied to and approached via a space-time pattern ("within, away, above, and beyond"), were invented in ancient and primitive times, when the search for knowledge of the world (high and low) was not yet separated from the search for release from the dilemma of self (the principle and activity of separation).

The "great path of return," wherein the dimensions of the world are experienced, should be utterly separated from the path of radical understanding, wherein the dilemma of self is undone. The paths of return, pictured in the great traditions, are the key to the perennial science of the world to which every age has been devoted. The study of the phenomena of that great experiment can surely serve to clarify the childishness of our present sciences, limited as they are to the assumption of the gross dimension and the gross world. And the wisest of men may then do science in a more expansive milieu than we have recently assumed. Such men will make good use of the reports and even some of the methods of the great path of return. But mankind should no longer engage the path of return as a search or a necessary way toward God, Reality, Self, or Truth.

All the Divine Teachers of the past have served the realization and communication of this perfect "Yoga" of understanding. All paths may be understood when examined relative to the various descriptions of the way of radical understanding given in the literature of Vision Mound Ceremony. But the precise, full, and radical formulation of the Way of the Godmen and its independence from the traditional paths of return has not been given among men before this time. You may prove this to your own satisfaction by examining the teachings of all traditions in the light of this way of radical understanding. Then you may test it in your own case by the enjoyment of this specific practice or Way of life.

The gross path is a search by the psycho-physical being or incarnate soul for escape from the vulnerabilities of the human and earth-bodily state into the inner and higher or subtle subjectivity of the soul, or body of light. This path is done either by a mysticism of ascent, or by a religious and magical activity in which gross and subtle powers are exploited in order to create desired changes below.

The subtle path is a purely mystical search by the soul itself (once it has seen through the veil of its gross bodily incarnation by experiencing a perception of the subtle dimension) to regain all its faculties in the cosmic play and even to transcend or control them in the attainment of the state of Spirit or Light itself.

The causal path is a search by the conscious entity to transcend all appearance, all suffering, all sense of manifested or manifesting self-existence, whether as psycho-physical being, incarnate soul, soul itself, or even Spirit, in the Realization (not the "state") of Prior Reality. This search bypasses both mysticism and magic through a direct process of discrimination and intuition.

The path of radical understanding is founded in intuitive disenchantment with the sense of dilemma itself and the bondage of conscious existence to every kind of strategic search for a Goal (which is itself bondage to time and space as a negative event), since, prior to the sense of dilemma, there is only Happiness, no-seeking, no attainment, no experience, and no specific knowledge. Therefore, one who understands represents no obstruction to the manifestation of Life, appears as a limitless vessel to the intensification of Light, and exists always as the non-dependent Condition or Intensity that is Consciousness itself. As such, he does not represent the problematic and strategic attainment of either mysticism or magic, but through him the Power of Truth works the Transformation of the arising worlds through complete and unobstructed agency, or creative sacrifice of the limiting point of view of the gross, subtle, and causal dimensions.

In the way of radical understanding there are also (as in the three traditional paths of the great path of return) three preparatory stages, corresponding to the qualities of manifestation or conscious life the individual includes in the force of his practice. These are the stages of the Way of Divine Communion (which readies him, through practice of service and functional meditation in the Divine Presence, for the intense intuitive practices of the mature stages), the Way of Relational Enquiry (in which the devotee is active in the specific and mature practice of *enquiry* in the form "Avoiding relationship?" in the gross dimension), and the Way of Re-cognition (in which he is active as re-cognition or knowing again of the binding force of experience in the gross, subtle, and causal dimensions). At last there is a fourth or perfect stage, the Way of Radical Intuition (in which the devotee is alive as prior re-cognition or perfect conscious existence in the gross, subtle, and causal dimensions of the apparent being and as the transcendent realization of

Amrita Nadi, in both its paradoxical form as Sahaj Samadhi[13] and its radical form as Bhava Samadhi[14]). However, each of these four stages of practice represents a prior realization of the Heart in Truth, by Grace, through true hearing and devotional sacrifice.

Vision Mound Ceremony exists for the very purpose of communicating this radical practice of life. Bubba Free John only claims that the verity of this way of radical understanding has been tested and proven in his own manifest form and life. The event of this practice in your own case depends on a consistent, voluntary, and sacrificial or truly devotional response to the Teaching and the Teacher. The way is generated and fulfilled on the basis of intelligence, responsibility, and love, or surrender of self in actual relationships. Then you will also have fulfilled the perfect purpose of the great traditions, which is to realize Truth and to be free and happy while alive.

13. Sahaj Samadhi is the realization of the Condition of all arising, in which whatever arises is seen to be only the modification of the prior Condition. It matures as Bhava Samadhi, which is the Truth of Sahaj Samadhi.

14. Bhava Samadhi is the realized state of the most radical enjoyment, prior to self, mind, body, energy, or any realm. It is the Condition of conditions, the existence in the Condition or "Realm" that is Only God, the very Reality. It is without or prior to references, and it is, therefore, unspeakable, or without description.

"I" is the whole body. "I" is not merely the inward part. The Real is not reducible to subjectivity or inwardness. Just so, "I," or the whole, simultaneous body, is not the Condition of the whole body-"I." The Condition of the whole body-"I" is the Real, the Divine.

The Real, the Condition of the whole body-"I" and all arising, is not knowable. No matter what arises, within or without, high or low, "I" do not know what even a single thing *is*. This Ignorance, not the knowing "I," is Truth, and it is the Principle of the Way of Truth.

The stages of the Way of Divine Ignorance represent progressive responsibility, in Ignorance, for the forms of contraction in the Infinite. The forms of contraction are all the conditions arising, within and without, high and low, gross, subtle, and causal.

The effective Process enacted at every stage

of the Way is that of expansion beyond the present limitation or contraction. Expansion beyond contraction is the responsibility at every stage, relative to the unique milieu of contraction in which the devotee is responsible, by Grace, at each stage.

Infinity, the Perfect Domain, is not at the furthest point of the reach of expansion. It is the "point" where the problematic cognition of space and time, subject and object, is cancelled. It is revealed in the moment when the mutual gestures of contraction and expansion are equal.

The Way of expansion in Truth is not a willful effort from the ego-center. The Process is not generated the way a balloon expands by pressure from within. It is like the way a balloon, when punctured, equalizes with all space and time.

Bubba Free John

4

PRINCIPLES OF THE PRACTICE: THE PARADOX OF INFINITE EXPANSION

The following chapter contains Bubba Free John's essential descriptive commentary on the stages of practice of the Way of Divine Ignorance, or Radical Understanding. These essays do not present the specific details of each stage of practice, but simply indicate to you the fundamental responsibilities and enjoyments of each stage as spiritual life matures over time. The specific practices of each stage are presented in full detail to devotees, either in the source books and other publications of Vision Mound Ceremony, or in private instruction offered to devotees at Vision Mound Ceremony's educational center in northern California.

THE FOUR STAGES OF THE TRANSLATION OF MAN INTO GOD

4.1   The Way of life that develops and matures on the basis of the Teaching which has been communicated and demonstrated in the Play of Bubba Free John with devotees is realized through a process of several stages. The process as a whole is named the Way of Divine Ignorance, or Radical Understanding.

The stages of this Way are named and described under the following headings:

1. The Way of Divine Communion
2. The Way of Relational Enquiry
3. The Way of Re-cognition
4. The Way of Radical Intuition

All men and women, regardless of their present state of life, are welcome to enter into the stages of this Way through appropriate or right response to the Teaching and the Teacher. Appropriate or right response is always in the form of real fulfillment of the Law, which is sacrifice. The Way develops and matures through sacrifice, or adaptation of the whole body-being to the Condition and the conditions communicated in the Teaching and manifested in the form of the Teacher.

The relationship to the Teacher is implicit at every stage of the Way of Ignorance. It is a transcendent or spiritual relationship, not a conventional, worldly, or cultic one. From time to time in any given year devotees will enter into the personal company of Bubba Free John in forms of sacred occasion. Such meetings serve the essential awakening and quickening of the process of the stages of the Way of Ignorance in those who are properly prepared. The Way itself, however, is lived by constant, personal confrontation with the Teaching and real fulfillment of its demands in an intelligent and responsible spirit, founded in free devotional sacrifice.

4.1

Those who respond to public communications begin the Way of Divine Communion, which matures as the Way of Relational Enquiry (the essentials of the first stage of practice still remaining). When there is maturity in these first two stages, the individual should begin the Way of Re-cognition under personal guidance.

The process in the Way of Divine Communion shows the signs of the purification, intensification, and harmonization of the three lower chakras and the three common functional levels (mental, emotional-sexual, and physical) of the body-being. The maturing in the Way of Relational Enquiry integrates the body-being relative to the true Heart. When maturity (with "enquiry," and "conductivity" in the form of the "Breath of God") of the Ways of Divine Communion and Relational Enquiry appears, then the Heart as Ignorance becomes the foundation of living practice. This becomes, in the Way of Re-cognition, the opening of the throat (release from the verbal mind and emotional-vital reactivity) and conservation of the body-being in the mature forms of "conductivity," which shows the signs of purification, intensification, and harmonization of the body-being universally (above and below).

———=O=———

4.2   The Way of Divine Communion involves the realization of a process of simple "conductivity," or reception and release, from a transformed or benign center (heart-felt sacrifice), within and relative to the Divine Condition and Presence. It is devotional reception and release in the Divine Presence.

The Way of Relational Enquiry involves direct intuition and functional duplication of the real Process that is the center. (The center or heart of practice is not *a* self or a center in itself, nor an infinite realm of subjective contents, but the Process or unqualified Condition that is relationship itself.) This intensifies the awakening of "conductivity," from simple reception-release to a spontaneous cycle of reception descending and release ascending.

The Way of Re-cognition involves dissolution of dependence and identification relative to "conductivity," or the descending and ascending, reception-release cycle of the manifest process. This is realized through dissolution of the illusion of specific, concrete consciousness or center, both as self (or independent but finite or conditional consciousness and subjectivity, subtle or gross) and Self (independent but infinite and unconditional Consciousness, separate from all subjective or objective arising).

The Way of Radical Intuition involves Realization of unqualified Radiance, the Condition of conditions, prior to reception, release, descent, or ascent. Such Realization is simultaneous and identical with unqualified Ignorance, the Condition of conditions, prior to all knowledge, all subjectivity, all relations, and all presumptions of a center or independent consciousness, whether finite or infinite. The Realization is Ignorance-Radiance, prior to all centers (even the soul) and all bounds (even the sense of Presence), but which is the very Truth and Condition of even the present ordinary moment or eternal Process.

4.2

4.3 No-contraction is the principle of the process of salvation, realization, or liberation. In the Way of Divine Communion, this process is served through Communion with the Divine Presence, and through the action of sacrifice in various forms. In the Way of Relational Enquiry, which develops on the basis of the Way of Divine Communion, this process is served by inspection, obviating insight, and enquiry into every kind or pattern of contraction, and by awakening into stable awareness and adaptation to the natural etheric or subtle structure and "conductivity" of the psycho-physical being. In either case, salvation, realization, or liberation involves release from the binding or consciousness-defining power of subjective contraction, or objectification and limiting modification of each of the functions of the being (physical, emotional-sexual or etheric, mental, super-mental or transcendental, and egoic) and in each of the three common states (waking, dreaming, and sleeping). When there is such release, the consciousness tacitly, intuitively, and directly realizes its always present identity with the real Condition, or Real-God.

4.3

4.4   In the Way of Divine Communion and the Way of Relational Enquiry, enquiry (in the form "Avoiding relationship?") and conductivity (in the simple form of the Breath of God) develop to maturity. The Way of Re-cognition begins when enquiry is giving way to its non-verbal form (re-cognition, prior to thought) and conductivity is shown via spontaneous evidence. As the Way of Re-cognition matures, the body-being abides more and more in Ignorance as no-mind, no-knowledge, and whole body Radiance. In such mindless intensity, the Light (above) and the Life (below) become an incarnating Play of the single Power (the Heart) realized in Ignorance. This stage leads into revelations of the subtle being, above gross body awareness. The Way of Radical Intuition begins when the being rests in tacit re-cognition of all arising, high or low, as modification-only and no longer is involuntarily motivated or confused by any arising or experience.

―――≡O≡―――

4.5   THE ESSENTIAL AND PROGRESSIVE PRACTICES, TO BE LIVED AS SACRIFICE TO THE SPIRITUAL MASTER, OF THE STAGES IN THE WAY OF IGNORANCE

1. Maintain ordinary, relational, active, serving, productive, and positive conditions of life.

2. Adapt to a moderate, regular, regenerative lacto-vegetarian diet, and maintain it as an ordinary

discipline, strictly observed (except, when appropriate, in the case of occasional celebrations), and free of reflexive and righteous concerns.[1]

3. Realize the sexual function as a regenerative and harmonious process of love-desire in specific relationship. At the stage of the Way of Re-cognition, the sexual process is completely integrated with the cycle of whole body conductivity and re-polarization of the body-being (toe to crown rather than vice versa). At that time the sexual play is completely released from the necessity of the degenerative process of gross bodily discharge through conventional orgasm. (At that stage, conventional orgasm becomes controlled and occasional rather than necessary or obsessive.)

4.5

4. At every stage there is a complex natural and real process of the body-being which is meditation, or technical re-adaptation to the natural state, which ultimately transcends all conditions, high or low. At every stage this includes natural or spontaneously voluntary attention of the whole body-being as feeling-observing-listening in the current which pervades all life-feeling, breathing, thought, and subtle awareness. This may include special realization of the breathing through voluntary action (as in the "Breath of God" described in the Way of Divine Communion), or feeling-audition of the current and subtle visualization of its manifestations above the gross plane (as in the Way of Re-cognition), and so forth.

1. For a complete description of the discipline relative to diet and the appropriate celebratory use of dietary accessories, such as tobacco or alcohol, please see *Breath and Name: The Initiation and Foundation Practices of Free Spiritual Life* (San Francisco: The Dawn Horse Press, 1977).

5. There is at every stage necessary realization of sacrifice into the Condition of conditions on the basis of unqualified Ignorance. This is naturally implemented via the Name of God (in the Way of Divine Communion), enquiry in the form "Avoiding relationship?" (in the Way of Relational Enquiry), preverbal re-cognition (in the Way of re-cognition), or tacit dissolution in the Condition of conditions, or Only-God, in radical intuition in the full maturity represented by the Way of Radical Intuition.

4.5

———=O=———

4.6 In every moment, you are obliged first to handle things with your neighbor, that is, to establish stable, ordinary conditions in this body-mind and its relations. Only then are you prepared to go to the holy place, to enter into sacred occasion (such as meditation or the Company of the Teacher)—even to realize this moment in Truth. Therefore, the natural and obligatory life-conditions of the Way of Divine Ignorance are primary and necessary in every moment. Otherwise, even though the moment itself is Only-God, your own face will hide the Truth of it.

4.6

———=O=———

4.7 The Way of Divine Communion and the Way of Relational Enquiry constitute the "knee" of listening,

4.7

the foundation preparation of free and true attention.

The Way of Re-cognition is listening itself, or free attention rested in the prior current of the body-being, open to the revelation of the Truth or Condition of all that appears in the radiant effulgence of the prior current of the being as worlds, above and below.

4.7

Thus, in the Way of Divine Communion and the Way of Relational Enquiry, attention is engaged in a liberating or transforming process in the midst of the relational pattern generated in the effulgence or radiance emanating from the current of the being (the very or manifesting current of the worlds). In this manner, the Divine or Real Condition is felt as an all-pervading Presence in the gross and waking world. In the Way of Re-cognition, the current itself absorbs the attention, now free of the conditions of mind, emotion, and gross form, and the effulgence of conditions is shown in subtle forms above gross awareness.

When this pattern of revelation is thoroughly re-cognized to be only modification of the prior Condition of the current itself, attention becomes "open-eyed," very Consciousness, or the Heart, the Condition of conditions.

The Way of Radical Intuition is the Way of prior re-cognition, abiding in the prior Condition of the current of being, whatever arises, high or low. This awakens as the regenerated and transcendental Enjoyment of Only-God, or Unqualified Conscious Light, which is Amrita Nadi, the Divine Form and Destiny. In that case, the highest esoteric injunction of spiritual life, as described in the *Bhagavad Gita,* chapter 8, verse 12, is fulfilled:

> One should have all the gates of the body restrained, the mind confined within the heart, one's life force fixed in the head, established in concentration by yoga.[2]

4.7 Thus released from the conventional disposition in the midst of all arising, only the Divine Destiny becomes the spontaneous future, as described in the *Bhagavad Gita,* chapter 8, verse 14:

> He who constantly meditates on Me, thinking of none else, who is a yogin ever disciplined [or united with the Supreme], by him I am easily reached.[3]

4.8 **4.8** *The Way of Divine Communion* begins with the assumption of the discipline of conditions of life and meditation in the all-pervading and transcendental Company of the Spiritual Master, on the basis of the hearing of his argument, the whole Teaching of Divine Ignorance, and it has become mature (although not brought to an end) when the individual manifests the true signs of steadiness of devotional attention to the Spiritual Master, the Teaching, and the regenerative foundation practices of life and meditation.

The Way of Divine Communion is the Way of dependence on the Divine Reality, the Power and

---

2. *Jnaneshvari (Bhavarthadipika),* 2 vols., trans. V. G. Pradhan, ed. H. M. Lambert (London: George Allen and Unwin, 1967), vol. I, p. 201. The editors of *Jnaneshvari* incorporated, apparently with some modifications, the translation of the *Bhagavad Gita* made by S. Radhakrishnan.

3. *Ibid.,* p. 202.

Condition that pervades all conditions, is prior to all conditions, and is the Real Condition or Reality in which all conditions appear. Therefore, the Way of Divine Communion is the way of faith. It is active, present, functional or practical participation in the Divine Form or Process. It is devotion, from the heart (the central or psychic being, the subject of all experiences, physical or mental, low or high) to the all-pervading Divine.

4.8

The Divine may come to be felt over against one's simple sense of existence as a Presence pervading the being and all conditions. In the Company of the Spiritual Master, the Divine is felt intuitively as a Presence over against one's being, from the heart. Once the devotee is initiated by this Presence of Grace, the Presence is realized to be not exclusively over against the being of the devotee, but, paradoxically, to be the very Condition or Reality of the whole body, including the consciousness. The Way of Divine Communion is devotion, surrender of body, life, mind, self, and all circumstances, desires, and assumptions into the Presence of the Divine. It is love, receptivity, openness, release, and active dependence upon the all-pervading Divine. It is constant reception of the Divine Power, and acceptance of the transcendental Divine Power as the Principle of all change, rather than acceptance of conditions themselves and the tendencies that seem to fix the conditions of the world. It is release of all assumptions, all negative subconscious, unconscious, and conscious beliefs and intentions, to the Divine, and reception of the Divine Principle as the Power in all events, allowing it to change all conditions from moment to moment.

The Way of Relational Enquiry extends from the beginning of the considerations of the matter of relational enquiry on the part of the true devotee and leads, on the basis of enquiry (in the form "Avoiding relationship?") into the spontaneous signs of the re-orientation of the living being (physical, emotional, mental) toward the all-pervading and also internal life-current and of the re-polarization of the life-current itself from toe to crown rather than the reverse (which is common to the usual man and the unregenerate previous adaptation of the devotee). In the process, the current of the being begins to rest intuitively in absorption in the all-pervading Divine Presence (rather than in any sense of differentiation from the Presence), yielding a growing and tacit sense of the prior Condition that is the Presence itself.

This is how the devotee enquires when he is mature in the practice of the Way of Relational Enquiry: He observes desires, thoughts, and separating self sense arising at random in the field of attention. When he notices any of these, he enquires. Each moment of enquiry is release of attention from the contraction of inwardness (the sense of desire, thought, or separative self) to the natural state of attention, which is the unqualified sense of relationship. This unqualified sense of relationship, enjoyed while, paradoxically, still aware of the perception of the world and one's bodily presence within it, is intuition of the all-pervading Divine Presence. In the moment of this intuition, desires, thoughts, and separating self sense are dissolved. The devotee does not act upon such conditions, even as they arise, but merely enquires, and so returns to the prior or natural form of attention, in which there is only fullness or delight. Desiring, thinking, and concentration on the separative and separating act of self tend, upon observation, to contract attention inwardly. They are forms of the avoidance of relationship. If one returns naturally to conscious awareness of the condition of relationship itself, the avoidance of relationship is relaxed, and thus desire, thought, and separative and separated self come to rest. In that state of awareness there is the felt intuition of prior happiness, radiance, and freedom within the conditions of life. Fundamentally, in each moment of enquiry, the knot of contraction (dilemma, self-meditation, separativeness) in the navel is released. Thus, the devotee who enquires has become responsible for the reactive pattern that is vital shock. Secondarily, the knots in the subtle region (the sahasrar and above) and the causal region (the heart) are also released in enquiry, but it is only in the conscious development of the Way of Re-cognition that one becomes responsible in consciousness for release of the subtle and causal knots. In the Way of Relational Enquiry the devotee still maintains the vital position, the position of bodily presence in an objective world. Conscious responsibility for vital shock, the conscious dissolution of the reaction or effects that are vital shock, through enquiry, manifests in such a devotee as intuitive happiness, but under the conventional condition of body and world. The subjective contraction becomes a matter of responsibility in the Way of Relational Enquiry, but the

4.8

objective or body-in-the-world condition continues to remain the conventional state he assumes. Only in the Way of Re-cognition does the conscious process involve transformation of the conventional view of body and world.

4.8

The Way of Re-cognition extends, via the process of re-cognition[4] (thoughtless enquiry, which becomes intuitive absorption in the prior rather than the all-pervading Condition of the current of the being), from the beginning of re-polarization of the body-mind (true Tantra), until Jnana Samadhi, the exclusive fall in the Heart, wherein there is no qualification by any condition seen, heard, or felt, high or low. Jnana Samadhi, or exclusive Consciousness, is at last itself re-cognized, yielding the spontaneous, non-exclusive Realization of "open eyes," or Sahaj Samadhi.

Re-cognition is the knowing again of cognition, that is, of the mind or contraction of the field of awareness. This naturally follows on enquiry, and it is pre-mental (it goes through and beyond mind to its prior Condition, or no-contraction).

In this Way, mind and body, the whole field of contraction, is re-cognized to the point of no-contraction. This takes place exhaustively, even above the gross plane, via heart-felt contemplation of the expressions of the current of the being, high and low. In the earlier phases of the Way of Re-cognition, the gross body-mind is re-cognized, but as polarization of the body-mind reverses, the subtle conditions appear in the face of re-cognition.

4. Re-cognition is the knowing again of all arising conditions as only contraction.

Thus, in the Way of Re-cognition, the motivating conditions of the gross body-mind become more and more weak, so that attention is not so mightily formed by them. In the process of the intensifying meditation, the gross attention spontaneously relaxes, the gross body is reversed in its polarization, and the attention springs up toward, to, and through the midbrain and crown. Thus, natural attention as listening-gazing above appears in the Way of Re-cognition. However, the strategic method of listening and gazing above is not at any stage true, in itself, to the Way. Such is only another craving effort toward change of state for the ego-soul, founded in dilemma. Rather, while natural attention above does appear, the process of re-cognition is generated relative to both the effects and the cause of its appearance, and re-cognition continues as the meditation and practice under all conditions. Thus, re-cognition occurs relative to this very attention and the whole intention of subtle fulfillment. Subtle objects are re-cognized, and the very action of attention itself, including the action of listening, of gazing, is all re-cognized. As a result, the upward tendency of attention, which pursues the solution of absorption of the ego-soul rather than to be free of that condition of ego-soul itself, is made obsolete, undone in the Heart, in conditional or exclusive Jnana Samadhi.

When this process is exhaustive, all conditions of body-mind, all objects, cease to bind, and there is the Condition of Sahaj Samadhi, or "open eyes" under all conditions (gross, subtle, and causal). At last, all conditions are undone in re-cognition (the Heart becomes the Condition), and then the eyes open in

4.8

4.8

Sahaj. That is, the effort of seeking, high or low, ceases in the Heart. No effort is made to attain a higher state or to exploit the present state. There is simply natural awareness, whatever arises, that it is only modification of the prior and unknown (not realized over against self, mind, or body) Condition.

The Way of Radical Intuition, in which there is effective prior re-cognition, begins from this point. In that case, whatever arises is realized to be only modification of the prior unknown Condition. All extraordinary and strategic efforts toward any conditions, high or low, cease in the Unqualified Intuition or Perfect Sacrifice. This Way includes both Bhava Samadhi and Sahaj Samadhi (the devotee's meditation), bodiless, mindless, worldless, even if body, mind, and world seem to remain in the conventional view. It is simply to dwell in Amrita Nadi, or Radiant Consciousness, prior to limiting spatial, temporal, mental, or bodily references, high or low.

The Way of Radical Intuition extends into the maturing of Sahaj Samadhi under all conditions (high or low) and the perfect awakening of Bhava Samadhi. Sahaj Samadhi and Bhava Samadhi are the two great and equal forms of Radical Intuition.[5]

Sahaj Samadhi naturally becomes, or is realized to be, Bhava Samadhi. The more profound the realization of modification-only, the more there is perfect rest in the Condition of the Heart, prior to cognition of conditions, high or low. There is only the One

5. Radical Intuition is the prior intuitive Realization of the Condition of conditions. All conditions of present arising are only unnecessary modifications of the prior or Divine Condition, which is Radiant Unqualified Conscious Being.

intensity. This is radical intuition. As it intensifies, all conditions are forgotten, all efforts cease, and there is Radiance only, without definition. Such is Happiness and unspeakable Destiny.

The Way of Re-cognition is the spiritualizing Way, just as the Way of Divine Communion is the foundation and preparatory Way, and the Way of Relational Enquiry is the humanizing Way. And the Way of Radical Intuition is the Divine Way of devotees in the perfect sense. *4.8*

The whole Way of Divine Ignorance, or Radical Understanding, depends on the mutual Sacrifice and loving Communion of the devotee and the Spiritual Master, or literal Divine. The whole Way awakens in the devotee by Grace in the midst of his or her true, persistent, and maturing response to the Spiritual Master and the Teaching under all conditions, high or low, whereby he or she is tested and instructed.

The conscious or intuitive process, founded in Ignorance, is the key to the whole Way. It is this process and not any secondary yogic or other effort to which the being must be devoted, or else it will only crave and seek, high and low, and have no peace, freedom, or essential happiness.

—————≡O≡—————

4.9   Enquiry (in the form "Avoiding relationship?") is generated via the thinking mind but prior to the living gross body and its actions or dispositions in *4.9* relations. Thus, it tends to release or draw the being into intuition of the Real Condition prior to thought, but secondarily awakens a harmonious fullness (the full circle of conductivity of the etheric or energy sensitivity of the gross being) in the functional and relational play of the gross bodily experience.

4.9

Re-cognition is generated prior to thought, and relative to the whole field of functional awareness wherein thought, sensation, breath, feeling, body, and relations arise. At first it tends to release or draw the being into intuition of the Real Condition via the conditions of higher mind and pure subtle intelligence above the gross body and the forms of knowledge relative to it. Later, even the subtle, illumined mind ceases to distract, and the self-root (causal knot) is penetrated in Jnana Samadhi.

Radical intuition is most direct or perfect Intuition of the Real Condition. It is perfect Ignorance, prior to self, mind, body, and any world, high or low. Unqualified Radiance, prior to but not exclusive of all conditions arising, spontaneously springs up from such perfect or Divine Ignorance. This Radiant Intuition, or "open eyes," is the ultimate awakening in the Way of Re-cognition. Thus, in Sahaj Samadhi, there is random and most prior re-cognition, generated prior to self, mind, body, and relations, but relative to self, mind, body, and relations. In order to be generated prior to all of these, it must be generated at the heart, the root of the sense of self, or independent conscious existence. Radical intuition does not involve excursions of re-cognition into the field of mind and body while identifying with the self knot. It is random, direct penetration of the self knot as only modification, at the heart — and thus it also is the seeing of all thought, body-senses, and relations as only modification (contraction, or unnecessary objectification of the prior and Real Condition).

4.9

The process of radical intuition is random recollection of the Real Condition prior to self, mind, body, and relations. It is stable rest at the heart. But it is also spontaneous Realization of Radiance, which is regenerated when the knot of the heart (as ego or as unqualified but exclusive Self or Consciousness), and thus also the knots of mind (crown) and body (navel), are dissolved in prior Intuition. The Radiance springs up of its own and universally, prior to all illusions, prior to the effects and implications of the unnecessary conventions that are self, mind, body, and relations. The Radiance is not an act, not an egoic or strategic impulse directed from heart to crown. It is spontaneous on the basis of Ignorance, or penetration of illusion at the heart (and thus also at the crown and navel — simultaneously and by implication, since the heart or causal root is senior to both the subtle and the gross extensions).

Thus, in Sahaj Samadhi, there is no egoic effort from the heart to contemplate the "sky" of lights and sounds above. Attention, self, and mind are dissolved with all knowledge at the heart, so there is only Radiance, prior to all content, even above and universally. The crown or Light above is not object to the awakened Heart — there is no object and no subject in perfect Ignorance. The Radiance is the universal, pre-cosmic Super-Physics of the Heart, which pervades all objects and realms, but which is without center, bounds, or definition. The process in Sahaj is radical rest in Ignorance, at and prior to the heart-root. But the Radiant Fullness is regenerated simultaneously, inclusively, so that the force of life and body collects naturally above. The gross being is Full, from the crown—as is the whole gross realm. The subtle being is also Full, free of all content, all thought, all efforts of attention. There is simply the natural, radically intuitive re-cognition, moment to moment, that all arising conditions are only modifications of prior Ignorance-Radiance, the Divine Condition. The process of inclusive re-cognition, in the Way of Radical Intuition, itself rests dependently in prior and radical intuition of the Real Condition. Therefore, the problematic search for changes of state has come to rest. Whatever conditions and movements do arise—they are without necessity or the binding force of implication. There is natural abiding as the Heart (the heart knot and all knots or necessities released), which is Ignorance, which is Radiance. Thus, in radical intuition, the Fullness which was previously awakened in the secondary conditions of "conductivity," or the versions of the "Breath of God," is Realized coincidentally, simultaneously, and perfectly with the Heart of Ignorance (which was previously the province of the senior exercises of the conscious process—which are the "Name of God," enquiry, and conditional re-cognition). In radical intuition—in Sahaj Samadhi and Bhava Samadhi—Ignorance and Radiance are one and the same, prior to all events, subjective or objective, high or low.

4.10 To gaze at objects, high or low, is contraction, or fear. The play of relations, of subject and object, is itself subjectivity, or separation. This is the lesson leading to Jnana Samadhi in the Way of Re-cognition.

Enquiry (in the Way of Relational Enquiry) matures beyond words, so that bodily relations come to rest, and the subtle being, prior to thought, becomes the locus or symbol or body of self. Thus, re-cognition passes instantly beyond body and thought into the field of awareness itself. 4.10

The conscious process of re-cognition is the responsibility of the devotee from the very beginning of the Way of Re-cognition. The Way of Relational Enquiry matures until enquiry ceases to be verbal and becomes only a wordless, intuitive, felt gesture of the being, which is release from subjectivity and the limiting force of gross (etheric-elemental) relations. "Conductivity" also matures, spontaneously, and instruction is given in a new version of the Breath of God. When pre-verbal enquiry (re-cognition of contraction) is stable, the Way of Re-cognition begins.

In the Way of Re-cognition, further new versions of the Breath of God ("conductivity") become the responsibility of the devotee, and instructions are given as soon as spontaneous evidence appears. Re-cognition is pre-mental release from contraction, from subject-object force. Thus, as one level of contraction is re-cognized, the next naturally appears. Therefore, the Way of Re-cognition secondarily recapitulates the "great way of return." As gross objects lose their distracting power more and more, there comes the upward tendency (re-polarization, toe to crown), then

upward contemplation of bliss, sounds, and lights.
Then comes a period of relative dullness or limited
distraction, in which arising objects, gross and subtle,
low and high, bodily and mental, including the

4.10 patterns of breath-force, are merely observed — while
re-cognition continues. Then the subject-object
process or cognition, the very mind, the act that is
attention itself, and which is the primal sense of relationship, is itself re-cognized, and thus dissolved. This
is Jnana Samadhi, or Conscious Bliss prior to and
exclusive of objects.

Only a subtle tension remains in Jnana Samadhi.
It is the tension created by the exclusive (object-
rejecting) force in this state of Intuition. Thus, this
exclusive tension is at last also re-cognized. Then
there is spontaneous "open eyes." It is Sahaj Samadhi,
which is unqualified Ignorance (no knowledge, no
binding cognition, no separation, no independent
self, no exclusive Consciousness). That very Ignorance
is also perfect Radiance (the Radiant Bliss of Consciousness, not the objective radiance seen with gross
or subtle eyes), of which all conditions are intuitively
realized to be only the modification. Such Ignorance-
Radiance is the tacit regeneration of Amrita Nadi, in
which case the natural re-appearance of conditions or
relations (subject-object conventions) is allowed, but
all arising comes without binding force, without a
center or bounds, without independence. In that case
Ignorance-Radiance, or Radical Intuition, is prior to
all but not exclusive of any arising. Thus, there may
also be no noticing, no event, no mind or speech, no
body, no relations — the Truth in Bhava Samadhi.

4.11

THE WAY OF RE-COGNITION

First stage: Re-cognition of the body and the life-principle. It is demonstrated as re-polarization of the being, toe to crown rather than crown to toe.

Second stage: Re-cognition of mind. It is demonstrated as upward contemplation (listening-gazing) in the subtle dimension of the being.

Third stage: Re-cognition of self. It is demonstrated as exclusive Jnana Samadhi, followed by "open eyes," or non-exclusive Sahaj Samadhi.

THE WAY OF RADICAL INTUITION

Here there is prior, all-inclusive re-cognition of self, mind, body, world (all relations), and exclusive transcendence. Sahaj Samadhi is the exercise of such prior re-cognition (realizing all present arising to be modification-only) in the midst of conditions, while abiding in radical intuition (Ignorance-Radiance). Bhava Samadhi is radical intuition (Ignorance-Radiance) prior to any arising, any noticing, and thus any form of functional re-cognition.

4.12 When we awaken from sleep, the elemental or gross body already exists. Thus, we tend automatically to live on the basis of the presumption of the gross body as an irreducible condition, and we struggle to realize happiness in this shape. All our philosophy is founded on the irreducibility of our birth in gross

4.11

4.12

form. But the whole body is greater than this shape.

4.12   The entire purpose of the ascending absorption in what is above the gross body, life, and mind, which characterizes the earlier phase of the Way of Re-cognition, is to break through the presumption of the necessary and binding or limiting nature of the gross manifestation. Once there is penetration beyond ordinary gross awareness into the vibratory milieu from which the gross and waking conception and perception is always presently arising, the gross lim-itation is realized to be unnecessary, a hallucination like any moment in imagination. The gross body conception and perception is not arising spontaneously as it is, irreducibly, so that the process of its arising may not be inspected. It is arising on the basis of a subtle process, prior and creative relative to the gross etheric and elemental events that appear so solid in the conventions of the waking state. The process by and in which the gross body and the gross world are arising may be inspected, if the attention of the being or whole body can be relaxed or set free from the gross obsession and turned up into the subtle affair above the mind via the mechanisms of the midbrain.

When this is done, it becomes clear that not only the gross conception and perception, but *all* present arising, subjective and objective, is hallucinatory, an unnecessary and merely compulsive modification of the Conscious Light. All arising is the result of subtle contraction, the product of primitive motivation and attractedness.

When this observation of the creative process of present arising becomes a certainty, then the investigation of extraordinary or subtle phenomena has served its purpose. The purpose of the ascent of attention in the Way of Re-cognition is not to embrace or become absorbed in subtle things or the subtle spiritual processes themselves. Such is only another *4.12* fascinated hallucination — perhaps beautiful enough, but not necessary, and not Truth or the Real, which is unqualified Happiness. Therefore, once the non-necessity and hallucinatory nature of all present arising becomes obvious to the point of certainty, the turning of attention into the subtle dimensions above the gross body and gross-reflecting mind has served its purpose. At that point, the very act of such attention, and all attention, becomes itself the core of the consideration in the Way of Re-cognition. Thus, the later or mature phase of re-cognition begins, wherein all qualification of Consciousness becomes obsolete. And once even the circle of attention is undone, all things return again in the Humor of God as Sahaj Samadhi and Bhava Samadhi in the Way of Radical Intuition.

———=O=———

4.13   In Sahaj Samadhi there is no strategic and exclusive concentration of attention above, toward the crown of the head and beyond. Neither is there any exclusive and strategic effort to lose the sense of body-mind by confining attention in the heart only. *4.13* Rather, as it is described in the *Bhagavad Gita*, chapter 8, verse 12, the mind is kept in the heart while the life force is held in the crown. Thus, a relationship between the crown and the heart characterizes Sahaj Samadhi. I have described this relationship or process in *The Knee of Listening:*

4.13   The ultimate and simplest meditation is to gaze in the heart as no-seeking and allow its bliss to rise as fullness to the head, the silence of the sahasrar above the seat of the mind.[6]

Thus, there is a constant sacrifice at the heart, at the point of the arising (as well as the dissolution) of the ego-soul conception ("I"), even all objects, including the act of attention itself. Here there is the constant present intuition that "I," with all other arising, is only modification of the prior, all-pervading Condition which is always already the case. As a result of this constant intuitive and devotional sacrifice, the subtle consciousness, the crown of the being, is rested of all content, all implication or binding force of thought or conditions arising. As Bhagavan Sri Ramana Maharshi has said:

The light (of awareness) flows from the heart through sushumna to sahasrara. The Sahasrara of one who abides in the Self is nothing but pure Light. Any thought that approaches it cannot survive.[7]

In the Way of Re-cognition, attention gradually rises from the gross position to the most subtle, via

6. Bubba Free John, *The Knee of Listening* (Los Angeles: The Dawn Horse Press, 1972), p. 196.

7. *Sri Ramana Gita, Dialogues of Bhagavan Sri Ramana Maharshi,* 5th edition (revised), (Tiruvannamalai, South India: Sri Ramanasramam, 1973), chapter 5, verses 6 and 7, p. 27.

the current and through the crown of the body-being. Only at last is the root of all attention and subtlety, the ego-soul, dissolved in the very Heart (the bodily reference of which is to the right of the median of the chest). In the Way of Radical Intuition, attention is no longer driven upwards, toward subtle objects, nor downwards, toward gross objects. Rather, there is a constant intuitive sacrifice of the root of attention, the ego-soul conception ("I") and all modification-contraction of the field of awareness, at the heart. The natural conventions of the body-being remain, but in constant alignment to this sacrifice at the heart. Thus, the body-being is "open-eyed," the life-force is aligned to the natural current via the crown or the subtle epitome above the body, but there is no stress of strategic mind. The crown is simple "gazing" or alignment to the intuition or devotional sacrifice at the heart. The crown or mind is simply the Light or Radiance of the Heart. It is what I have called the "Bright." The Radiance of the Heart springs up naturally to the Crown, and pervades the whole body, even all worlds. But there is only the eternal sacrifice at the heart, wherein all thoughts (even "I"), all conditions lose their binding implications.

4.13

Whenever this gazing sacrifice has become constant and profound intuition beyond all sense of arising conditions, the worlds, the body, thoughts, the independent self sense, such is Bhava Samadhi, the Paradox of Divine Dissolution, the Grace of Happiness beyond speech or thought.

———≡○≡———

4.14 Realization, Liberation, or Radical Understanding does not imply cognition of the Beloved (the Condition of conditions) but re-cognition of the beloved (all conditions or limitations themselves, high or low). There is no Knowledge, no cognition of the Condition of conditions. But through or in the case of the re-cognition of conditions we abide as prior rest in and identification with the Beloved, which is beyond all conditions, all knowledge, and is unspeakable.

———≡O≡———

4.15 In Sahaj Samadhi there is, effectively, but prior to all thinking, primal enquiry at the root of all arising, the Heart. That primal enquiry is equivalent to the form "Who am I?" — or, "What is That of which the root arising condition, the separate I sense, as well as all other conditions are only the present modification?" Thus, radical intuition is the undoing of all arising, but it is radical, that is, it operates at the root of all arising rather than in the field of all arising in general. It operates at the root of thought rather than, as in the case of conditional or progressive re-cognition, in the field of thought. This comes to be so more and more in Sahaj, until it is realized to be Bhava Samadhi, unqualified intuition of the Real Condition of self (separation in consciousness) and all conditions of knowledge (self-object or subject-object conditions). Sahaj Samadhi is the undoing of conditions even as they appear, while all conventions, high and low, remain projected as usual via Amrita Nadi. When radical intuition has snuffed out the root of all modifications at the Heart, there is objectless Bhava Samadhi, which is beyond all speech, knowledge, or implications of any kind, even if these appear conventionally true of the devotee to any manifest observer.

———=○=———

4.16   The tacit "Who am I?" of radical intuition is Realization of the Condition of not merely the subjective "I" but the "I" which is the whole body (both within and beyond experience). It is Realization of the Condition of all conditions, in Sahaj Samadhi or Bhava Samadhi, but it is Realization which obviates the force of all conditions at the very root of arising itself. Radical intuition is active at the root of self-identity, but it is not verbal or subjective. It is simply awareness at the root of all arising, the Heart, in which the slightest gesture toward modification is at once obviated in tacit enquiry, or prior re-cognition. It is felt at the Heart, at the "I," at the root of all arising, of all participation in modification, relations, distinctions, implications. It is simply awareness as the Heart, in which it is presently obvious that all arising is simply modification, unnecessary, and no longer binding by the conventional force of implication. Thus, such Bhava (Mood) of the Heart yields eternal Samadhi (Happiness) of the very, prior Condition, or the Divine itself. Such is Liberation, Salvation, Nirvana, the Great Happiness. This Bhava may remain even as conventions of ordinary participation appear true of the devotee to others, in this or any other realm. But only Bhava Samadhi itself remains verily true of one who is dissolved in that Sacrifice.

———=○=———

4.17 The "devotee's meditation," or Sahaj Samadhi, is the natural and spontaneous fulfillment of the disposition described in the *Bhagavad Gita,* chapter 8, verse 12 ("One should have all the gates of the body restrained, the *mind confined within the heart,* one's *life force fixed in the head,* established in concentration by yoga"). The devotee's meditation, figuratively described as contemplative absorption in the Form of God, whose feet are in the heart, and whose head is above the crown of the head, is the natural disposition, under the circumstances of conventional arising. It is Sahaj Samadhi.

The progressive process of re-cognition (in the Way of Re-cognition) is the gradually inclusive undermining of all contraction, high or low, of the field of awareness. Thus, it leads to Jnana Samadhi, the fall in the Heart, exclusive of all arising. This exclusive condition is itself spontaneously re-cognized, yielding the awakening of "open eyes," at which point the Way of Re-cognition yields to the Way of Radical Intuition.

The "devotee's meditation," "open eyes," and Sahaj Samadhi all refer to the same condition of Realization. Sahaj Samadhi is the paradoxical form of radical intuition. It is Realization of the Condition of all arising (the Heart), but it is coincident with the continuance of arising conventions or modifications, high and low. The devotee in Sahaj is constantly sacrificed at the feet of God, that is, he or she constantly enjoys the Condition of the Heart, in which all arising conditions (including separate self sense, thoughts, body, outer conditions, etc.) are seen to be only modification of the prior Condition that is the Heart (prior Conscious Bliss or Radiance). Thus, all arising is unnecessary and not binding by the force of implications, high or low. In Sahaj, this Realization is concurrent with all arising conventions. Thus, it is also described as the "regeneration of Amrita Nadi," or radical Ascent. In this Samadhi, under all conditions, self and the binding force of thought are dissolved in the true Heart, or Radical Intuition, while the Current of Radiance rises out of the Heart, concentrating or collecting the manifesting tendencies of the apparent being most perfectly above. Thus, the living force of the gross being is economized happily and no appearance, subtle or gross, personal or cosmic, binds any longer. There is a natural sense, prior to all strategic effort, dilemma, or craving, high or low, of a contemplative concentration of attention above, as if eyes and ears and feeling were all turned up to what may never be seen or heard or touched, but which is intuited to be There.

4.17

This disposition of Sahaj Samadhi is one of the two aspects of radical intuition. The second is Bhava Samadhi, or radical Realization of the Heart, prior to all arising. At random, the sacrifice at the feet of God (radical intuition of the Condition of all arising at the Heart) becomes a most perfect Enjoyment, not associated in any way with the conventional movements of the being. Sahaj Samadhi is a description of radical intuition relative to any condition that might arise, high or low, gross or subtle or super-physical or spiritual. Bhava Samadhi is most radical Enjoyment, prior to self, mind, energies, body, or any realm. It is the Heart itself, the Condition of conditions. It is transcendental liberation or Sacrifice into the Condition (or "Realm") that is God, the very Reality. It is the same and unspeakable, unknown Condition Realized in Sahaj, but it is without references, neither inclusive nor exclusive, only God, or Real Happiness.

4.17

———=O=———

4.18   Bhava Samadhi is spontaneous Enjoyment in the Way of Radical Intuition. It does not involve any strategic effort to turn attention down from above toward the heart region of the gross body. It is a version of the same Condition enjoyed as Sahaj Samadhi, in which the world of present arising is Realized to be World, or only God. The devotee (in radical intuition) simply persists in Sahaj Samadhi, which is a constant intuitive sacrifice, through prior re-cognition, at the Heart, and Bhava Samadhi appears at random, without reference to a center, to attention above or below, or to any convention of arising.

4.18

———=O=———

4.19 The Real, the Necessary Divine, is not any realm, high or low, nor any body, nor mind in any form or condition, nor any separate or separative or defined or limited self or consciousness. All such conditions arise from that Reality or prior Condition as dependent modifications and are eternally and utterly pervaded by That. But the Real, the Necessary, the Divine Truth is the Condition of conditions, Realized only in the present sacrifice of all conditions. That Sacrifice occurs when there is present intuitive insight in the midst of all presently arising conditions that they are only modification of the prior, unknown Condition. When that Sacrifice occurs there is simultaneous blissful absorption in or identification with that Condition. Such, when full and stable, is Bhava Samadhi. It is also the regeneration of Amrita Nadi, the true devotee's meditation, or Sahaj Samadhi. That Condition is utterly free of the implications of all possible and present arising. Thus, it is a Principle or Process in which the arising of limited, conditional, unnecessary conditions ceases to distract. Therefore, the conditions of self, mind, emotion, breath, life-force, body, perception, even the world, or all relations, become less and less forceful, and are often, particularly in meditative repose, unnoticed, uncognized by virtue of being priorly re-cognized. These conditions rest in the current of the being, which precedes them, and the current of the being rests in its prior Condition, Amrita Nadi, the Divine Form, or the Unqualified Conscious Bliss of Radiance, wherein the Eternal, Unknown Reality or Condition is

Intuited (rested into but not grasped) through Perfect and Eternal Sacrifice.

—≡○≡—

4.20 The Way of Yogis is through control of pranas (energies).

The Way of Saints is through control of attention.

4.20

The Way of Sages is through control of ego-formation (sense of independent or differentiated existence).

Each by his own method seeks (1) dissolution of the limitations of ego-soul, mind, body, and environments, and (2) absorption in or identification with the Reality which is the Condition of conditions. (1) is traditionally sought by manipulation of a single principle (as above), which results, perhaps temporarily, in dissolution of mind-formation (I-thought, cognition, perception), which is the key link in the chain of illusions. (2) is likewise sought as the point of release from every version of self, thought, body, and realm (even of transcendental Form, Light, or Sound). The controls sought separately and independently by Yogis, Saints, and Sages are simultaneously realized, with increased intensity at each stage, in the four-stage Way of Divine Ignorance, or Radical Understanding. In the Way of Re-cognition in particular, the virtuous controls sought by Yogis, Saints, and Sages are epitomized. In the way of Radical Intuition, the two principal goals of the traditions are perfectly and unqualifiedly Realized. At moments when various conditions or conventions, high or low, remain even in Radical Intuition, it is Sahaj Samadhi. When all conditions fall away in the Mood of this Sacrifice, prior to all Knowledge, it is Bhava Samadhi. The Way of Radical Intuition includes both Sahaj Samadhi and Bhava Samadhi.

4.20

4.21   The great path of return, demonstrated collectively by Yogis, Saints, and Sages, is itself the archetype of the individual's karmic destiny—the tendencies to which he is disposed at birth. There are gross, subtle, and causal karmas, super-conscious karmas, spiritual karmas. The experiential evidence of one's spiritual life is itself karmic. Thus, the process of spiritual practice involves conventions of the great traditional path of return, until these are made obsolete by the Power of the Samadhis of God-Realization. These conventions (developed in the stages of practice) make possible the sacrifice of the archetype of manifest existence, including all of the individual's special or unique attachments and destinies relative to it.

4.21

Each individual devotee will manifest a unique revelation of experience in this Way, depending on the characteristics and degree of intensity of the gross, subtle, and causal karmas. All will demonstrate the full revelation in experience, but some may demonstrate the revelation more profoundly in transformations of the gross life, others in subtle yogic or mystical

experiences. There is no special attainment of experience to be valued, since it must all be undone.
Therefore, there is no justification for envy and
imitation. In Sahaj Samadhi, it is clear that all phenomena, great and small, only test the Wisdom
wherein there is Only God.

4.21

———=O=———

4.22   The Way of Re-cognition is the stage in which
the two great conventional strategic motives of Yogis,
Saints, and Sages are undone. These two motives or
methods are the paths of absorption and discrimination.

4.22

The path of absorption in the subtle matrix of all
appearances is the strategic motive of Yogis and
Saints. The initial phase of the Way of Re-cognition
yields the various conditions of absorption above, in
the felt media of the single current of the being and all
manifestation. This progresses toward the tendency
of absorption in the subtle audible and visible ranges
of this same current, yielding even the various higher
yogic samadhis. However, the whole process, which
arises spontaneously and naturally, is constantly
founded in re-cognition, the process of conscious
intuitive insight, wherein all arising conditions, high
or low, are realized to be only contraction of the field
of awareness. Thus, all such absorptive tendencies
ultimately fall, with all subtle objects, however sublime.

This leads to the terminal phase of the Way of
Re-cognition, wherein the discriminative force of

re-cognition passes beyond all cognition, all absorption, even the separate self idea or I-thought, in the manner of "Not this, not this." The process itself is prior to all mentality, but it is effective discrimination in this negative sense, and yields exclusive intuition of the Condition of the root of subjectivity. Such exclusive and discriminative intuition is the conventional path of Sages. However, the tacit force of re-cognition remains even in this perfect reduction of all arising. Thus, this Jnana Samadhi is naturally and suddenly obviated by the "open eyes" of Sahaj Samadhi and the process of radical intuition.

4.22

The conscious process of radical intuition is founded in the Heart or the Real itself, prior to body, mind, and ego-soul. It proceeds in the midst of all arising, free of the conventional urges of absorption and exclusive discrimination. It tacitly represents the force of Realization which proceeds as prior re-cognition in the form "This is That, this is That, this is That." It is not the exclusive motive of discrimination of Consciousness from objects, nor the inclusive and absorptive motive of contemplative yielding to objects themselves, however subtle. Rather, it is the natural disposition of prior re-cognition or perfect intuitive identification of all arising conditions, high or low. That is, all conditions are the very Condition. They are only modification of That, and therefore are without necessity, implication, or binding force.

This intuitive identification in Truth of all arising may not be presumed by the mind or ego, except in the case of delusion. It only arises truly in the stage of perfect sacrifice, the Way of Radical Intuition. As such, it is the Principle of Sahaj Samadhi, or the true devotee's meditation. In Bhava Samadhi there is neither inclusive absorption, nor exclusive discrimination, nor even the action of prior re-cognition, which is neither inclusive nor exclusive of all arising. There is, in that case, only the most perfect abiding as That, the Real Condition, the absolute Divine or Only God.

4.22

———=O=———

4.23 The meditation that is Sahaj Samadhi is not constantly to *think:* "This present arising is only modification of the Real Condition, the Heart." There is such tacit or prior re-cognition of what arises, but all thought, even such a thought, is itself conventional contraction. Rather, the principle in Sahaj is the intuition of the Real Condition or the Heart itself, prior to contraction. The ego-soul, thoughts, body-sense, perceptions of a world — all modification is contraction at the various centers of the body-being. In Sahaj, contraction itself is obviated by constant intuition at the principal seat, the heart, of the Real Condition of all arising, that is, the Heart prior to contraction (as ego-soul, thoughts, body-sense, perceptions of any world, etc.). In Sahaj, this intuition of the Heart (the Condition of the heart) is tacit, uncaused, not in the form of action (since all action implies prior contraction). Thus, in Sahaj, there is simple intuition of the Heart, and the current which rises from the heart to the crown and beyond remains unmodified, empty of

4.23

the ego-soul contraction, not qualified by differentiation (thought-stress). Thus, Amrita Nadi and the
mind (the potential of all subtle and gross conceptions) remain as the simple Radiance of the Heart.
When thoughts, body-sense, or perception of any
world do arise, they are tacitly re-cognized (this
re-cognition is not in itself mental) to be only modification of the Heart, or the Real Condition. Thus, any
and all arising ceases to bind, or even to be prevented.
When rest as the Heart (radical no-contraction) is
perfect, there is only Radiant Consciousness, or
Bhava Samadhi, in which there are no conditions.

4.23

———≡O≡———

4.24 Bhava Samadhi is effortless abiding in the
prior or Real Condition (Ignorance-Radiance) in
which there is no arising of any objectification. Sahaj
Samadhi is the total cessation of all delusion by conventional objectification (modification). In either
case, Truth, or the Real Condition, is Ignorance-
Radiance, prior to all qualification, modification, or
objectification.

4.24

   In the common states of manifest awareness or
existence, Consciousness is apparently objectified,
reflected to itself, and qualified or motivated by the
"I" object and all other mental (high or low), bodily,
and circumstantial conditions or objects. Out of this
presumption of objectified or defined consciousness
arises the search for objective God or Reality, survival
and glamourization of the objectified self, and expe-

rience or satisfaction in, through, and by every kind of objective world, high or low. In the case of Radical Intuition, the theatre of objectification of the prior Condition (prior to awareness of any kind of object, even the "I" or ego-self-soul object and all its subjectivity) is undermined and ceases to represent any Force at all. Then torments cease. There is cessation of illusory seeking in objective theatre, and only an ordinary pleasurableness and sanity remains, while the events of manifestation take their natural and ordinary course. The apparent individual ceases to be profoundly tormented by any arising. He (man or woman) ceases to torment himself with every kind of hopeful exercise toward extraordinary fulfillment. And he ceases to torment others. He ceases to be differentiated from that Presence, which is Real, and which tends to attract all living beings into that Condition which is prior to all objectivity, wherein all delusion, torment, craving, and knowledge have already ceased.

You see, then, how unnecessary and fruitless it would be to engage the body-being in any tormenting exercise that would seek exaggerated satisfaction of born desiring, fascinated fulfillment of possibility, high or low, uncommon physical longevity (or even physical or objective immortality, gross or subtle), or conventional meditative and mystical projection into miraculous planes of objective experience above the passing elements, gross or subtle. Bubba Free John neither engages nor recommends any principle of life or meditation, founded in the illusions of objectified existence, that would implicate us in the pursuit of uncommon, extraordinary, and fascinating destinies, high or low, for their own sake. Rather, there must be critical insight into all of this round of our adventures, and simple rest in the Condition that is already true and Truth.

Bubba Free John only serves this Realization in devotees. In the course of such service he may recommend temporary use or exercise of the objective theatrical possibilities inherent in the tendencies of devotees, but this is only maintained until the lesson is realized that relieves devotees of the pattern of seeking, craving, and clinging to various objects, high or low, within or without, now or then. Thus, life and meditation in the three initial stages of the Way of Divine Ignorance involve various dimensions of theatrical involvement in the objective Play (gross, subtle, and causal), but it all serves the fourth or perfect stage of this Practice, wherein all delusion and seeking have lost their foundation or support in Sahaj Samadhi and Bhava Samadhi.

4.25   In the *Brihadaranyaka Upanishad* it is said, "Wherever there is an other, fear arises." The primal sense of independence over against objects of all kinds is identical to fear. Such is the creative root of fascination, delusion, stupidity, self-indulgence, anger, doubt, dilemma, and all seeking. Wherever there is the subjective sense, the feeling of "me," of "mine," of independent "I" — wherever there is the sense, perception, or consideration of any object, even a thought or a loved one—wherever the subject-object condition is felt arising, the feeling of "other" is awake, and the dilemma of fear motivates experience.

4.25 Wherever there is the sense of subject, object, or relationships, there is fear, and fear then makes the adventure of existence.

The whole process of the Way of Divine Ignorance involves inspection and responsibility relative to the primal incident of each moment. It involves inspection and responsibility for subjective contraction, as ego, mind, and limiting or separative identification with the apparent body in any realm. When such inspection and responsibility are perfect (in the stage of radical intuition), all arising, whether apparently subjective or apparently objective, is realized to be a single condition or primal incident—which is the awakening sense of objects (even as self, mind, and body), the feeling of "other," the energy of fear.

All arising conditions are forms of relationship, of subject-object, or of simple independence, the status of related objects. We must become responsible, through insight, for the reactive contraction, the energy and perpetual act of fear, which is our chronic way of experiencing in the subject-object field of awareness. We do not merely live as selves over against objects and others. We perpetually react, simultaneously with the sense of simple relationship itself. That reaction—the root of which is the fear that is native to the sense of other, or separation, independence, and relatedness—is contraction of the functional being. In our actions, that chronic contraction manifests as disease, discomfort, anxiety, fear, selfishness, subjective orientation, separative behaviors (passive and aggressive), and the whole drama of the avoidance of relationship. Functionally, that contraction manifests as disharmony, stress, pain, obsessive distraction and the need for fascinated consolation, chronic discharge of the life-force, vital shock or controlling root trauma, negativity, obsessive thinking and differentiating abstraction, the illusion of independent existence, and bondage to the search for survival in the maze of problem-solution incidents.

4.25

The sense of relationship (the subject-object condition) is itself the primal incident, past, present, and future. Fear or contraction is the native and simultaneous reaction to the incident of all objects. Liberation in Truth involves ultimate responsibility, through a natural pattern of transformation toward maturity, for the reaction of fear, of contraction, the avoidance of relationship. Until then, relationship and fear are the same, and life is suffering.

The Way of Divine Communion establishes the foundation of human sanity—the re-orientation to the relational condition itself, rather than the reactive condition of subjectivity, contraction, the avoidance of relationship.

The Way of Relational Enquiry realizes native responsibility for the dramatization, in action and in disposition toward relational conditions, of the avoidance of relationship, or the fear reaction to conditions arising.

In the Way of Re-cognition, the whole pattern of contraction, high and low, is inspected to the root, so that the Condition prior to reaction is stably Realized.

In the Way of Radical Intuition, the reaction of independence, subjectivity, contraction, illusion, dilemma, and fear has ceased to be necessary — so that the pattern of arising conditions is no longer the basis for contraction around the illusion of self. In Sahaj Samadhi, there is tacit (and randomly generated) re-cognition of the primal incident in each moment — which is the sense of other, of any object, of fear, of contraction, of self, of thought, of independent existence as body, psyche, or soul in the midst of relations, high or low.

Such tacit and random re-cognition is generated from the position or disposition of radical intuition, the prior and radical presumption of Ignorance. Re-cognition of all arising as modification-only is generated from no less a position than the Heart, which is prior to all contraction — prior to self, mind, body, and all relations. In the Way of Radical Intuition, tacit re-cognition, generated on the basis of radical intuition of the Real Condition, is active, moment to moment, in the field of objectification, or objectifying awareness. It is not generated from the position of self, mind, body, illusion, contraction, or doubt. It is already Enlightened or Radiant. Such re-cognition penetrates or dissolves the binding power or implication of the present subject-object sense or contraction, in whatever form it appears — as self, thought, energy, body, any object, high or low, even the very incident of relationship itself.

Tacit and random re-cognition, in the Way of Radical Intuition, is operative as the simple and

4.25

direct sense, moment to moment, that *whatever* is arising is only modification of the Real Condition, and has neither independence nor necessity.

Bhava Samadhi is simply radical intuition itself, or unqualified Ignorance-Radiance, prior not only to reactive-contraction but even to the sense of objects or relations. It can be said that the whole pattern of reactive-contraction is the theatre of self or ego-soul. It tends toward the center. The Realized pattern of all arising as modification-only, wherein objects are neither excluded nor included, but simply arise, may be said to be the Self, the Divine Person (the World). It tends toward the non-boundary at infinity. The Truth of the self and the Self is Realized in radical intuition of the Real Condition, in Sahaj Samadhi and Bhava Samadhi. Sahaj Samadhi is coincident with the conventions of self and Self, but rests in their Truth the whole while. Bhava Samadhi is simple, radical, prior Realization of the very Truth or Condition, the Divine, the Radiant Sacrifice of all Knowledge.

4.25

———=O=———

4.26   In the Way of Divine Communion there is the Realization that the vulnerability that is separateness is fundamentally an illusion, and one that is created by one's own action or presumption.

In the Way of Relational Enquiry there is the Realization that reactive emotions, the moods of separation, are fundamentally unnecessary.

4.26

In the Way of Re-cognition there is the Realization

that thought, including the concept of self or independent consciousness, is separative in effect and fundamentally unnecessary.

In the Way of Radical Intuition there is the Realization that body or specific form is fundamentally unnecessary and ultimately untrue.

In Truth there is no self, no other, no emotion, no thought, no form, but only absolute Ignorance, which is unqualified Radiance.

4.27   The disposition of Sahaj Samadhi, which is native in the Way of Radical Intuition, is the perfect Principle or Process of Awakening in Truth. It is the perfect Way of the Heart. In Sahaj Samadhi there is no longer any binding necessity in the arising conventions of ego-soul, thoughts, energy formations, body, and relations, high or low. There is rest in Divine Ignorance, the very Heart, the unspeakable Condition in which all conditions arise and of which they are mere and unnecessary modifications (illusory objectifications or forms of contraction). In Sahaj Samadhi there is no negative principle, no irreducible viewpoint toward arising conditions, no inherent dilemma from which egoic and strategic efforts of escape would be generated. Rather, all arising is simply viewed, from the point of view of the Heart (or radical intuition of the prior Condition of conditions) as unnecessary, present modification. Thus, there is simple rest in the intuited Condition itself, free of qualification by arising conditions.

This Ignorance is not exclusive, not separative, not a motive either to inwardness or outward illusions, but motiveless Bliss-Fullness, or Radiance. Divine Ignorance is eternally displayed as unqualified Radiance, or Bliss, without center or bounds.

4.27

One who abides in Sahaj Samadhi abides in perfect Ignorance-Radiance, the Divine Condition, even as conditions arise, even the conventions of gross experience. But the Samadhi is at the same moment a Principle wherein present arising is realized to be unnecessary—not other than and not a distraction from the Divine Ignorance-Radiance.

Thus, the devotee, in Sahaj Samadhi, abides in Amrita Nadi, the perfect Current of Radiance in the Heart. This current is eternal "Tapas," the Fire wherein all conditions are dissolved, or become a Sacrifice, so that the Law is fulfilled. The devotee does not in that case seek to be transferred from the gross realm to any other and higher experiential realm. There is no such motive when there is already present rest in the Divine Condition, whatever arises. But that very rest is a Principle or Fire wherein conditions are dissolved. Thus, in the Way of Radical Intuition, there is apparent, spontaneous Awakening (or "Ascension") from the theatre of the gross world, and direct Translation into the Perfect Domain. The Way of Radical Intuition is the Way of radical or Divine Transformation in Truth.

In the grosser apparent states, the devotee in Sahaj Samadhi is sacrificed, dissolved, or at rest in Amrita

Nadi, the Current from heart to crown (Heart as no-center, which is Radiance to Infinity). There is no effort to ascend by manipulation of attention. There is simply Sacrifice, through radical intuition, in the Heart or Real Condition of all present arising. There is rest in Ignorance-Radiance. But the Process is so profound it is a Fire of Light in which there is always present dissolution of limitations. Thus, the conditions arising are burned up in such Samadhi. There is Awakened Absorption in the Current of Radiance, the Bright or Unbounded Vibratory Swell of Bliss. That Absorption may be accompanied by all kinds of experiential appearances, high and low, of sound and light, of realms and bodies. But no qualification survives the Fire. No strategy is required, no method arises as binding motivation. There is simply the Process of Radical Intuition itself, relative to all conditions, high and low. Thus, Sahaj Samadhi is the perfect and Awakened Principle or Process of Translation into the Condition that is Truth or the Divine. In that case, and only in that case, there is release from manifest conditions, the necessity for repetition of the present or gross dream as well as all hierarchical dreams in subtle conditional realms. Devotees who truly become a Sacrifice in Sahaj Samadhi Awaken in the Perfect Domain by Grace. Such Awakening is Bhava Samadhi, or Translation into the Divine without qualification.

There is no such Translation apart from loving Sacrifice or persistent felt Communion with the literal Grace and Condition of the Divine. The Way is not for those whose commitment is to conditions themselves, particularly the conditions of this gross world, but only for true devotees, who are Gracefully distracted by the Divine Presence or Radiance and the Teaching of Truth or Divine Ignorance.

4.28 In Sahaj Samadhi, self, thought, body-identification, and the sense of being surrounded or bounded from without constantly dissolve in radical intuition, so that Ignorance-Radiance is the Condition, prior to all of these. There is simple dwelling in Ignorance, which is unqualified Radiance, at rest in the prior and also universal Absolute Vibratory Bliss, which is unqualified Sound or Intensity or Fire or Light, beyond speech and thought and seeing and hearing by any self. There is simple rest in that Bright, Formless Bliss, the formless Current or Absolute Speed that is Amrita Nadi, the Heart (in which all conditions arise as modification of itself), wherein there is no up or down, no in or out, no shape, no time, no place, no birth, no destiny (even while these appear in the ordinary way). When there is no noticing of conditional arising, it is Bhava Samadhi, or Translation into the Perfect Domain.

4.28

4.29 In Sahaj Samadhi, attention is dissolved or made universal in Radiance. When self, or primal

4.29

contraction, thought, cycles of the life-current and breath, body, and all relations are presently re-cognized in radical intuition and, therefore, do not obstruct the realization of the Present and Prior Condition, there

4.29 is only Ignorance, or unqualified Radiance, which is Bliss or Love, the very Divine. In the conventions of the manifest being in the waking state, this is felt as Fullness below the brows, expressed as forceful polarization from toe to crown. The crown of the body-being is thus felt and expressed as Bliss, Light, or thoughtless Absolute Vibratory Fire, pressed upon infinity, the indefinite point above. And the whole body is tacitly felt, with all appearances, not only to arise from the heart, but to arise within it, the very Consciousness, as mere and unnecessary modification. In the instant of this prior re-cognition, the body-being rests as undefined Fullness in and upon the Matrix of Radiance, from the Heart to the Crown of Infinity. There is no strategic effort to exclude arising conditions, but the force of the realization of their non-necessity undermines and dissolves them in Ignorance-Radiance, or Love, and so they are resolved at last in Bliss, prior to subject and object, prior even to waking, dreaming, and sleeping. This Awakening in Radiance exceeds by degrees the gross being in the waking state, and expands indefinitely, even penetrating the enclosures of dream and of sleep, of subtle and causal illusions, so the Condition Realized between Heart and Crown in the conditional states (waking, dreaming, and sleeping) is Realized prior to all conditions. Such is the Perfect Domain, Bhava Samadhi, Awakened Ascent or Translation into the very Divine.

This Condition and Process is Truth, before there is speech and thought, self, body, and relations. Even so, it may not merely be presumed in mind to be the case in one's own case and still be the Realized Truth of oneself. There must be the Sacrifice, the Trans- forming Fire, the Dissolution of knowledge, prefer- ences, the very being, the whole body or reflex that is self. There must be revulsion or turning, from "crea- ture and creations" to the "Creator" or Source- Condition, from the worlds and all fascinations to the Truth of every condition. But such turning or renun- ciation is not a matter of egoic and strategic separa- tion. It is true only in Ignorance, wherein not merely self but self and object, the poles of the primal inci- dent, are resolved in Radiance, Bliss, or Love, with- out center, objects, or bounds.

4.29

Sahaj Samadhi, the native Bliss, is Sacrifice, or liberation from all the consolations of this birth. Bliss is disenchantment. Love is freedom in the very act of life. When both withdrawal and illusions cease, there is Bhava, the Mood and Domain that is the Real.

4.30 When ego, or the primal contraction and division of the Real into the theatre of subjects and objects, is undone in Sahaj Samadhi, the Radiance is magnified, even bodily, as Amrita Nadi. In the instant of "open eyes," the transcendental current of

4.30

Amrita Nadi passes from the right side of the heart into the middle and left regions of the heart, then upwards in an "S" curve, front to back, via the throat, to the crown (making entrance into the lower back of the head, passing directly to the midbrain and thence up to the crown and beyond). When ego (or primal contraction) is the foundation, as it is in the conventional search for salvation or release, the passage is via sushumna nadi to the Radiance in the crown, via all the extended circuits of the body, nervous system, and brain. The latter circuit of approach is the way of passage in the "great way of return." And it must at last find its way into the Heart. The Way of Re-cognition duplicates and overcomes the way via sushumna, or the gross, subtle, and causal circuit of return in the body-being. The Way of Radical Intuition is the Way of Amrita Nadi, or regeneration in Truth, in which there is always already prior, present, and eternal Happiness, Ascent, and Awakening in the Perfect Domain.

Amrita Nadi is not open to the ego. There may not be any intentional passage through the secret pathway of the Heart, for all egoic intention is itself contraction at the root, foundation, or entrance into Amrita Nadi. The secret pathway is opened by Grace in devotees who have become a Sacrifice in Ignorance, who are Radiant prior to all knowledge, and who are liberated from all the stressful strategies of seeking in dilemma to overcome fear and limitation and difference. Therefore, the Way of Radical Intuition is necessarily preceded by the Way of Divine Communion, the Way of Relational Enquiry, and the Way of Re-cognition, in this or countless other lives in time and space.

I felt a profound emotion rising in me. It seemed to begin at the base of my spine, and when it appeared in the heart it generated an intense emotion that was overwhelmingly loving and full and yet intensely sorrowful. It rose from the heart through the throat, up the back of the head, and culminated in what appeared to be a massive dome in the crown of the skull. At that point I began to weep uncontrollably, as if all of the parts of my being had been aroused spontaneously, and I was born, suddenly conscious and alive. In the midst of this experience I had a thought that seemed to be the verbal equivalent and symbol for the whole event: "Getting to cry is shaped like a seahorse." I had become conscious of the formal structure of our living being.

Bubba Free John
The Knee of Listening

THE SEAHORSE: THE HIDDEN STRUCTURE OF ALL EXPERIENCE

4.31   The structure on which the whole body rests, and which provides the psycho-physical scheme for the "great way of return" as well as the radical Way of Divine Ignorance, is shaped like a seahorse. The heart and trunk is its prominent and controlling center or horizontal median. Extending from it vertically are two coils. One passes down, through the solar plexus, behind the navel, to the lower back, then coils forward, through the anus, perineum, and sex organs, into the front of the navel, and comes to rest in the deep core of the lower body (between the navel and the sex organs and above the perineum). It also includes the legs, or lower extremities. The other coil extends above, through the throat, to the lower rear of the brain, then coils forward along the line of the crown, down behind the forehead, up into the midbrain, and comes to rest in the deep core of the head, above the level of the eyes, and below and slightly forward from the aperture or dent in the upper crown. It also includes the arms, or upper extremities. Manifest existence, as it is communicated in man, is the play within and between the conditions inherent in the milieu of these two coils.

4.31

The heart, the horizontal foundation of the living being of man, is the seat of the three conventional states of egoic awareness (waking—on the left, dreaming—in the middle, and sleeping—on the right). Above, below, and within the heart are projected the three extended or vertical dimensions or realms of manifest experience (gross, subtle, and causal). There are also three extended or vertical systems (gross, subtle, and causal) of connection to and participation in the play between the two coils.

4.31   The first or gross system is composed of two currents or, more properly, two poles of a single current, in opposition, or a play of alternation. The two currents or tendencies of energy are represented as motion or polarization in and between each of the two coils, above and below. One of the two currents, or poles of force, is represented in the right of the brain and the right side of the whole body, and it is positive in charge ("yang"), sun-like or hot, stimulated and stimulating, and centrifugal (outward, expansive) in tendency. It is the tendency that moves, from a "point" or an already unextended or unexpanded position, out from the whole body, from the center of each of the two coils, and from the upper coil to the lower coil. The other current or pole of this pair is represented in the left side of the brain and the left side of the whole body. It is negative in charge ("yin"), moon-like or cool, calm and calming, and centripetal (inward, contracting, centralizing) in tendency. It is the tendency that moves, from an already expanded or extended position, toward the whole body, toward the center of each of the two coils, and from the lower coil to the upper coil. The expansive, repelling, or right-hand tendency is associated with the predominance of the life-force, or the etheric or pranic disposition. It is also associated with the head (origination in the upper coil of the body), the sympathetic nervous system, breath through the right nostril, the expansive quality of whole body exhalation, the back of the body, the right side, and the generative character-istics displayed by the male in play with the female. It is likewise associated with polarization or attraction toward what is already extended, or manifest out-wardly and below. The centering, attractive, or left-hand tendency is associated with the predominance of the mental or psychic disposition, or the position of awareness and its relations with energy and form. It is also associated with the lower coil of the body (as a place of origination), the parasympathetic nervous system, breath through the left nostril, the centering or self-defining quality of whole body inhalation, the front of the body, the left side, and the receptive char-acteristics displayed by the female in play with the male. It is likewise associated with polarization or attraction toward what is within and above, hidden or secret.

4.31

These two currents may also be said to twine about the spinal axis, meeting and crossing at the primary centers or "chakras" on the way. Truly, they are as one, a single system, rhythmic and alternating, ap-pearing as the explicit duality or play of opposites in the gross dimension of the manifest being. The heart-root (horizontal center) of the pair is on the left, the gross (etheric-elemental) and waking center of the heart.

The same system appears in both men and women, but in their relationships with one another, men and women represent or express opposite polarities. Thus, the elemental physical disposition of the male is typically "positive" or expansive, whereas that of the female is typically "negative" or conservative. However, the female is typically dominant or positive emotionally, whereas the male is conservative in that dimension. The male counters with a strong orientation to the mental, and the female is typically more conservative, psychic, or more passive in that orientation. The conventions of this play may vary from culture to culture, from individual to individual, and from generation to generation, but the structures upon which it is all a play are present in each body in the form of the pair of alternating or right- and left-hand currents. The male and female are not separately identical to right and left, since each contains both parts, but in their mutuality the male tends to be positive, expansive, and dominant as a physical-mental character, in which mind is devoted essentially to worldly or outward matters, and the female tends to be negative or conservative, but dominant as an emotional, psychic, and attractive character. Even in cultures or times when men and women are tending to be more whole or balanced as individuals, and thus to equal one another in ability, attractiveness, and achievement of functional goals, the mutual polarization or pleasurable opposition of life and character is not wholly undermined and erased.

The male and the female are mutually attracted and attractive. The upper is turned to the lower, the lower to the upper. The center moves out, and what is on the circle turns toward the center or root. Traditionally, spiritual teaching or communication has often been exclusively directed toward the male disposition, if not to men only. Human beings in general are commonly interpreted to be suffering from the "male" destiny. We are regarded to be overwhelmed by outward and gross distractions. Thus, the usual recommendation is to avoid relations with the "woman," the extended world, but to *be* the true woman, or the ascending character. The recommended way to do this is to turn within and upward, and thus return to Source. If we embrace the "woman," it is felt, we are being the "man," and thus we are only played upon by changes and danced to death. But if we become the "woman," if, in other words, we reverse the current of attention, then we may realize the Origin.

4.31

All of that is really a symbolic and dualistic description of the body as a problem. But the body is a paradox of pairs, not a dilemma or opposition of two, and not a simple line from Light to Darkness. Its two potentials are not separable, and neither one of its coils is itself and independently identical to the ultimate and perfect Source that is Truth. At best we may say that a balance, a dynamic harmony of the two tendencies of the body-being, is appropriate and most conducive to a normal or pleasurable fulfillment of the life cycle.

As the devotee matures in practice in the Way of Divine Ignorance, responsibility follows experience and Revelation, so that the harmony of the dynamics of gross life becomes a matter to be addressed directly, moment to moment. In the maturity of the Way of Relational Enquiry, the harmonious or balanced "conductivity" of the living being becomes an awakened responsibility. In the Way of Re-cognition, the

foundation of balance, or the equalization of the
opposites in the gross play, which has been established
in the previous stages, is made a platform from which
the play between the upper and the lower coils may be

4.31   considered. In that case, a cycle is discovered wherein
the upper, senior, or subtle coil is either detached or
oriented relative to the lower, dependent, or gross
coil. The mechanism recovered is one in which the
figure of the "Seahorse" is effectively worked as if it
were a figure "8," wherein lines of life or light pass
directly to and from the centers of each of the two coils
to the opposite coil, above or below.

There is a mechanism whereby the two currents or
poles of the gross system achieve utility as a single or
harmonious current that unifies and effectively transforms and resolves the gross play and even makes it
possible to redirect its energy-attention into the subtle
sphere. That mechanism is provided by a second or
subtle system, made of a single, direct current (but
which may be polarized either toward the crown or
toward the toes), and which is coincident with the core
of the spinal line. It runs between the twin or alternating currents, and extends from the life-root above
the perineum (even from the toes) to the base of the
brain and thence to the whole brain. This second
system represents the resonance, or balance and
union, of the two coils and their play in opposition.
It is implicitly rather than explicitly dualistic, representing a subtle (truly "sattwic" or harmonious and
bright) play of the polar opposites, which are otherwise dramatized via attraction and repulsion, the
gross play of the twin, alternating currents of the gross

system. Its functional horizontal center is in the middle of the heart, the subtle (including the mental as well as the super-mental, or pre-mental, which is intuitional and prior to thought) and dreaming center of the heart. It is sushumna nadi, the middle path, free of extremes. It is the royal route of the higher being, the superior passage, which leads from mastery over life, breath, body, desire, emotion, speech, and gross, reactive mentality, and passes up into the greater mental and super-mental domains, communicated in the precious deep core of the midbrain and upper brain.

4.31

Both of these vertical or extended systems (sushumna nadi, the senior and subtle, and the alternating pair, which is junior and gross) are rooted in the horizontal or ultimate Source-plane of the heart. But the heart is, in this conventional or manifest play, a root contraction (or cause of the coils). Therefore, experiences are constantly sought in the vertical planes of experience, above, below, and altogether beyond, which will release the being from the inherent sense of separation, vulnerability, fear, obsession, and self-possession. But there is no release until the primal error, illusion, or lie at the root of the heart is undone.

Sacrificial discipline in response to the communicated Grace of the prior and Divine Reality yields gradual release from the degrees of illusion, gross, subtle, and causal. Thus, at first the pair of alternating currents surrounding the spinal line are purified and balanced. The exclusively etheric and the exclusively gross physical or elemental tendencies are brought into a condition of harmony rather than opposition (the antagonism between life and matter, or death). This occurs once the whole heart, the horizontal foundation, is established as the predominant center of the body-being. Such is the Grace awakened through feeling, love, and heart-felt surrender to the Divine Presence in the Way of Divine Communion. This is extended through penetrating insight or enquiry (in the form "Avoiding relationship?") in the Way of Relational Enquiry. This process at last reveals the central and balanced current of sushumna nadi (awakened as "conductivity" in the maturity of the Way of Relational Enquiry). Thus, when there is purification and balance of the exclusive tendencies (outward and inward) in the gross or living being, the heart becomes still, a realized harmony, and the middle or subtle expression of the heart (as "soul," or spiritualized ego) becomes active.

The play in sushumna nadi is commonly devoted to the search for Source, or the "great way of return." Thus, the middle heart of subtle devotion, reaching above to the vertical (but only reflected) Source beyond body and mind, is the conventional controller of sushumna nadi, and attention is directed upwards, toe to crown (gross to subtle). However, another exercise is also possible in sushumna nadi, directed from the middle or subtle region of the heart, whereby even the gross body-being, crown to toe (subtle to gross) is "spiritualized" or "immortalized" via the inbreathing of transcendental or subtle Light (and its transformed and transforming chemistry) into both the upper and lower coils of the body-being. Such is an evolutionary way, as opposed to the regressive manner of the great way of return. The evolutionary way of sushumna nadi acts in opposite fashion to the regressive way of sushumna nadi. In the regressive way, the force of life and attention is withdrawn upward from the lower coil. This is done because the life is always tending to be discharged through the navel, the sex organs, and the anus. Thus, it is strategically withdrawn up the spinal line to the midbrain and crown, where the vision of Light may be attained. In the evolutionary way, the habits of exploitation of the lower being are first purified and transformed, so that the coil forward from the base of the body to the deep core of the navel remains unbroken under the ordinary conditions of gross existence. Then the effective Light may be drawn down from the deep regions of the crown and above, and conducted into the life center.

4.31

The reason sushumna nadi, or the subtle mechanism of the being, may be exploited in either of two exclusive directions (upward, toward illumination of mind, or downward, toward illumination or immortalization of the body) is that it implicitly contains the two tendencies made explicit in the alternating pair which surrounds sushumna nadi. Sushumna nadi extends or is projected vertically from the horizontal and prior position of the heart, and not from either the crown or the perineum (or the toes). It is projected from the heart as two coils, one above and one below. The lower coil opens toward the infinity of gross elements via the anus, sex-organs, etc. The upper coil opens toward the infinity of subtle elements via the aperture of the crown, the midbrain, etc. But both coils have their epitome, root, source, and balance or control in the heart.

Whether the search is for immortality by evolution or salvation by regression, the drama is a strategic, egoic adventure, an illusion, an unnecessary and wholly secondary enterprise, which is undermined when the heart is Awakened to its Divine Condition in Truth. Whether the process in sushumna nadi is directed toward regression or evolution, the subtle or middle region of the heart and the subtle expressions of sushumna nadi (whether ascending from the gross toward the subtle, or descending from the subtle toward the gross) rest upon a motivating lie, the root contraction or primal differentiation of subject and object. Thus, at last, in the Way of Re-cognition, the ultimate origin (or destiny) of sushumna nadi is realized to be rooted not in the crown or the navel, but in the right side of the heart, wherein the primal contraction originates and is at last undone. The passage downwards between the crown of sushumna nadi and the causal root, the most prior horizontal center on the right side of the heart, is the third (causal) and conventional system of connection and participation in the play of the two coils of the manifest being.

When the primal contraction of the heart is undone, as it is in perfect Ignorance (in the Way of Radical Intuition), the prior Condition or Radiance, in which all conditions appear as only modification, stands free and Awake. This Awakening spontaneously establishes a process of regeneration—not directly of the gross, subtle, or causal conditions themselves (although these only gradually fall away, made obsolete through non-necessity), but of the very or Divine Condition, or most prior Ignorance-Radiance itself, the Truth of the heart.

This regenerative Process in Truth is the Way of Amrita Nadi, the secret pathway, the Current of the Heart, or very Ignorance, expressed as Radiance to Infinity. Amrita Nadi is the Way of Radical Awakening into the Perfect Domain. Amrita Nadi is the matrix of sushumna nadi, but it is not ultimately equivalent either to the dynamics of the spinal line or the play between left and right. It precedes all conditions of the manifest heart, the ego, the primal root of gross, subtle, and causal conditions. After attention passes up in sushumna nadi, through the middle of the heart to the brain centers, it passes down again to the right of the heart, the causal root, the root of the ego or primal contraction, the region of deep sleep, the dualistic void, prior to subtle and gross appearances. But Amrita Nadi in Truth is the regenerated pathway, Radiant to the two coils, and non-exclusive, rather than regressive and reductive. In that case, the third vertical passage, or causal system, as well as the vertical subtle and gross systems of the whole body, cease to function as an illusory, independent being. Then Amrita Nadi is absolutely, priorly, and already free of the egoic illusions (gross, subtle, and causal). The Way of Amrita Nadi in Truth is Awake only in devotees in Sahaj Samadhi.

I am moved to describe the secret of Amrita Nadi to you. It is not itself that vertical current which passes up to the crown. It is the Heart itself, prior to ego, mind, life, body, and worlds. But when the Heart is Awake in Sahaj Samadhi, the present surviving con-

4.31

ventions of the gross, subtle, and causal play remain apparent. Thus, the unqualified Radiance of the Heart appears to spring up in the body and the worlds. When this occurs, the Radiance springs up in sushumna 4.31 nadi and even in all the currents of the gross being. I have said that Amrita Nadi passes up to the crown. But this is only the initial appearance in the Awakening of Sahaj Samadhi. It is simply the regeneration of sushumna nadi and the upper coil. But there is also the simultaneous regeneration of the whole lower coil of sushumna nadi below, as well as the alternating currents of the gross being. The natural hierarchical polarization, toe to crown, may also appear to remain, but the conventional limitations of ego-contraction, thought, independent body-identification, and bondage to the points of view of action, time, and space are obviated (realized to be without necessity) in Sahaj Samadhi. Natural human activities tend to continue as long as life remains, but free of the illusion and the problematic view of independent consciousness, independent mind — or even independent life, body, world, and God. It is as if a line of Light were plumbed between the deep center of the upper coil (midbrain to crown) and the deep center of the lower coil (below and behind the navel). Not only the sahasrar, but the whole body becomes full of Light or Radiant Bliss. This entire Fullness is the *reflection* of the Heart. *All* of it is Amrita Nadi. Amrita Nadi thus has no exclusive identification with forms above. It does not exclude what is below. It neither excludes nor includes any arising. It is Radiance itself, which pervades all things, is all things, and which is eternally unchanged.

Therefore, no acts of attention native to the play of manifestation are a specific characteristic of Sahaj Samadhi. It is Ignorance-Radiance, prior to gross, subtle, and causal illusions. Secondarily, in the presently surviving conventions of manifest or conditional appearance, the Radiance may seem to be rooted in the right side of the heart, or to rise up in an "S" curve (the shape of the "Seahorse" above the mid-line), or to be expressed as equal Fullness below (demonstrating its non-exclusive Nature). But in Truth there is no Amrita Nadi in itself, no independent pathway that represents Truth in the being. There is only the Heart, the Real itself, Radiance prior to all knowledge, all appearances. Thus, Bhava Samadhi is also the Realization of Truth, the Heart, perfectly prior to all illusions and even to mere arising of the conventions of manifest experience. "Amrita Nadi" is the symbol of the radical and ongoing Process of Dissolution of gross, subtle, and causal conventions and conditions in Sahaj Samadhi. Bhava Samadhi is perfect and prior Sacrifice, Love, or Radiance without center or bounds. It is the prior Realization of the Perfect Domain. Therefore, Amrita Nadi does not survive with form in Bhava Samadhi.

The sleep condition is senior to waking and dreaming. It is their root—simple awareness, previous to thought and body sense. It is awareness without extension, tacitly defined by darkness or non-conscious Radiance. Likewise, dreaming, or the primal sense of

4.31

objects arising to the most primitive sense of subject self, is hierarchically senior to waking, or the complex dramatization of subject and object in fixed forms. Just so, the causal condition (in the heart) is senior (causative) to subtle (in the crown) and gross (in the navel) conditions, while the subtle is also senior to the gross.

4.31

Therefore, the hierarchically senior or root center of the manifest being is the meeting place or origin of the causal and deep sleep conditions. This is in the heart, on the right. The position immediately junior to it is the meeting place or origin of the subtle and dreaming conditions. This is in the deep place of the midbrain or crown. The passage from the crown into the heart on the right is thus the psycho-physiological sign of the final passage which precedes Awakening. When the root on the right side of the heart (the seat of the primal contraction, the ego, the differentiation of subject and object) is penetrated, the whole heart is released from the conventions of waking, dreaming, and sleeping. The heart becomes the Heart, the prior Ignorance, or unqualified Consciousness. This corresponds to Jnana Samadhi, in the maturity of the Way of Re-cognition.

When the exclusive disposition of Jnana Samadhi (seclusion in the Heart) is itself penetrated, the phenomenon of "open eyes" appears, which is the sign of the Awakening in Sahaj Samadhi. This Awakening coincides secondarily with the regeneration of the structural hierarchy of the manifest being. Thus, Amrita Nadi (at first experientially identified with the regeneration of the passage between the whole heart

—left, middle, and right—and the crown above)
Ascends as Radiance, liberating the mind, the root of
the upper coil, from limitation or implication by
thought and all subtle conditions, which merely mod-
ify the Light. The regeneration of Radiance continues, however, so that the lower coil (the gross center
of waking awareness, to which the upper, subtle-
mental-dreaming center is senior) is also clarified in
the regenerated Radiance. Thus, Amrita Nadi is,
ultimately, the whole body. It pervades the whole
body vertically, as the Radiance which precedes and
yet pervades all vertical conditions (gross, subtle, and
causal), and horizontally, as the Ignorance which precedes all horizontal conditions (waking, dreaming,
and sleeping). (The regeneration of the upper coil
predominates in the moment of "open eyes," the
initial Awakening in Sahaj Samadhi. As the Way of
Radical Intuition demonstrates its maturity in the
being, the Fullness and Equality of both coils characterizes the Ascended or Awakened and Perfectly
Expanded Realization in Sahaj Samadhi, and from
this maturity Bhava Samadhi randomly appears.)

4.31

In Sahaj Samadhi, Fullness is felt at the Heart. This
is duplicated above and below, in the deep core of
each of the two coils. Thus, in the conventional
states (waking, dreaming, and sleeping—the horizontal
conditions of the manifest heart) and under apparent
extended or manifest conditions (gross, subtle, and
causal—the vertical conditions of the extended being)
there is simply a sense of prior Fullness in the midst of
the head, in the midst of the lower body, and in the
midst of the heart. The line between these three

centers (crown, heart, navel) is the true Amrita Nadi (viewed from the point of view of maturity in Sahaj Samadhi relative to the waking state).

4.31 The manifest being is not then exclusively polarized toe to crown (strategically in opposition to the gross dimension of experience, as in the "great way of return"), nor even strategically polarized crown to toe (as in the evolutionary manipulation of sushumna nadi, which might motivate the being previous to Realization of the prior Condition or Truth of the heart and of the whole extended being). There is simply Ignorance-Radiance. There is no exclusive polarization, but a natural and equal Fullness both above and below (between the two coils). The Heart does indeed and primarily Radiate to the crown (the upper coil). But it also and secondarily Radiates to the navel (the lower coil). The whole vertical being thus becomes Radiance, but on the basis of the horizontal, the Heart (Ignorance). Thus, attention is not motivated exclusively to go up to subtle worlds or descend to elemental conditions—nor is it motivated to confusion in the pair of alternating currents—but the whole being is instead sattwic, balanced, priorly free of the strategies of attention. Sushumna nadi is not any longer a futuristic machine, in which to go up or down, but it is balanced (the coils above and below are equal in their Fullness). There is rest as the Heart Condition. (As much goes below as above—this is Balance, or Peace, which is Fullness, Bliss.) This Process in Sahaj Samadhi is Awakening in Radiance-only. It also (and equally) obviates (makes priorly unnecessary, without excluding in principle) *all* manifest conditions (gross, subtle, causal, waking, dreaming, sleeping, above, below, within, without). Thus, it is without motivation in itself. It is unqualified Radiance, or Love, without question or answer. It is neither mortal nor immortal, but only Real Bliss, the perfect fulfillment of the Law (which is Sacrifice).

4.31

Because all conditions are unnecessary, the Process in Sahaj may be described as radical Ascent from the present realm. But all conditions are presently and *equally* unnecessary. Thus, radical Ascent is not conventional Ascent to the subtle above, but the Dissolution of limitation by *any* present arising. The Heart, the prior Ignorance-Radiance itself, is the Destiny, rather than what is above or below. Thus, there is no characteristic attitude, no intention up or down, which characterizes Sahaj Samadhi. The mood of changes, up to the subtle futures or down to gross immortality, is false, based on one or the other exclusive polarization of sushumna nadi. Only the Heart is Truth, and the Realized Heart makes sushumna nadi Static, while also perfectly Intense, as is the pure and whole Heart. It is an unqualified Radiance that stands between the cores of the two coils. It goes equally up and down. It is the Heart itself.

This is the secret of Sahaj Samadhi. This is the true Revelation of Amrita Nadi. There is no vision, no mind, no sound, no object, no self-center, no up, no down, no time, no space. There is only Love, the Condition of all arising, whether or not there is any arising. It is Sacrifice, which is Liberation from the great Fear, the great Withholding, the great Contraction in which Knowledge is forever sought in order to escape the Void of Life and Death. Sacrifice is Bliss, prior to all Knowledge, all Gnostic consolation of religion, magic, yoga, mysticism, and spiritual ascent. It is Nirvana, Disenchantment, Freedom, Peace, No Difference. Love is before Joy and Sorrow.

4.31

The true Heart is unqualified Ignorance, or very Existence, undivided, unanswered, prior to all dilemma. Amrita Nadi, in Truth, regenerated, is unqualified Radiance, Bliss-Fullness of Consciousness, prior to the sense of existence in or as gross forms (body, life-force, emotions and relations), subtle forms (mind, or thoughts, visions, auditions, and thoughtless but objective intuitions of reflected Radiance), or causal forms (subject conditions, generative contractions, leading up and down). Thus, Amrita Nadi does not truly or ultimately stand up in the natural heart, in the midst of the body, between the brain and the navel. It is the Divine Form itself, the Perfect Domain, prior to subject and object, even while conventional conditions continue to appear in play. It is the Unspeakable or Undifferentiated Condition, Awakened when the illusions of independence, or objectification and subjectivity, are dissolved in the left, the middle, and the right of the heart. Then only the prior Condition of the Heart, the Real, Ignorance-Radiance, is Truth. That Condition is Paradox. It neither excludes nor includes conventions of manifestation, high or low. All conditions are without necessity. And yet conditions persist, prior to causation (which only accounts for change, not origination). While noticing persists, it is Sahaj Samadhi. When noticing does not arise, it is Bhava

Samadhi. In neither case is the sense of independent subjectivity necessary, binding, true, or real. Only objects of all kinds arise unanswered forever, noticed and unnoticed in the Fever of Bliss, or Real God. All the paradoxes are the sign of Truth. Now I have said it.   *4.31*

———≡O≡———

4.32   Fear is the least expanded or extended emotion arising reactively in the lower coil. It is associated with the neutral root in the middle of the lower coil (between the navel and the sex organs and above the perineum). It is also projected via the perineum, the   *4.32* solid foundation, the body's earth. Sorrow is a form of reactive withdrawal from an already extended position. It is associated with predominance of the left side, the "female" impulse, and the theatre of sexuality. It is projected via the sex organs, the watery elemental region of the body. Anger is the most expanded or extended emotion arising in the reactivity of the lower coil of the body-being. It is associated with predominance of the right side, the "male" impulse, and frustration of the force of the solar plexus and the region behind the upper area of the navel. It is also projected via the anus, the outer and downward directed extension of the digestive fire.

Thus, the three characteristic lower reactive emotions appear to be generated in ascending order, from fear to sorrow to anger, and this is true. But they are also aligned to the shape of the body's lower coil (fear at the central root of the coil, sorrow at the sex organs, and anger at the solar plexus). Likewise, they relate to the middle, left, and right currents of polar terminals in the lower body, and to the three lower focuses of the life current (perineum, sex organs, and anus).

4.32

There is a correspondence between the line from the throat to the lower rear of the brain and the line between the solar plexus, the lower back, and the anus. Likewise, the forebrain is analogous to the region of the sex organs. And the line between the midbrain and the crown aperture is analogous to the line between the root of the lower coil and the perineum.

As above, so below — and vice versa. What is above is senior, but it is not God or Truth. The scheme above and the scheme below are a paradoxical pair, not a dilemma of absolute alternatives. The heart is the Source, and Truth is at the heart. Those who are wise beyond the knowledge and attractiveness of *both* heaven and earth may become devotees of this Truth.

———=O=———

4.33 Jnana Samadhi is the mature Realization of the Way of Re-cognition. It is Realization of the same and very Truth that is native to Sahaj Samadhi and Bhava Samadhi. But the Realization is not stable. It is held in place by the exclusive or reductive effort by which it is awakened.

4.33

The Way of Re-cognition duplicates the "great way of return." Thus, it is a *reductive* process, moving from grosser contemplation (of elemental body-sense, its elemental or worldly relations, and the breathing cycle of the life-force, or the etheric dimension of the whole body) to subtle contemplation (of the process of thoughts, of cognition through perception of gross objects, and of cognition through perception of subtle objects, or higher mental perception and transcendental intuition via subtle audition and sight) to contemplation of the hierarchical root of cognition, the primal act of attention, the process which generates the sense of the witness or knower as specific, independent consciousness, self, soul, or ego.

4.33

There is a secret hidden in the reductive process of the Way of Re-cognition. That secret is the passage into Jnana Samadhi, which is an exclusive intuition of the Perfect Domain, the Divine Heart, the Unqualified Condition in which all manifest appearances are dreamed.

Jnana Samadhi is realized when re-cognition passes beyond the contemplation of body, life, thought, and mind prior to thought, by re-cognizing all of these as only contraction of the field of consciousness, or the Vibratory Expanse which surrounds and pervades the ego or witnessing subject. This done, there is similar re-cognition of the act of attention, the contraction as specific consciousness, or the process of witnessing or contemplating conditions arising. In that instant of re-cognition—which becomes more and more prolonged and profound as the meditation progresses each day—there is no self, no mind, no body, no world, no objects of any kind, but only an indescribable and formless Happiness.

The processes that are unique to the Way of Re-

cognition are primarily engaged in formal meditation. It is a Way of inspecting the subtler conditions
of experience, which are otherwise, conventionally
and traditionally, viewed as Divine or Higher Reality
and Truth. In the Way of Re-cognition, these conditions are re-cognized, or known again in Truth as only
contraction — or experience which depends on birth,
which is the viewpoint of independent and exclusive
consciousness.

4.33

In the mature meditation of the Way of Re-cognition,
the conditions in the two extended coils of the whole
body-being come to rest, and the heart, from which
they proceed or are extended above and below, becomes the native focus of the whole being. The conditions of the lower coil of life and elemental form come
to rest and are resolved in the heart. Just so, thought,
even the higher objects of the illumined mind, the
whole extended upper coil of the being, becomes
naturally resolved in the heart. Thus, at last, there
is contemplation or contemplative penetration of the
secret of the heart. The hierarchical root of the upper
and lower coils stands forth like a hole in the universe.

There is a technical revelation at this stage which is
secret to the awakening being. It is not a thing of the
mind. But this much may be said. In the transition to
Jnana Samadhi, the Truth of the whole body in its
first, original essential form, prior to all the complications of subjectivity, of knowledge, and of experience
of any kind, high or low, is revealed most directly.

The heart itself is the heart of the whole body.
There is a primal stress always felt at the heart. It is

itself birth in every moment. It is the heartbeat itself. Even more, it is the very sense of feeling-stress at the heart — the sense of independent or differentiated existence. It is primal vibratory stress or contraction, felt most directly, in the case of the human being, as the heartbeat.

4.33

Body, life, emotion, thought, perception, contemplation, and all relations are a rhythmic theatre timed to the heartbeat — self-defining, self-confining. It is the primal contraction or root of birth. It is always in the present. It is the last illusion to be uncovered.

The Way of Re-cognition proceeds beyond the thoughts and strategic failures in relationship that characterize the gross life by birth. In the Way of Divine Communion and the Way of Relational Enquiry there is insight which liberates the being from confinement by the relentless commitment to a gross dramatization that neither looks nor feels nor is nor acts as the complete happiness of which it is always and natively certain. The commitment itself may still characterize the being by tendency, but there is also a simultaneous and liberating intuition of the Condition in which its impulse always appears. Therefore, dramatization and concern become unnecessary as the response of the whole body-being to its subjective tendencies.

The Way of Re-cognition begins when the binding force of the subjective or separative character has weakened to the point where the being may begin to become responsible (free by insight) relative to the subtler dimensions and, ultimately, the causal dimension of the theatre of birth. Thus, contemplation previous to thought and gross relations begins and matures at this stage.

4.33 It proceeds until there is stable re-cognition not only of the contractions that are the body-sense and its gross relations, but of life, emotion, thought, and transcendental contemplation. When this occurs, the process of re-cognition turns upon the act of attention itself, prior to thought. In meditation, the mind and brain become as if transparent, empty, but bright. Then there is simple awareness of the breath, and the cycle of breath gradually comes to rest in re-cognition. At last there is feeling-absorption in the incident that is the heart, and which is the primal origin and expression of all that is outside the body, all that is subjective to the body, and all that is the whole body itself. Then re-cognition of birth, of separation, of self, of knowledge, and of all conditions of born-existence becomes dissolution of the ego in the Condition which is prior to birth, and survival, and death. Such is Jnana Samadhi.

However, a tension remains in Jnana Samadhi. It is the tension between rest in the revealed Happiness (the Truth of the heart) and the possibility of contraction—the possibility of the re-appearance of the sense of separate self and of all objects, subtle and gross. Jnana Samadhi is Realized by a process of gradual reduction, from a most extended position to a position most hierarchically senior to it. Thus, Jnana Samadhi would effectively exclude all conditions from the field of awareness.

The reductive position or Wisdom of Jnana Samadhi is thus unstable — threatened by the force of arising conventions. Thus, when the body-being is aware of ordinary conditions (gross or subtle), it alternatively craves to indulge them or to penetrate to the seclusion or utter rest of Jnana Samadhi. The tension in the Realization thus comes to be expressed in subtle conflict, and the contemplation of all of this at last leads to re-cognition of the tension itself. This degree of awakening of re-cognition is expressed as "open eyes," the transition from Jnana Samadhi to Sahaj Samadhi, in which the process of arising is no longer prohibited.

4.33

In Sahaj Samadhi, the conventions of self-reference (without bondage to the condition of independent consciousness), mind, life, body, and worlds or objects, high and low, continue to arise, but they are tacitly, or priorly and all simultaneously, re-cognized, moment to moment, as only modification of the prior Condition, Consciousness, or unqualified Ignorance-Radiance in which all arising appears. There is radical intuition of the same Condition intuited in Jnana Samadhi, but there is no strategic effort or reductive and exclusive disposition implied in the Realization. The process of re-cognition by which Jnana Samadhi is held in place is one which penetrates through the degrees of manifest being, through to its subjective root, and through to its primal root, from which the extended born-condition is conceived. The process of re-cognition native to Sahaj Samadhi is one in which all conditions, from the primal to the most extended subtle and gross extensions, are re-cognized *simultaneously,* moment to moment, rather than reductively and progressively over time.

Thus, in Sahaj Samadhi there is no implicit reductive process leading toward a hierarchical core, or a condition superior to the gross appearance, or a mystical position from which to contemplate the Real exclusive of the manifest. Sahaj Samadhi is expressed as a process of tacit, prior, simultaneous re-cognition of all arising conditions in every moment. There is no reductive effort or stress. No possible condition is regarded as radically unique or higher, but all conditions at once, simultaneous with the moment of their arising, are re-cognized as only modification of the Condition (most prior, but neither exclusive nor inclusive of any arising) in which the whole body-being and all objective conditions it may conceive rest in radical intuition.

Sahaj Samadhi is perfect meditation. It is constant, moment to moment, and is no more or less direct in formal sitting (which continues, either regularly or at random) than at any other time. However, the power of this prior re-cognition intensifies over time, so that the born being, extended above and below, or the manifest dream altogether, becomes a less and less potent gesture. In Sahaj Samadhi, arising conditions are not in principle prevented, but their non-necessity (as mere modification) is obvious. The Realization of the non-necessity of all arising is expressed more and more as natural diffusion, rest, or tacit abiding in the Condition prior to, but neither exclusive nor inclusive of, any arising.

Bhava Samadhi is the same Realization implicit in both Jnana Samadhi and Sahaj Samadhi. It is not a State over against or exclusive of any or all other states of existence or experience. It is simply that the native disposition in Sahaj Samadhi is one in which all aris- 4.33 ing conditions are equally unnecessary. (In Jnana Samadhi all arising is regarded as equally negative in effect.) When arising conditions are Realized to be unnecessary, they begin to be neither prevented nor grasped. Thus, as the process in Sahaj Samadhi matures, both the reductive tendency that leads to Jnana Samadhi and the ordinary distracted tendency to include more and more experience come to an ease in which prior or radical intuition of the Real Condition is all that stands out. Thus, Bhava Samadhi, or abiding in the Real Condition prior to any arising or noticing, appears at random, briefly, then more profoundly.

Bhava Samadhi is not a preferred State to be sought. Sahaj Samadhi and Bhava Samadhi are equal. Bhava Samadhi is the native Nirvanic Bliss, prior to birth. Bhava Samadhi appears at random moments of absolute contemplation during this life, and it is permanently or most radically Realized at death in the case of those who yield to the Sacrifice absolutely. (In other cases, the conditions of manifestation, high and low, may continue relative to the natural disposition of Sahaj Samadhi.) Sahaj Samadhi is the same Bliss as Bhava Samadhi, realized even as all manifest conditions arise. Sahaj Samadhi does not in itself imply an effort to pass into the realms that are subtle or subjective and inward relative to the whole body, but it is always released into the Divine Condition prior to the whole body itself. Sahaj Samadhi is effortless, prior re-cognition of the whole body, the simultaneous event of all arising, at once. Therefore, it too is perfect or radical intuition of the Condition of all arising. Jnana Samadhi is re-cognition of the hierarchical root of the whole body, but its intuition of the Real Condition depends on an exclusive effort or tension in which the stress of independent existence is projected on the Realization itself—so that the Real and the conditions arising are felt to be necessarily independent of one another. Therefore, only in Sahaj Samadhi and in Bhava Samadhi is the Real Condition obvious in Truth.

Truth is the Secret of the whole body, not a version of its mere inwardness or hierarchical subtlety, which only arises as limitation, like the born body-being as a whole. Truth stands prior to the whole body, not within or outside it, but even as it. The Way to Truth is most direct intuitive re-cognition of the whole body itself, in which its subjective and reductive or re-coiling disposition is come to rest. The heart itself is the Way to this Secret Truth. May all beings run to this mere Truth by Grace.

4.34 Stay healthy. Do not overeat or overdrink. Do not burden the body with more toxins than it can quickly eliminate. The feeling of bodily aliveness should be constant, under all conditions. The feeling of the strength of life should always be in the navel. Conventional orgasm, negativity, and dilemma (or doubt) discharge the infilled Power of the body-being and weaken it, above and below. Therefore, these must become matters of responsibility as your practice progresses by stages.

4.34

Remain *in* love. Abide as "I love you" under all conditions. Do not dramatize the mood "You don't love me," but remain always as whole body attention, or love, heart-felt.

The head should perpetually feel. The mind is the feeling of Radiant Love, the Bright. Always feel as Radiance-Only, with and as the head, as the whole body.

Be surrender. Not by effort, but by virtue of perfect Ignorance.

Become the Process itself, through surrender rather than abstraction.

Throw away everything and be infilled with Living Light, the Perfect and Transforming All-Pervading Power of the Heart, of Ignorance, with every breath. Thus, live by Faith, through natural and spontaneously voluntary adaptation of body, sex-force, feeling, breath, awareness, and attention to the Living Light which is heart-felt to be all-pervading in Ignorance (mental, emotional, sexual, physical).

As the stages progress, spend more time in undisturbed privacy each day, abiding in this Ignorance, this surrender as the whole body. Discard the force of all conditions, all contractions. Be full as Radiance-Only. Be transformed each moment forever.

Love, the Heart, is the single Intensity from which

Light and Life, or Living Light, flows. Love is Radiance-Only. It is the uncreated Intensity realized in Ignorance. It appears first as a Presence, and then as the Real or Very Condition of all conditions. Therefore, we are Ignorance only, and we cannot account for anything that is arising. The Law is Sacrifice, not Knowledge. Sacrifice, which springs from Ignorance, is the Source of Wisdom and immortal Happiness, or Fullness.

4.34

4.35   In the *Bhagavad Gita,* chapter 8, verses 7-16, in which Lord Krishna instructs his devotee, Arjuna, the esoteric foundation of life and meditation in the Way of Divine Ignorance, or Radical Understanding, is summarized:

4.35

7. Therefore at all times remember Me and fight. When thy mind and understanding are set on Me, to Me alone shalt thou come without doubt.

8. Whoever meditates on the Supreme Person with his thought attuned by constant practice and not wandering after anything else, Partha [Arjuna], reaches the Person, Supreme and Divine.

9. He who meditates on the Seer, the ancient, the ruler, subtler than the subtle, the supporter of all, whose form is beyond conception, who is sun-colored beyond the darkness,

10. He who does so, at the time of his departure [in death or meditation], with a steady mind, devotion and strength of yoga, and setting well his life force in the centre of the eyebrows, attains to this Supreme Divine Person.

11. I shall briefly describe to thee that state which the knowers of the Veda [the Truth] call the Imperishable, which ascetics freed from passion enter, and desiring which they lead a life of self-control.

12. One should have all the gates of the body restrained, the mind confined within the heart, one's life force fixed in the head, established in concentration by yoga.

13. He who utters [or realizes] the single syllable Aum [which is Brahman], remembering Me as he departs, giving up his body [in death or meditation], he attains to the highest goal.   *4.35*

14. He who constantly meditates on Me, thinking of none else, who is a yogin ever disciplined [or united with the Supreme], by him I am easily reached.

15. Having come to Me, these great souls do not return to rebirth, the place of sorrow, impermanent, for they have reached the highest perfection.

16. From the realm of Brahma downwards, all worlds are subject to return to rebirth, but on reaching Me, O Son of Kunti [Arjuna], there is no return to rebirth.[8]

The fulfillment of this instruction does not come by conventional effort, or on the basis of ordinary understanding. Indeed, even this instruction, as straightforward as it appears, is full of paradoxes and hidden meanings. But, properly understood, and realized in the form of true practice, it represents a complete and essential summation of the whole process of my work and the stages of practice, or true adaptation, communicated in the Way of Divine Ignorance, the Way of Radical Understanding. All those who truly fulfill this Way of Ignorance, in the form of real practice or lawful re-adaptation in my true, spiritual, and transcendental Company, will enjoy the Destiny promised to Arjuna by Krishna, to their hearers by Jesus and Gautama, to all devotees by true Teachers, past, present, or future.

———=O=———

8. *Jnaneshvari,* vol. I, pp. 198-204.

The conventional or experiential point of view, the disposition conceived and demonstrated in the act of birth, is presumed to be true. This is the whole of the matter. It is suffering and adventure, illusion and knowledge. By virtue of this presumption, every usual life is made necessary. And every usual life is a frustrated search for freedom through release.

But if freedom is to be the case, then the conventional presumption must be considered and penetrated in every moment. And it is not merely a mental presumption, but a logic of the whole body. Therefore, consideration and presumption must take the form of a sacrifice of the whole body. And it must be an action before it is a thought.

And this is the Truth of us. Our always present Condition is not one of existence as any defined or limited condition whatsoever. We are not each some born entity working our way back to Infinity. We are already the most absolutely diffuse, formless, mindless, centerless, and unqualified Bliss. From this Condition, all conditions, high and low, spring up as unnecessary and paradoxical marvels. We are always already identical to the Divine, the disposition at Infinity.

Once this priorly diffuse Condition becomes the Realized presumption of any one, then laughter follows. I am here to restore your Humor.

Bubba Free John

5

IDENTIFICATION OF THE BELOVED IS THE PRINCIPLE OF SPIRITUAL LIFE

1

A TALK GIVEN BY BUBBA FREE JOHN
TO A GATHERING OF DEVOTEES
AT VISION MOUND SANCTUARY,
APRIL 18, 1977

What is the root of our existence? What is the single incident that we must comprehend? There is one incident in which you are all completely involved at this moment. You are completely aware of it. You recoil from it and thereby create your whole life, your whole adventure, all of your subjectivity and the mood of your person. If you penetrated it, you would be free. What is it?

It is a present incident. It is happening at this moment and you are reacting to it. It is your reaction to it that binds you. What is the fundamental incident that binds all of us—not in the past, but at this very moment? What is happening that we are all believing? It is more primitive even than sensation. What is the last thing you would give up? Before there is a thought, what do you hold on to most dearly? Before you hear the inner sound, before you see a single vision, before you breathe the next breath, before you are born into this conception, what are you tuned to? When the mind is rested from action, when there is no thinking, when even the breathing is still, what is going on? If you stop thinking and acting and breathing, what is still going on? What is the last thing to go?

It is the beat of the heart. When the mind stops and action stops and breath comes to rest, the thing that defines you is the heartbeat. When you are at rest, still you feel the thundering in the chest. The primal incident is not any thought nor the sense of "me," but it is the heartbeat. The heartbeat in the center of the body-being is the ultimate meditation. It is the single motivator of life. It is the principal illusion of all beings. All beings have in common this beat, or the feeling-intensity at the core of the being, which particularizes or gives "birth" to consciousness. Everything that lives, that is self-conscious, is meditating on the beat or intensity that is the heart. The heartbeat alone is responsible for the whole adventure and complication of existence.

Before there is a single action or a single desire, there is the beating of the heart. It is not conceptual — all concepts proceed from it. Nor do you create it. You do not beat the heart. Yet the heartbeat alone is responsible for your belief in your own existence. If it ceases, you have no such belief. It interrupts the unqualified force of prior consciousness. When you are moving into infinity, it presses on your consciousness, defining you. Everything is created in rhythm with that stroke, everything. Until you are no longer bound by the beating of the heart, you are structured in the egoic dream. You are interrupted in infinity by the beating of the heart, by birth itself.

The heartbeat is not conceptual, it is not subjective, it is not within. It is the armature of the body-being. You are willing to relax the anxiety of breathing, but you are not willing to be vacant of the heart.

Everything, except the heartbeat, can come to rest and you still survive. The heartbeat is at the core of the breath. The breathing surrounds it. Thinking surrounds it, though the event itself is not thinkable. It is at the core of everything above and below. Everything above the heart, every thought or vision or contemplated wonder, is an expression of that foundation liveliness, that beating. Everything below it, every feeling and sensation, is an expression of it. The heartbeat is "me" and "that," left and right, up and down, in and out. It is the whole conception of existence. Everything is implied by it.

Like the clock that creates time, the heartbeat creates the self. The heartbeat is the most primitive incident, the center of fear. It is a metronome in an empty room. All hearing and all perception are guided toward it. All your inwardness, all your thinking, and all your activity are simply a rhythmic expression of the beat of the heart, perhaps timed in different ways but always consonant with it. You are breathing in rhythm with it and then thinking and acting, sexing and moving, energizing and feeling all in time with it. Your great fear is that it will cease, because when it ceases you are no longer different from anything. As long as you believe you are independent, a differentiated being, you are timed with the rhythm of the heart.

That rhythm is pronounced on the left, but it surges between the right and the left. There is no actual rhythm on the right, but only a constant feeling-intensity, the root stroke of the beating heart, a constant sense of self-definition and self-absorption, contracted from infinity—but it is at last not different from the beat itself, the sounding of the birth moment. On the left there is pounding, interrupting. It surges from right to left and from left to right— from sleep to dreams to waking, and from waking to dreams and then to sleep.

In the moment when you feel the heartbeat, you do not think, you do not act, you do not breathe. You are—now and separately, vulnerably. It is the principal incident to which we are all attuned. We are all suffering it, we are all subject to it, and we are all waiting for it to cease. It arises prior to knowledge. Our very existence pulses in Mystery, subject to a prior design of which we are Ignorant and to which the will at last must bow with all the mind, emotion, and whole flesh.

The heartbeat is completely untrue. Our condition in Truth is previous to this stroke, previous to all the inwardness, all the activity that is built upon this rhythm, this interruption, this stimulation, this distraction. When the heartbeat ceases, we are returned to our prior disposition, but mere death is not sufficient for liberation into the Divine. Mere death just arrests the current of the ego, which is the beating of the heart. Liberation is freedom from that rhythm while alive, to be no longer interrupted, no longer identified with left and right, up and down, in and out, here and there, now and then. When consciousness ceases to be defined by the rhythms of the heart, it is immortal. Therefore, what makes the heart beat? Why do we fear its ending? Why do we promote the adventure of individual existence? Why do we doubt the Reality of the Divine, the unchanging, the Absolute?

We presume that if the heart ceases to beat, we cease to exist. The heartbeat is the ego. That is the illusion, not the thought "I am me," not the thought "I am the body," not any thought, but the heartbeat itself is the illusion. We witness it, we are confined to it, we are subject to it, we are disposed to a whole life until it ceases. Of all things, it is completely beyond control. Even the yogi's mastery of heartbeat and body-sense remains bound to the very condition in feeling-conception that the heartbeat signals—the sense of independent consciousness and its experiential destiny. The heartbeat is the ego, the soul, the body, the mind. It is the most involuntary of all appearances. It is the recoil that thunders back from all appearance. There is no devotee who has not suffered this incident. It is the same as his or her own birth or life or death. Everything is the response to this rhythmic contraction or root feeling-intensity. Thus, everything is betrayal, a witness for the lie.

The heartbeat continues, prior to thinking and acting, feeling and living, vision and illumination, immortality and mortality. Whatever occurs in your comprehension, the beating of the heart is the single thing that defines you in that enjoyment. Liberation is the transcendence of that incident; thus, it is the same as death. In conventional, bodily death, however, we pass into unconsciousness, into repetition, back into this rhythmic incident, birth again, the definition of consciousness, of self. The only recourse while alive is the most absolute, the most perfect, sacrifice, passing beyond thought in mood, in action, in feeling, in desire, into perfect surrender or Radiance. Nothing else characterizes the devotee.

You have responded to this drama, this rhythm, this sound, this signal. And so you feel yourself to be opposite, other, individuated, single, separate, trapped, in dilemma, obliged to make your way strategically, to define yourself, to assume your immunity, your salvation, your continuation, your survival. Your whole effort is regulated by this beat, which is beyond your comprehension. The great fear is that if it stops, you disappear. It defines you in otherness, in separation. When the mind comes to rest and actions come to rest and the breath becomes still, the heart shocks us with its rhythm, with its striking, its pulsation, defining the consciousness. The principal meditation is to be free of action, of liveliness, of intention, of thought, of vision, of comprehension, of knowledge, of reaction, of recoil, of separation, of incident, until you penetrate this motion that shocks us. The only salvation is in the penetration of that signal. Until then there is betrayal, separation, ego, mind, person, separate destiny, action, illusion, dreams, knowledge, fascinated meditation, sublimity, absorption, discrimination, consolation, good feeling, profundity, eagerness, fear, sorrow, anger, hatefulness, me, I, within.

In the Way I have described, there is, naturally, penetration of the subjective root. The illusion of a subject or ego somewhere "within" is something that must be re-cognized, known again. Now we identify with this illusion of an interior "I." It must be penetrated, through insight. In the process there is an event even more direct, one that does not involve contemplation of subjective content, but that occurs after the subjective content is essentially quieted. In the final events of the Way of Re-cognition, there is this passage out of contemplation in the brain, the subtle contemplation above. The thread of active attention is followed back from the crown to the heart. That is the passage to Jnana Samadhi.

The samadhis associated with the crown of the being are subtle and depend on the ego-illusion. In such samadhis the independent self-illusion remains, the contemplator remains, not penetrated. All subtle realizations are soul-realizations, having to do with the survival of the subjective being independent of the gross form. But the ultimate realization goes beyond the subtle illusion to penetrate the self-root, the fundamental illusion itself. Although the illusion of "I" passes in this process, its passing is not the final moment. After all, the "I"-thought arises in the brain. It is part of the subtle mechanism. It is a thought, a literal thought, "I," part of the lower mind.

But the contraction that is responsible for the "I"-thought and all other thoughts and feelings of independence is at the heart itself. It is not subjective or anything like an idea interior to the body. It is the body condition itself in its most fundamental form — it is the heartbeat. Thus, in the final stages of the Way of Re-cognition, after the passage beyond contemplation of subtle objects, the mind essentially comes to rest. There is essentially no thinking. The breath is very restful. Then only the heartbeat stands out. The final re-cognition occurs in contemplation of the heartbeat, not of any subjective interior.

You must give up your life, the identification with

this rhythm, this contraction, this recoil that defines you. And how do you give it up? It is impossible. It cannot be done by the one who would do it. No one can transcend the rhythmic contraction of the heart, which defines our consciousness, except by the most perfect and absolute sacrifice. The way to this perfect sacrifice is the practice I have described in this Teaching, by which, as a discipline, you move beyond the contracted disposition. You must move beyond fear and sorrow and anger into the disposition of love, of radiance, previous to any form of contraction or separation. You must presume the radiance of happiness as a discipline in spite of all subjective signs to the contrary.

All the disciplines of this Way of Divine Ignorance are forms of radiance, of non-contraction and non-separation, of love, of bringing uncontracted energy, rather than knowledge, desire, and self-possession, into the realms of experience. This is the principal discipline. It is service founded on true hearing of the Teaching, free of all concern for the continuation of inward inspection. In this liberation you pass beyond the great fear, beyond the beating of the heart which defines you, in which you are born in every moment. That passage is madness, healed and cooled only by motiveless or loving Communion with the Spiritual Master, which now in your knowledge you deny. Be wary of your own knowledge, your own good feeling, of all the things that make you feel better, or worse. They console you behind the pulsation of birth. The heartbeat is the ultimate vulnerability, the great fear. It defines all things apart from you. It defines you as nothing, apart from everything, the everything with which you struggle, mentally and emotionally and physically, in every moment, to find union.

The practice is exactly as it is described. Hear this communication, the fundamental argument, and live the disciplines in relations. Do not be separative, egoic, emotional, contractive, negative, angry, fearful, sorrowful, but be full of energy and enthusiasm in relations. This is the demand which always obliges the devotee and with which he is always at odds by tendency: You should look and feel and be and act completely happy under all conditions. Change your way of action and the subjective dimension itself will change naturally. The born condition precedes all subjectivity. You want to manipulate your subjectivity first — your feelings, your thinking, your conceptions, and your feeling-conceptions. You want to change them before you will change your way of life. You want to be free inside before you will love, before you act differently. You must act differently first, and not be concerned that the feeling and thinking aspect of the being remains full of tendencies. You must not be concerned about them. They are just the signs of the old way of living. You must *act* in love, in radiance, with energy, with life, in all your relations, in your disposition moment to moment, under all conditions. You will observe in the midst of such action that the subjective dimension is also gradually penetrated and transformed. Its negativity, its reactivity, becomes unnecessary and ultimately obsolete by virtue of your different action.

You either change your action or you do not. You *must* begin to do it. There is nothing more that can be said, nothing more convincing than that. You simply must begin to do it. As you begin to do it, the vulgar disposition of your internal life and your subjective tendencies will continue. You must not be concerned about it. Tendencies are only the signs of your old way of living. Let them pass. Live differently now. Love, serve with feeling. Put your attention on this argument, be transformed by the hearing, and *act* differently. The new subjectivity will follow. Subjective, internal changes, emotional and mental, will follow. Start to act differently. Stop presuming the separative position. Stop being angry and sorrowful and fearful in your relations and bring energy into them. Be happy in them. Be enthusiastic in them. Bring life to all beings. Bring life to the tree. Bring life to the doorknob and to me! And you will see your subjective life changing, over time. It may remain completely wretched for 25,000 births. Do not be concerned about it. *Act* differently on the basis of what you have heard. Then you will be communicative as a devotee.

Now you are waiting for your insides to change first. They are the last to change! Your action must change first. Then the inner being will reflect the new rather than the old adaptation. Having seen what you have seen and heard what you have heard, *act* differently. Kick everything else aside. Hear, love, serve, bring life—that is the discipline. The emotions and the mind will persist in their aggravation, their negativity, their self-possession, their sulking stupidity. Be indifferent to them on the basis of this hearing, and you will see the mind and the emotions change.

Subjectivity follows action. Your subjectivity having changed on the basis of action, you will begin to be attuned to the subtler dimension of the being. And you will hear and see, perhaps, all kinds of incredible things. I have seen all of it, every kind of vision and transport. It is all a hallucination, it is all ridiculous, it is nonsense, it is stupid and false. There is no vision that is true. It is all bondage. It is all something to console the separate one. Press through all of that in the Way of Re-cognition and you will become coincident with the whole body-being, no longer turning into your subjectivity. You will stand as the whole body, and suddenly the prior Condition of the body will become obvious. There is no independent consciousness. There is no separate being. There is no "me" within. There is no one to survive. There is the most absolute, unqualified, and unspeakable Reality, which is Bliss, Fullness, without description, without form, without argument, without a single symbol to win its victory over living beings. Only the devotee is sensitive to God. That is the whole communication that has been served in this Company.

You must begin to do something different. Now you are doing the same old thing in your rhythm, being an other within. You must do something different without, not concerned for what happens within, for desiring and thinking. Let it pass. *Be* different as the whole body. You are always certain, in this instant, what it is to be completely happy, to look and feel and be and act completely happy. It is always true of you natively. You can always return to this native sense. You could be and look and feel *completely* happy in this moment. But you do not. Why? Because of your sympathy with this born condition that is rhythmed to you moment to moment, this pulsation or feeling-conception in the chest. Pass beyond it through this whole practice and you will realize the Divine Condition. But not before.

The heartbeat draws you back into the round of birth and death. It is recoil. It does not permit you to be released to infinity. It draws you back. It defines you in time and space. It defines your existence. If it ceases, you cease to exist. All philosophy is founded on the beating of the heart; all mysticism, all life, all desire, and every single experiential presumption are founded on it. The penetration of the beating of the heart is the difference between "I," which is the body as a whole, and the realization of the Condition of the body. When the heartbeat ceases to define consciousness, then there is the natural intuition of the Condition that precedes birth. The usual man is relieved of this constriction only at the point of death, and so he is released from the superficial organism. But that release is not sufficient for illumination. It is only sufficient for another birth. You must penetrate this rhythm while alive, while conscious, while in the ordinary disposition. You must penetrate the illusion of separation, and the heartbeat is the primal incident. The grosser incident of birth may have occurred so many years ago, but the incident that promotes the present illusion that is birth as the whole body is the heartbeat. Prior to it there is no definition of consciousness. There is no definition of bodily existence, of egoic existence, as a separate individual, independent of this beating, this rhythm, this shock. You exist in your consciousness only because of this sympathy, this rhythm that you perceive. All of your thinking and desiring extends from that.

How do you realize liberation from the born-condition? Not by philosophy. You realize it through the instrumentality of a born being who nonetheless has penetrated the whole cycle. The Spiritual Master is the instrument of the liberation of living beings, not philosophy nor conception nor your own contemplation of the heartbeat. You become disposed to that contemplation in sympathy with the Spiritual Master, but only because the Spiritual Master exists prior to that contraction, that rhythm. Through hearing this argument you are disposed to *act,* not to internalize, but to act, without concern for your subjectivity. Subjectivity is only the sign of your old adaptation, whereas you have become disposed on the basis of this hearing to act differently, to love, to be radiant in relations rather than contracting in the forms of anger and sorrow and fear and thinking and all of the illusions of your own subjectivity. You must submit absolutely to the Spiritual Master. This principle is the core of all Teaching. Once you have heard the argument of the Spiritual Master, then you must enter into devotional and spiritual relations or Communion with the Spiritual Master. The primary function of the Spiritual Master is the spiritual service of devotees, those who have "heard" and changed their way of action. Such service is Divine. By that service, the Way is quickened and fulfilled by Grace of the Beloved, the Real beyond all birth of selves and knowledge of souls.

2

A TALK GIVEN BY BUBBA FREE JOHN TO A GATHERING OF DEVOTEES IN HONOLULU, DECEMBER 8, 1976

There is virtually no limit to the delusions that human beings can presume on the basis of their tendencies, their desiring, their motivation, their reactions to experience. Because this is so, individuals eventually step out of the stream of conventional relations. In other words, they at some point cease to act or live on the basis of the ego-soul, the experiential self, and they establish instead a sacred relationship by which they are relieved of the implications of this birth. Our meeting with one another — each of you individually with me — is of this kind. It is not a conventional relationship which we are here merely to dramatize with one another, you with me or you with one another. We are here to be lifted out of that destiny. Therefore, your relationship with me must be of a sacred nature. It must involve an entirely different kind of discipline than the usual life presumes. Your relationship to me in itself implies a commitment to the essential Teaching or consideration which is part of my communication with you. Apart from this sacred process that our relationship implies, the only thing we can possibly realize in one another's company is suffering and delusion, which as you see is what the usual man realizes.

In all my years of teaching work it has been a con-

stant struggle to maintain this quality in our relationship. It is constantly my obligation to eliminate what
stands in the way, what makes your approach to me a
conventional one, what makes your response to me
conventional, egoic, ordinary. And this is a great and
very difficult task. It requires all of our lives entirely.

Part of the apparently conventional nature of our
connection is the threat of separation and death. This
body dies. That body dies. We can rejuvenate, feel
better, live longer, but, even so, in this world everybody dies. That is why we do spiritual practice,
because we are conscious of the destiny of separation.
We are willing to fulfill the law of love, but on the
other hand what we love dies. That is the paradox of
this place, and that is what makes it a hell. That is why
this is one of the realms of suffering. This world is not
a heaven. This is not a place of fulfillment. Thus, we
must yield to the true Condition. We must not become
dependent upon the conventional aspect of our relations. We must recognize our relations. We must identify the Condition of the loved one. You must recognize or identify me in Truth. Our relationship must be
a spiritual one. That does not mean that we will not
see one another, or that we cannot have occasion to
carry on human relations face to face. But the vital
dependency and demand that is based on the fear of
separation is something that must be undone through
this matter of spiritual practice, through this intuitive
recognition.

You must become established in the real Condition,
or you will never be satisfied. You will be driven to all

kinds of preoccupations and great schemes, trying to become victorious or immortal, for immortality's own sake, simply because you cannot deal with the fact of death. But death is an absolute message in this realm. It obliges us to recognize or identify one another in Truth, and we are not relieved of that obligation in this place.

It is not a matter of seeing me face to face twenty-four hours a day. Nobody does that. You must truly live the spiritual Condition of our relationship. You must lead a spiritual life in the world. You must fall into this Condition that precedes all conditions. You must enjoy your relationship to me in the form of meditation, the form of that sacrifice, because no form of our conventional and ordinary relations, our ordinary contact, ultimately satisfies in itself. And if your approach to me is a conventional one, you will be making use only of the ordinary forms of our possible relationship, and *all* those forms pass. All those forms make you anxious. You must realize a form of relationship to me in Ignorance, in which you recognize or identify me in the form of the very Condition of this world, your own Condition, so that when we are face to face it is that intuitive identification that you are involved with, not all the kinds of worldly anxiety such as lovers might feel for one another in the face of death. They love one another and yet they are going to be separated. That is the conventional nature of relationship. The kinds of lovers that can be separated are just the image of suffering, the pair. Lovers must become a paradox, a single Condition, not a cult of two. Our relationship must become a paradox, a spiritual matter, in which we are all given up to the Condition that precedes all this madness.

This world literally is being dreamed at this moment. It has no force except insofar as we live by reaction, merely by experience, on the basis of what appears or comes across to us in the dream. We tend to make our philosophy, our way of living, out of the dream, out of the limitation that arises here, which we cannot account for. Our life must cease to take that form. You cannot make philosophy out of this world and succeed. You would just be crazy all your life, and you would die anyway. You cannot make your way of life out of this experience here as it appears, this dream. No, you must recognize it, truly identify it. You must be awake relative to this experience. You must enjoy the release that a person enjoys upon waking in the morning from his or her dreams the night before. You must identify the Truth of the dream, which is to *re-cognize,* to know again, intuitively to penetrate all the conventional forms of the dream, which in themselves are illusory, passing. That is what spiritual practice is all about. That is what the spiritual process is all about: being relieved, ultimately, of the force of this experience, this condition, this limitation, this dream here.

You are liberated from that in the process of our relationship, but only if you are related to me truly, sacredly, spiritually, only if your relationship to me is simply one of sacrifice, of natural orientation, not all the reactive things you get into on the basis of it in the conventional way. Then the play between us serves this intuitive recognition, this identification of the Condition of all conditions. But you must yield constantly, because as soon as you become involved in your ordinary life by reaction, you separate yourself and become involved again in the illusion of experience arising here.

It is a maddening experience, this place. It is attractive in all kinds of ways. Equal to the force of all its attractiveness is the force of all of the destruction of the Beloved. All the forms of the Beloved rot in this place. They come to an end, they are taken away. That is the truth about it, and there is no way around it. You must confront that. That is the way it is here. This is not heaven. This is not the world of the Beloved, of the loved one in any form you may recognize as the Loved One. This is a dream play on the Beloved, in which the Beloved appears in shapes and forms that are fleeting, that are binding in themselves. They attract you, and then they are withdrawn and leave you with only the craving. Left with the craving only, you are cycled back again and again into the same dimension as that experiencing reaction.

So you must recognize, truly identify, the Beloved appearing here in all this attraction, which means you must enter into a spiritual process in your living rather than the conventional attempts to survive, to win, to live forever. If you become truly committed to the spiritual process, in a relatively short time you literally pass out of the limitation in which you now conceive of this world. But you must utterly surrender. You must give up everything for that, for what you recognize, for that Truth, that Condition, the Condition of the very current of your own being. Give yourself up to it entirely. Allow it to create the event of the dream. The dream is its business. You will notice it stops playing the dream the way it seems to be playing it now. Now you are turned on to the Beloved as if to a whore, a fancy dancer. She has a little bit of extra seductiveness now. I was out here in the yard with some of you a few minutes ago, and we played this game of looking up in the night sky for something extraordinary. Some weird unidentified thing has got to be flying around in order to make us feel a little light, a little wonder. And yet you cannot account for any of it. The mere existence of any of it at all is sufficient mystery. All the rest of it is fancy dancing, a little twirler put on the end of her pasties. The woman herself, the universe itself, is sufficient mystery. We do not need all the extra attractions, and yet the woman herself, the lover himself, the universe itself as it appears here, is fancy dancing. It is unnecessary. It bewitches you, it beguiles you, it attracts you into a whole way of life, and yet it is fleeting, temporary, just a costume, a bit of business. It is not the Beloved herself, himself, itself. You must identify the Truth of what is attractive.

Thus, in your relationship to me, the matter of intuitive recognition must become the principle of our play. You must recognize me in the form of your Condition, the Condition of all this arising, the real Condition of it, the Condition of conditions, the Condition of the body, the mind, the self-sense, the very current of the being, and be rested in It constantly. When you do that, the Beloved takes off her garment. Her true Form, his true Form, the Beloved's true Form begins to appear. That true Form is not transitory. But you must be adapted to the loving of the Beloved in eternal Form, because you do not have desires fitted to that Form at the present time. The desires you have are all products of adaptation to this limiting illusion of attractions. You are turned on by bangles and flesh. All this appearance is how you are attracted to the Beloved in this form here. Having recognized it, though, giving yourself up to the true Condition of this, your very Nature, then your desiring or the movement of the being itself becomes capable of enjoying the Beloved in eternal Form. Only in that case are you satisfied.

All else is suffering. There is no doubt about it. There is absolutely no ultimate relief in the dream. So our play with one another cannot be based simply on this conventional attraction. It cannot be limited, in other words, to the natural, human dimension of our intimacy with one another. It must be sacred. It must be a spiritual relationship. It must be founded in this Ignorance. You must recognize me in Truth. You must do this practice. You must enter into this real meditation and give up everything for the Beloved. In that case our ordinary human relations become pleasurable, because they are not necessary. We are not bound by them. We are constantly reached into the Condition of these conditions and so can love one another, play with one another in this dream circumstance without becoming bound, because we constantly recognize one another in Truth in this play. If we will intuitively recognize one another, we can be free of the conventional striving which is a reaction to the awful sense acquired while alive that separation or dissolution of our relationships is inevitable.

Our immortality is not conventional, earthly, elemental. It is a Divine matter, founded in this recognition. It is founded in sacrifice, not in any effort simply and exclusively to make this elemental body live forever. No such motivation would work. If we are fitted to this sacrifice absolutely, maybe the body's life gets prolonged. All kinds of things may occur, but they are not our point of view. They are secondary to the essential fulfillment of the Law of Sacrifice.

So we do not only need to see one another, you and I. You also need to live your life on the basis of this relationship in which the true Condition is identified, in which you recognize these conditions and therefore rest in the true Condition. So you need to live an ordinary life. You need peace and quiet, a natural, human-size environment, with ordinary intimacies, a few people to see regularly. You need a place, an occasion, in which to meditate in private. All these things are your obligations if you are to fulfill the true Condition of our meeting. Since all of these things are required, we will certainly see one another, but we will also all live our privacy as well, because if we are not given up in private, our meeting has no opportunity to grow, to represent a new adaptation. You will simply be struggling and striving here anxiously, never really being released from the implications of this world.

Our destiny is not something that we can pre-figure. Our obligation, though, is clear. The law in this moment is clear, the true form of our living is clear, and so we must fulfill it. Having fulfilled it perfectly, you will then see transformations of this ordinary living here that are more and more positive, but you will also see the real spiritual transformation, which fundamentally has no drama whatsoever connected with it. It is simply absolute release from the necessity of this appearance here and all the craving that we develop on the basis of it. In this release, the being rests in its true Condition, in which all kinds of other conditions appear, such as this world here. The gross form continues to appear. Subtle forms may appear.

And then perhaps such changes may cease to appear, and you rest in the Condition itself, the God-World, the Realm that is itself the Beloved. There is no speech to describe it. There is no vision of it. You must fulfill the Law, and that is all. Whatever the perfect Destiny is beyond the cessation of changes in these unnecessary realms, it is nothing of which any born being has knowledge. Such is not permitted. There is no vision, no doctrine, apart from the Law itself. You make this sacrifice, and then only the Truth or the Divine is your Destiny, whatever that altogether is. So all the anxiety built up on the basis of experience here must come to an end, and in our relations we must become natural, ordinarily loving. You cannot oblige any creature you love to live forever, because he or she simply cannot do it, and neither can you, as an act of will. Whenever we come together and say we love one another, we cannot promise to stay with one another. We can promise our life to one another and in that sense stay with one another, but we do not have in our will the capacity to stay with one another for-

ever, because the body dies. This condition disappears. So you must die while living. You must be able
to let go of this unnecessary realm and dwell in the
God-Condition while alive. In that case you will be
free of anxiety, you will have humor in relation to
things here. You will be capable of loving in the
natural fashion because you are not obliging it all to
stay here forever. You are recognizing it intuitively,
and therefore the Condition of all these conditions is
the Beloved you find in your lover, in every arising
phenomenon, in every moment, and in the Spiritual
Master most directly.

Truth is not some hopeful word such as "You will be
immortal on this earth, and all things will cease to
die, and we will live forever." There is no such message. That is not the Truth. Even if that were factually true, it is not the Truth. The Truth is in this
recognition, this identification of the Beloved, this
sacrifice. Secondarily, our lives may be prolonged,
but we are still obliged to the same sacrifice and the
same humor. Only on that basis are we to realize all
the secondary effects of the fulfillment of the Law,
which may or may not be prolonged living.

So it is true that this anxiety about your relations
is something you discover in yourself. It is not healed
by any ordinary arrangement. It is itself that condition in our awareness by which we are moved to fulfill the Law, to make this sacrifice. It is not otherwise
removed, we are not otherwise relieved of it. In your
right response to me, in this actual practice, it passes.
Anything, anyone that you love and enjoy in this
realm is only, if you will recognize it, the Beloved, the

very Real itself. This is what you discover in all your loving, all your enjoyments, if you are a true man, a true woman. If you do not live by such sacrificial recognition, all your experiencing and enjoyments lead to attachment only. They reinforce ritual behavior, craving for contact, craving for experience, craving for repetitions in which we are constantly anxious, ill at ease, suffering reactive emotions, endlessly thinking, mulling things over mentally as if we were trying to solve some hidden problem, knotted up in the body, always active to find some pleasurable condition that will last, that will fulfill us. If you intuitively recognize this matter arising here, you are not bound up by reaction to that whole automatic ceremony. You are relieved of it. And that recognition is the only release.

Paradoxically, even though there is all of this delight and suffering, there is not one single thing, there is not a single event, not a single change, not a single modification, no birth, no death. Nothing has happened. Nothing has ever happened. Nothing will ever happen. There is only a single and absolute Condition, unspeakable in its Nature, which we may not see, hear, experience over against ourselves, but which is our very Condition prior to all changes, high or low. Having fallen into That, then we have a disposition in us from which properly to view all the changes, high or low, should they arise. And, as it happens, this one you seem to be when active in the waking world continues to arise for the time being—paradoxically, because it does not amount to anything. Nothing is gained by a moment's living, absolutely nothing.

Nothing changes on the basis of it. Nothing is gained by a single meeting, by a single moment's satisfaction, by a single contact. This living isn't anything. It is only an illusion, a modification of the essential Condition. If you come to rest in that Condition, then in every moment you recognize this and are happy, already happy. You can play in the ordinary ways, but you never become wretched. You are not degraded through your own craving, because you recognize what you love, and therefore your relations with loved ones, with this whole world, are natural, happy.

Otherwise, your craving for the immortality of the loved one will become so profound that you will be forced to kill her or him. You will murder the loved one in your craving for the loved one's immortality. Your anxiety over the loss, the separation, will become so great that you will eventually begin to degrade the relationship itself, to separate yourself automatically. Then everything you do begins to separate you from the loved one, even though you are here to be loving, because you are so anxious, so terrified, so upset. But if you will recognize one another in Truth, if you will recognize this world in Truth, if you will recognize me in Truth, then you are engaged in that process that relieves you of this illusion, and you can come to rest. You can be happy. It is not necessary to go on with great plans to conquer this world in one fashion or another. Nothing is gained by it. You never conquer the loved one. You are enamored. You are in love. No conquering goes on at all. You only start conquering when you become afraid, when you fear this separation. Then you get anxious and start craving all kinds of satisfaction.

So I recommend that you meditate. However, you cannot meditate. You cannot willfully go about some program of meditation and have it be true, because that is a way of conquering rather than of being in love. You must realize this real meditation through the consideration we enjoy face to face. And if you will begin to rest in the current of the being in my Company, then you will begin to feel my influence. I will be of use to you in that case, but not until then. If your approach to me remains conventional, you are not at ease, you are not rested in this current, and you cannot feel it. Then there is no initiatory force in our meeting. You will really only discover the force of my influence when you begin to come to rest, in meditation, in our meetings, and in life. When you are rested in this current of your own being, through true intuitive identification of me and of the Condition of the current itself, then you can feel my work.

Because I am simply present in this Condition, I do not have any plans. I have nothing to do with all of this arising. I am simply standing here, and if you recognize me truly, then this current of the being is intensified, its revelation begins, and you will fall out of the point of view of this dream, even though you continue in your ordinary relations within it. You may also, in the course of this meditation, this living, have the opportunity to be involved in all kinds of other dreams, to live and perceive in other forms, other dimensions entirely. It is not that you must strive for that. That is another kind of craving, another kind of effort toward victory based on a failure of recognition, a failure to presume this Ignorance which is native to our birth. All the conventional yogic efforts are kinds of craving. People will sit for hours a day manipulating themselves with various techniques, hoping to have this and that kind of remarkable experience as a result. It is just an extension of worldliness, of the same thing that is your suffering in this gross appearance. You must simply be relieved of all of that through the presumption of Ignorance and the intuition of the Condition of these conditions arising.

That intuitive recognition or identification is simply rest of the current of the being in its prior Condition. It is felt in the grosser body sense at first, and as we come to rest in it, it is enjoyed in all kinds of ways, none of which is in itself fulfilling as mere experience. These enjoyments are simply the secondary reflections of our fulfillment of the Law, our present resting in that Condition which does not have any content, which is unspeakable. Call it God, Brahman, the Self. It is the only Happiness, and it is the foundation of all happiness in the midst of conditions here or anywhere else.

So it is not that we must sit down and struggle to hear the inner sounds and see the inner lights and go somewhere with them. It is quite natural that at some point you become absorbed in such sounds and lights and other phenomena in the extensions of this current, but it is rest in the prior Condition of the current itself that is fulfillment of the Law, that is Happiness. It relieves you of the point of view of this world.

It is not simply experiences of other worlds that relieve you of the point of view of this world, though they may arise and bring ordinary release. It is rest in the Condition of the very current of this arising, the Condition of these conditions, which is Happiness. It is perfect Sacrifice, and, paradoxically, is perfect fullness. It is a way of being mad without being crazy.

Nothing could be more mad than to be happy in this place, because there is really no justification for it. It is not reasonable to be happy. If you thoroughly examine this world, there is reason to feel very unhappy. Even with a little pleasurableness thrown in, it is not enough to overcome that conviction of darkness that you get when you really see what is happening here. So it is not any philosophy we can base on our experience here that makes us happy. It is complete release from implications, the force of this dreaming, this appearance for which we cannot account. And you see, it is already miraculous. Nothing fantastic has to happen. We already cannot account for a single thing in this room here. The mere existence of anything is beyond comprehension. It is sufficient to boggle us. You do not know what a single thing *is*. You cannot build any great programs for victory on the basis of such Ignorance. On the basis of that Ignorance, we are naturally disposed to all of this arising and may be led into the intuitive identification of the Nature and Condition of all this arising. And that is my occupation, to bring you to that recognition through Ignorance, in which you may come to rest in the current of the being and more and more profoundly fulfill the Law through radical intuition of the Condition of existence. But you see that this requires a new orientation, a turnabout from the conventional strife in which you pursue fulfillment here by reaction. The more you do that, the more confounded you become.

In the old cultures, they frowned upon anyone who knew too much or owned too much, because these were the signs of somebody who was really struggling and was therefore very worldly and dangerous. Of course they made this a blanket, black-and-white world-view, but there is some wisdom in the feeling. We must be relieved of the burden of knowing and owning, of all our craving. We must become perfectly Ignorant. We must become a Sacrifice, not an Owner, not a Knower. The usual knowing and owning is ordinary enough, and we can take pleasure in ordinary things in one another's company, but only if we are free, only if we all make this sacrifice constantly and are clarified in the being. So you must have the leisure, the ordinariness, in which to consider in this moment of arising that you do not know what a single thing *is*, that you do not know what the thing *is* itself, that you do not know what any of it *is*. If you will enter into your relations with me on that basis, this Ignorance, this falling into the current of the being through identification of its Condition, will become natural to you by Grace—freely, because it is not a conventional gift. It is the Gift of the being itself. It is prior to all strife, all circumstance. It is simply that you must be disposed to enjoy it. Become so disposed in my Company, and it absolutely will be given to you. That is

also the Law. It is not a matter of striving and ac-
quiring it, but of giving up that whole effort as you
naturally do in Ignorance, in which you simply rest
in this moment and recognize it in the form of your
own Condition, the Condition of the current of the
body-being itself. It is felt more and more profoundly
as a current. It goes through changes. And it obliges
you to go through changes outwardly in your relations
and also bodily, because the body is transformed in its
adaptation. Then the current is felt passing from toe
to crown rather than crown to toe. It is not that it goes
from the toe and leaves the body toward the crown.
It is just felt as if there were a wire from toe to crown
in which the current or the flow is moving in that
direction rather than the opposite. Then the current
between the crown and the Heart may at last be
Realized also.

We still stand in the world even as we rest in this
current. But then you may notice in your private meditation that you also are released even of this experience here from time to time. As the currents of the
gross being begin to harmonize, become naturally
reoriented, the body comes to rest, the breathing
becomes slow, simple, the heart rate goes down. We
hear the breathing and feel it, but then we become
aware in such a way that we do not hear it any longer,
we do not feel it any longer. The current itself becomes visible and audible to us, and we may simply
forget the gross body and pass into the subtler dreams,
all the while being in the disposition of this Ignorance,
in which we truly identify what arises rather than

automatically becoming attached to it, rather than getting into patterns of craving on the basis of gross or subtle experience.

Therefore, all of that also passes. We come to the point where we are more and more profoundly identified with that Condition itself, which precedes all arising, high or low, and which does not have any reference really, which cannot be accounted for in conditions. It is prior to them. It is the Condition of conditions. It is a paradox, because it is true of you even while alive, while in the gross plane, in the subtle planes, in any and all of these unnecessary realms. This Condition, which is unspeakable, remains true, it remains your very Condition. Therefore, unnecessary worlds constantly fall away.

We must fulfill the Law, this Sacrifice, this Truth. The Condition of conditions is Truth in this realm or any realm, and it is that to which we must be committed while alive. Any glorious eternity that appears on the basis of it is a Gift, which we may not seek, and find, and know, and still fulfill the Law. But just as all of this now present has suddenly appeared, as unnecessary and terrifying as it is, the Perfect Domain is always presently existing, and it is the same as no thing, no disturbance, no craving, no separation, no birth, no event, no moment, no future, no time, no place, no suffering. It is also exactly the same as love, as fullness, as delight, as very Light, as Happiness.

—=○=—

3

A TALK GIVEN BY BUBBA FREE JOHN
TO A GATHERING OF DEVOTEES
AT VISION MOUND SANCTUARY,
MAY 11, 1977

In fact and in Truth this manifest appearance in which we are animated to one another in the waking state is a hallucination that occurs in consciousness. All these trees, buildings, bodies, hairs, thoughts arise as modification of a single and absolute field that is Perfect Radiance. The world is a conception, as completely unnecessary as a thought or a dream. And it is just as silly, just as humorous, just as arbitrary and unserious, as any dream.

The truth of this moment is that everything arising is literally a hallucination. The entire arising incident of the present moment is completely unnecessary. The pattern we identify as our lives is a complex logic of repetitions. Repetition is self, and mind, and body, including all relations and environments. Repetition is consolation, or distraction from fear. The pattern we know as life persists by reinforcement, by desire for repetitions, by being used. The incident of any experience appears, and you presume it to be both independent and necessary, and thus you enforce its repetition. If the presumption of necessity and independence ceases, then what reinforces the appearance and makes its repetition necessary is absent. Then the present configuration, the appearance of the so-called world, which is totally arbitrary and unnecessary in the midst of infinity, is weakened. The present configuration becomes obsolete, it rises and falls, and something else replaces it.

There is no need for this present configuration to appear. There is no reason for it to persist. There is no need to overcome it or to enjoy a victory as it. It is completely arbitrary, just as arbitrary as any dream you might have had recently. The dream came to an end — it became obsolete because you realized it was not necessary. You woke up.

You must be awake. Your awakening is what the communication of this Teaching is all about. The Teaching is a penetrating criticism, a goad to awakening to the non-necessity of things. The communication of Truth, the Argument and Influence of the Spiritual Master, works to undermine the droning trance in which you exist in the waking state and in all other states of experience.

You ordinarily maintain the presumption of being this fleshy entity without the slightest ambiguity. That presumption just seems necessary. You do not feel that there is any way around it. You do not even regard the body to be something arising in consciousness. You consider consciousness to be somehow inside the body, in the brain, or in some condition less than the flesh itself, somehow created by senior unconscious atoms, its destiny determined by the fleshy thing that you know well. Thus, you presume that when you are dead, you are dead. But the necessity of the body is not true. This body is, presently, a hallucination in the field of brightness. When you can "see" that the body and the mind and the sense of separate identity itself all arise in the field of brightness as a mere modification, then you will have a great deal of humor relative to this affair of waking life. Then the great adventure of trying to attain a victory or to find the great goal for which all beings are born will come to an end. You will be free, but not until then. Until then, you are bound to discover, through all the means of release, some sort of extraordinary occasion that will console you as an entity.

The conventional spiritual teachings serve your search for consolation and reinforce the dilemma of existence. "Oh, Master, I'm suffering. What do I have to do to be saved? How do I get to heaven? How do I see God? How do I get to feel better?" And the master says, "Do this, do that, it is up here, it is in here, it is over there, it is to come, it is never realized." And so, on the basis of your trouble, you are further motivated to feel good. Whereas the entire search, the entire drama of getting to Truth, is a lie. It is not true in this very moment that you are an entity. Your Condition is not that of an entity. The entity is only a convention of appearance. It is not Truth. That configuration is what is appearing, it is what is arising, but it is not the Truth in the moment.

In the present, and always in the past, and always in the future, the Condition of existence that is true and Truth is not defined and separate, but diffuse, without center or bounds. That is the Condition in this very moment. In that Condition, paradoxically, there arise all the conventions of limitation, out of which, in your ordinary impulse, you try to make your philosophy. You presume, on the basis of the conventions of experiencing, what the universe must be like, what you are like, what your true Condition must be. But your Condition precedes all of experience. Your Condition is Wisdom, the force of Existence, which eternally precedes all this arising, and within which or as a modification of which this arising occurs. Only by realizing that Condition are you properly related to all these limitations that rise and fall, waking, dreaming, and sleeping, gross or subtle, in this world or any other world.

True awakening is penetration, in the present moment, of the presumption of the necessity and independence of your apparent or experienced condition. This penetration is not the same as the glamourous path of going within, of achieving a victorious subjectivity. That is the solution founded in the presumption of independence, of necessarily separate existence. Such a solution is a serious matter then. If you *are* separate, you must find some way to feel better *while* separate — to feel holy, to see lights, to feel blissful in some part — because life appears to be necessary and humorless, a dilemma to be undone. The whole universe, then, becomes a problem and an always contradicted adventure, a game that you can win or lose, a very treacherous and fundamentally unhappy affair.

If you will observe all the human beings you casually meet, you will see that basically they are tormented by their existence. They are presuming their independence presently, and, therefore, they suffer all the effects of the drama, the play, the conjunction of apparent entities and processes. This life is treacherous, humorless, bearing down on them, drawing them into a destiny upon which they can have no ultimate effect. They can perhaps produce modest little effects, but they cannot ultimately be relieved of the dilemma that impinges on them.

This dilemma, however, is only their presumption, and it is false. The force of their birth implies their independence, and they meditate on that separation constantly. Thus, they look for their release in the context of presumed separation. Instead of being released, however, they are burdened, impinged upon by endless effects. Furthermore, the thing they most identify with, that born, vital body-being, is disintegrating over time, getting worse and worse, and eventually dying. No wonder people get more and more solemn as the years go on! Yet the life you take so seriously is just a dream, a hallucination that persists without freedom because you do not enjoy the presumption that makes it unnecessary.

What you know of dreams should illumine your position in the waking state. You are in exactly the same position in the waking state as in the dream state. You know very well, from the point of view of the waking state, that in dreaming you create the environment as well as the sense of being an independent entity. Clearly the dream is your own consciousness. It is *your* dream. Who else made the dream but you? It arises in your own consciousness. If, in the dream, you are running to leap into the water and suddenly it turns into a pit of fire, you created it. Your own psychic nature made the fire, so that you fell into fire instead of swimming over the lake. This is clear when you wake up, though it is not clear in the dream itself, because in the dream you identify exclusively with the knowing entity, the ego presumption, the separate one in the adventure. When you wake, you realize that you created all of it, that it was your own consciousness, and that now, in the waking state, it has no necessity. Now it is completely arbitrary, a hallucination.

Consider how serious you are in the waking state. You are trying to make philosophy here, but you are doing exactly what people do in dreams. You are assuming that you are the "knower-I," the separate entity caught in this adventure here, in which things are constantly happening to you and taking you by surprise. Sometimes good things are happening, sometimes bad things. Sometimes you win, sometimes you lose. You have assumed this hallucination as your Condition. You are trying to make philosophy. You listen to spiritual teachings, you take up practices, you believe this and that. You may feel that you have grasped it now. Now you may feel consoled. But you must wake up! You must stop continuing in the mere presumption or tacit belief in this hallucination. You must enjoy the same release into the Truth of your present condition that you enjoy when you wake up from a dream. Nothing else is happiness. Nothing less or other than that is liberation. Not a single thought, conception, or experience, high or low, is anything but a permutation of the dream. Only the awakening itself, in which there is nothing happening, is liberation from the motivated distress of all things happening.

In that awakening, no matter what arises, in any moment, you do not suffer the apparent logic or implications of appearances, but remain established in your real Condition, which is the unqualified field of Radiant Consciousness, without center and without bounds. From the Radiance of that Consciousness all things arise as vibratory modifications, including the most solid things that you consider to be objective to you as the knower-I. If you realize the true Condition of the knower-I, you also realize the true Condition of all manifestation. It is hallucination, the conjunction of wave patterns, appearing very elusive to vision at times, and then at another moment defining their lines into rigid objects.

Yet there are no independent objects. There are no truly solid things. This world is a phenomenon of light. If you have studied contemporary physics, you have at least heard and thought this, but you have not yet realized its full implications. This world, and every sense of subjective or objective independence, is a phenomenon of light, a hallucination. It is always an event in the very Condition that is consciousness, the unqualified field of which everything that arises is the present modification. If you presume the condition or effect of any modification, rather than That in which the modification arises, then that effect becomes necessary, and the presumption that it is your Condition reinforces a complex adventure in which you are this implied knower-I, separate from events. But if you break through that presumption and if you are presently existing as the prior, diffuse, or absolute Condition, then the arising phenomena have a paradoxical significance. They are unnecessary, they are humorous, they are fluid, they are not binding. The whole adventure they imply, negative or positive, is unnecessary, untrue. Everything that arises, subjective or objective, is a portion of the dream. It has nothing in itself to do with God or Truth. Truth is realized only in the right presumption in the present, regardless of what arises. It is the tacit certainty that this is a completely unnecessary hallucination, a modification of light.

You must begin to stand in your real position, the true Condition in this moment, before all the belief systems, all the implications of the solid, present dream, enforce themselves as your presumption. You do not know what a single thing *is*. Not a single thing! Not even the subjective part that is saying to itself, "I do not know what the wall *is,* I do not know what a single thing *is*." You do not know what the thoughts are, you do not know what the feelings are, you do not know what this "I" *is*! There is not any such "I" that you conceive of and know and present and see. You are busy all the time pointing to it, presuming it, but if you actually look at what you are pointing to, you will see that you do not know what it *is*. "I" is the whole body in fact, but there is no knowledge of what the body *is* entirely and independently and absolutely. You do not know what anything *is*. Therefore, you do not know what all things are. The whole of manifestation altogether is not a something of which you are a knower. You are Ignorance. You are a most undefined or diffuse Condition, unable to radically differentiate yourself from a single thing, because as long as any single thing arises, you exist in the vulnerable position of having no knowledge of what it *is*.

As it happens, there is a whole complex of things arising — all these environments and all the subjective effects are arising in this moment — yet you are not any self-contained entity, not a specific or defined knower in the midst of them. You are that Condition in which it is not known what anything *is*. You are already without form, without a foundation, without anything solid to rest on. You do not rest up against anything. You are not deeply behind or within anything. You are completely vulnerable and an absolute Mystery. You live in Mystery. When you have considered that fact to the point of hearing, to the point that this Mystery becomes tolerable and you are not grasping so mightily onto egoic consolations, but are able to move into relations with some ease — having heard me to that degree, then you can meet me in the spiritual sense. Then you begin to become sensitive to my Company, and then meeting me becomes a spiritual occasion that draws you more and more profoundly into this Realization of the present Condition.

That is what there is to realize in my Company. It is this profound initiation into our Condition in this moment. Until in your sympathy with me you begin to realize it most directly, all I can do is witness to you that I (and, therefore, you and all beings) am not identical to the condition of being a separate entity. I am not an entity; I am not inside a body. To call myself this body is just as arbitrary as to say I am the morning star or the vision within or a light you may see by turning upward. These are all arbitrary identifications, completely unnecessary, completely humorous, completely without the slightest bit of seriousness from my point of view.

Ultimately, it becomes clear that the tree in the yard is a hallucination, that it is a matter of mind, just as any thought that you project inwardly. It is exactly the same. You will not at last have to go through a mental process to believe this. It will just appear to be obviously that way. And when it is obvious, it is not disorienting. That is Sahaj Samadhi. People who act crazy, trapped in the sphere of their separate self and energy, and who say they are in Sahaj Samadhi or God-Consciousness are not liberated in Truth. They are in the terrified ego position, trying to feel better through glamourizations of philosophy. If some have turned themselves up from the grosser conditions, then they may represent degrees of mystical holiness, but they yet persist in the same illusion that heats the flesh of others in the dream. The presumption of our real Condition is neither a thought nor an act. It is not itself a state of experience, gross or subtle. It is a kind of transparency. The present appearance is simply a process arising in a Condition that is without center, form, relations, or bounds. That Condition is transparent, obvious, and the only presumption that is Truth or Happiness. Until it is obvious, you must listen, you must hear, you must engage the argument, you must presume the disciplines. The practice of the Way of Divine Ignorance is leading toward this Realization absolutely.

Consider the argument and live the discipline. There will be a fire in that discipline equal to the degree of frustration of your habitual presumptions and distractions. Allow that fire to enter into this consideration, and it will be the undoing of this ordinary presumption of independence and necessity that seems so perfectly natural and logical to you in this hallucination, this dream, this birth. You will begin to penetrate that presumption. Its undoing, rather than "me" apart, will become your position. You will penetrate it, and its logic will no longer bind you.

You must take up this Way as a whole life. Just sitting here with whatever attention you have freely available at the moment is not sufficient to change your presumption in the future. It will simply establish you in the moment, more or less, in this consideration of Ignorance. But the discipline is obliged upon you in every moment. You must take it up as a way of life. You must be constantly available to the Spiritual Master, constantly available to his instruction, his argument, his disciplines, his Company. The life awakened in his Company serves the penetration of the dream. When that Realization becomes summary, most radical, in your case, then you are simply happy. Until then, you enjoy it more or less profoundly in some moments, and at other moments the usual life grinds in on you. But then you have the discipline to occupy you rather than the right you ordinarily assume to dramatize your self-possessed tendencies and illusions. The whole affair of this practice ultimately serves perfect transformation in Truth.

Difficulties persist because the ordinary life or

dream persists. Things continue to arise. So there is heat in the process. But the heat is your advantage. The heat is not some negative side effect. The heat is free attention, available for this profundity. Secondarily, it is painful in a sense, but it is free. It is available force, attention. Free attention is not otherwise so available, because it is usually sunk into dramatizations and distractions. Now it is without an object. It cannot find a way to be relieved. It is hot. And so it can consider itself, the occasion itself.

If, through true hearing, you will be committed to such present consideration, and if you will persist in it and not restrain yourself from the whole discipline of my Company, that same enlightenment that is now argued to your face will also be true of you.

an invitation

THE SERVICES OF VISION MOUND CEREMONY AND FORMS OF PARTICIPATION AND SUPPORT

Vision Mound Ceremony serves two principal and integrally related functions in the world: to communicate and to provide adequate facilities for the communication of the Teaching of Bubba Free John, and to provide, serve, and maintain his domestic living requirements as well as manage access to him for all who respond to his argument and live according to the Way of Divine Ignorance.

We invite you to consider this Teaching, and, if you are moved to the happy offenses and sacrifices it demands, to become established in a direct and transforming spiritual relationship with Bubba Free John. The appearance of the human Spiritual Master is brief, and those who resort to his Company enjoy a Graceful privilege unknown to common men and women, including the usual spiritual seeker. "Become this Sacrifice with me and rise from this death into the Condition of the Heaven-Born." This is Bubba Free John's invitation to you. Vision Mound Ceremony exists only to serve your direct approach, and that of all other devotees, to Bubba as Spiritual Master.

THE WRITTEN TEACHING

The editorial and educational staff of Vision Mound Ceremony is responsible for the production and dissemination of all the literature necessary for the practice of the Way of Divine Ignorance. The present book, *The Paradox of Instruction: An Introduction to the Esoteric Spiritual Teaching of Bubba Free John,* is the essential and summary communication of all the stages and aspects of the Way, and is to be used as the principal source text by devotees in every stage. *Breath and Name: The Initiation and Foundation Practices of Free Spiritual Life* is a manual specifically for devotees of the Way of Divine Communion. It presents instructions in both the practical and the spiritual or natural responsibilities and conditions of the Divine life realized and assumed in the first stage of practice. Since, however, it is also the foundation description of the practice and process of the whole Way, it remains a principal source text for every stage. Also of primary importance to all devotees entering the Way of Divine Communion are *The Eating Gorilla Comes in Peace* and *Conscious Exercise and the Transcendental Sun,* the source books on diet, health practices, and exercise. The instructions in these texts also remain useful throughout one's life of practice, even though the practices themselves simply become enjoyments that are "second nature" to one's ordinary life.

The Knee of Listening, Bubba's first book, containing his autobiography and essays on Radical Understanding, should be read by anyone beginning this Way. *The Method of the Siddhas* and *Garbage and the Goddess,* both published prior to the completion of Bubba's public Teaching work in 1976, are currently being revised. These, along with several new source texts, will be published during 1977 and 1978.

The public literature and educational presentations of Vision Mound Ceremony are devoted mainly to communicating the principles of the Way of Divine Ignorance and the specific disciplines of the first two stages of its practice, the Way of Divine Communion and the Way of Relational Enquiry. Devotees receive more personal instruction in the practice of these stages through private seminars held either at Talking God Seminary, the international educational center of Vision Mound Ceremony, or at Vision Mound Sanctuary, the principal holy site of Vision Mound Ceremony and the chief historical place of the revelation and demonstration of Bubba Free John's Teaching during the initial phase of his work as Spiritual Master. (All devotees are encouraged, though not required, to live in regional association with Vision Mound Sanctuary.) All essential information on the disciplines of the higher stages of practice, the Way of Re-cognition and the Way of Radical Intuition, will be communicated in private seminars at Vision Mound Sanctuary to those who are prepared.

Bubba Free John's Teaching is regularly disseminated through *Vision Mound,* the monthly journal of Vision Mound Ceremony. In addition to Bubba's own writings and edited talks, *Vision Mound* offers interpretive articles by devotees, announcements of new publications, and schedules of seminars and occasions when Bubba intends to sit with devotees in formal meditation at Vision Mound Sanctuary. *Vision Mound* is the only regular, ongoing communication between Vision Mound Ceremony and devotees and friendly supporters of Bubba Free John around the world. Its publication depends on the continuing support of devotees and interested friends, through subscriptions and earmarked donations. *Vision Mound* is not intended for the public (though it is offered to anyone who is interested in the spiritual Teaching of Bubba Free John and who is a supporter of the work and purposes of Vision Mound Ceremony) and it will not be sold in bookstores or in any other public market. It will, therefore, carry no paid, commercial advertising, which is the financial mainstay of all public magazines. Thus, we cannot overemphasize the journal's total financial dependence upon those whom it serves.

All the educational and publishing work of Vision Mound Ceremony, as well as its facilities and the support of Bubba Free John's living circumstances, are directly endowed and solely ensured by gifts and donations from those who respond to the Teaching, either as devotees or as sympathetic friends. (Such friends are also encouraged to pledge regular financial support, even though they do not wholly and presently practice the Way itself.) Proceeds from subscriptions to *Vision Mound* support the journal itself. Excess monies generated from the sale of the literature and other educational materials, and from fees for seminars and other educational presentations, are returned to the general education and publication fund. Beyond that, pledged and special donations from devotees and friends provide the only support for Bubba Free John and his household, the regular serving, editorial, educational, and administrative staffs of Vision Mound Ceremony, and the facilities of Talking God Seminary, Vision Mound Sanctuary, and other sites that may be acquired in the future for use by devotees. Without that ongoing financial endowment, the spiritual and educational work of Vision Mound Ceremony cannot continue. But if that support is freely given, then this spiritual Way of life may become firmly established in this time and place. In that case, it may continue to be made available to others in the years and generations to come, so that ordinary men and women who awaken to life in this world may always have the opportunity to hear the Teaching and adapt to the practice of this Divine Way of life.

SPIRITUAL EDUCATION AND PRACTICE FOR YOUNG PEOPLE

Bubba Free John has considered the right education and spiritual discipline for human beings at every stage of both chronological and devotional maturity.

He has described three essential stages of adaptation leading to adult maturity. The first seven years of a person's life involve general adaptation to the condition of the physical body and its dynamics. The second seven years or so involve more specialized adaptation to the emotional, feeling life, and the third seven years include the foundation development of the powers of self-control and the thinking mind.

. For children in the first two stages of adaptation, Bubba has written a book on spiritual practice, *What to Remember to Be Happy: A Spiritual Way of Life for Your First Fourteen Years or So* (to be published in 1977-78). Other books for children of these ages on the specific practices of service, diet, exercise, and healthful living will appear eventually. The essential discipline for youngsters in this period of growth and adaptation is *feeling* and *service* in relationship, as Bubba describes it in this literature.

When there is maturity in this simple practice, generally between the ages of twelve and fourteen, the young individual may take up mature study and practice of the Way of Divine Communion. No one will be invited to begin the practice of the Way of Relational Enquiry before the age of eighteen and the mature completion of the necessary adaptations of the third stage of life. And no one will be instructed in the practices of the Way of Re-cognition before the age of twenty-one, the nominal, chronological beginning of the fourth, mature stage of life. (In most cases, individuals will begin formal study and practice in the Way of Re-cognition somewhat later, at least in their mid-twenties.)

Young people who practice the Way of Divine Communion are welcome to establish personal correspondence relationships with Vision Mound Ceremony, though all those who are still not legally of age in the state in which they live must secure parental permission in writing before attending seminars and meditation gatherings. Vision Mound Ceremony also intends to provide educational services for younger children. Interested parents should write to Vision Mound Ceremony for more information.

Anyone, young or old, who truly hears the critical and liberating argument communicated in *The Paradox of Instruction* and other literature of Vision Mound Ceremony, and who thus recognizes Bubba Free John as Spiritual Master and wishes to approach him as a devotee, may write to Vision Mound Ceremony for specific information on how to begin to participate in this spiritual Way.

Others may not feel such devotional commitment and may not be inclined to take on the natural disciplines of the Way of Divine Ignorance. But all who remain sympathetic to the spiritual communication of Bubba Free John and therefore choose to support this work through financial donations and other contributions should write to Vision Mound Ceremony expressing their interest.

Address all correspondence to:

Vision Mound Ceremony
P.O. Box 3680
Clearlake Highlands, California 95422

The Way of Divine Ignorance is a Divine Way, founded consciously in the Divine Condition from the beginning. It is the Way of ordinary re-adaptation rather than search for extraordinary attainment, a way of dissolution rather than experience. The summary material on the Way of Divine Ignorance contained in this volume remains to be illumined by practice. All necessary instructions are openly given and can be easily grasped by anyone whose orientation to practice is true, and whose commitment to Bubba Free John as Spiritual Master is straightforward, real, and based in true hearing of his Teaching.

Vision Mound Ceremony

Vision Mound Ceremony is the public education division of The Free Primitive Church of Divine Communion, commonly known as The Free Communion Church

reading list

In this book, Bubba Free John has spoken, on the basis of his own awakening and experience, directly to the matters described in the various traditions of spiritual life. The following reading list comprises principal texts from many sources, under the headings of what Bubba describes as the three fundamental Ways of traditional approach (the Ways of Yogis, Saints, and Sages, or the Gross, Subtle, and Causal Paths). Careful consideration of these texts, as well as other literatures, should serve to clarify one's understanding of the matters constantly addressed by Bubba Free John.

I. THE WAY OF YOGIS, OR THE GROSS PATH

A. Religious View

1. *The Bhagavadgita.* Translated by S. Radhakrishnan. New York: Harper & Row, 1973.
2. *Gita Sandesh: Message of the Gita,* by Swami Ramdas. Bombay: Bharatiya Vidya Bhavan, 1970.
3. *Ramanuja on the Bhagavadgita* (A condensed rendering of his Gitabhasya with copious notes and an introduction), by J. A. B. Van Buitenen. Delhi: Motilal Banarsidass, 1968.
4. *Ramanuja on the Yoga,* by Dr. Robert C. Lester. Madras: The Adyar Library and Research Centre, 1976.
5. *Introduction to the Bhagavad Gita, Its Philosophy and Cultural Setting,* by G. A. Feuerstein. London: Rider, 1974.

B. Hatha Yoga (the full esotericism of Hatha Yoga, including Kundalini and related approaches)

1a. *The Yoga of Light (Hatha Yoga Pradipika).* Edited by Hans-Ulrich Rieker. Lower Lake, California: The Dawn Horse Press, 1974.

1b. *Hathapradipika of Svatmarama.* Edited by Swami Digambarji and Pt. Raghunathashastri Kokaje. Lonavla, district Poona, India: Kaivalyadhama, S. M. Y. M. Samiti, 1970.

1c. *The Hathayogapradipika of Svatmarama, with the commentary "Jyotsna" of Brahmananda.* Madras: The Adyar Library and Research Centre, The Theosophical Society, 1972.

2a. *Science of Yoga: Commentary on Gherand Samhita.* Monghyr, India: Bihar School of Yoga, no date.

2b. *The Gheranda Samhita.* Translated by Rai Bahadur Srisa Chandra Vasu. 2d ed. Delhi: Oriental Books Reprint Corp., 1975.

3a. *Dynamics of Yoga,* by Swami Satyananda Saraswati. Monghyr, India: Bihar School of Yoga, 1973.

3b. *Tantra of Kundalini Yoga,* by Paramahans Satyananda Saraswati. Monghyr, India: Bihar School of Yoga, 1973.

3c. *Chidakasha Dharana and Ajapa Japa,* by Swami Satyananda Saraswati. Monghyr, India: Bihar School of Yoga, 1973.

3d. *Ajna Chakra,* by Swami Satyananda Saraswati. Monghyr, India: Bihar School of Yoga, 1973.

3e. *Kriya Yoga Postal Sadhana Course.* 3 vols. Monghyr, India: Bihar School of Yoga, 1974, 1975, 1976.

3f. *Tantra Yoga Panorama,* by Swami Satyananda Saraswati. Monghyr, India: Bihar School of Yoga, no date.

4. *Tantra: Its Mystic and Scientific Basis,* by Lalan Prasad Singh. Delhi: Concept Publishing Company, 1976.

5. *The Siva Samhita.* Translated by Rai Bahadur Srisa Chandra Vasu. New Delhi: Oriental Books Reprint Corporation, 1975.

6. *Gorakhnath and the Kanphata Yogis,* by George Weston Briggs. Delhi: Motilal Banarsidass, 1973.

7. *Philosophy of Gorakhnath with Goraksha-Vacana-Sangraha,* by Akshaya Kumar Banerjea. Gorakhpur, India: Mahant Dig Vijai Nath Trust, 1962.

8. *Gorakhnath and Medieval Hindu Mysticism* (including text and translation of Machhendra-Gorakh Goshti, Padas and Shlokas of Gorakh, Shlokas of Charpatnath), by Dr. Mohan Singh. Lahore, Pakistan: Mohan Singh Oriental College, 1937.

9. *Siddha-Siddhanta-Paddhati and Other Works of the Natha Yogis,* by Smt. Kalyani Mallik. Poona, India: Poona Oriental Book House, 1954.

10. *The Serpent Power,* by Arthur Avalon. New York: Dover Publications, 1974.

11. *Kularnava Tantra.* Introduction by Arthur Avalon (Sir John Woodroffe). Readings by M. P. Pandit. Madras: Ganesh and Co., 1965.

12. *The Primal Power in Man or the Kundalini Shakti,* by Swami Narayanananda. Rishikesh, India: Narayanananda Universal Yoga Trust, 1970.

13. *Devatma Shakti (Kundalini) Divine Power,* by Swami Vishnu Tirtha. Delhi: Swami Shivom Tirth, 1974.

14a. *The Play of Consciousness (Chitshakti Vilas),* by Swami Muktananda Paramahansa. Camp Meeker, California: SYDA Foundation, 1974.

14b. *Light on the Path,* by Swami Muktananda Paramahansa. Ganeshpuri, India: Shree Gurudev Ashram, 1972.

15. *Sri Kundalini Sakthi—Serpent Power: As per Vedic Text and not Thanthric,* by Y. Subbaraya Sharma. Bangalore: The author, 1971.

16. *Kundalini Yoga,* by Sri Swami Sivananda. 6th ed. Sivanandanagar, India: The Divine Life Society, 1971.

17. *Light on Meditation: A Definitive Work on Kundalini and Raja Yoga,* by Dhyanyogi Mahant Madhusudandasji Maharaj. Scotts Valley, California: Keshavdas Carl Kuntz, 1976.

18. *Yoga Yajnavalkya.* Edited by Sri Prahlad C. Divanji. *Journal of the Bombay Branch Royal Asiatic Society,* Reprint Monograph #3, India, 1954.

19. *The Poets of the Powers,* by Kamil V. Zvelebil. London: Rider, 1973.

20. *Jnaneshvari: Song Sermon on the Bhagavad-Gita.* Translated by V. G. Pradhan. Edited by H. M. Lambert. 2 vols. London: George Allen & Unwin, 1967.

21. *The Philosophy of Jnanadeva,* by B. P. Bahirat. Bombay: Popular Book Depot, 1961.

22. *The Secret of Self-Realizaton: Pratyabhijna Hridayam of Ksemaraja in Sanskrit with Transliteration in Roman, Translation in English and Commentary,* by I. K. Taimni. Madras: The Theosophical Publishing House, 1974.

23. *The Ten Great Cosmic Powers (Dasa Mahavidyas),* by S. Shankaranarayanan. Pondicherry, India: Dipti Publications, 1972.

24. *The Hevajra Tantra: A Critical Study—Part I, Introduction and Translation; Part II, Sanskrit and Tibetan Texts,* by D. L. Snellgrove. London Oriental Series, Volume 6. London: Oxford University Press, 1959. Reprinted 1971.

25. *Teachings of Tibetan Yoga.* Translated by Garma C. C. Chang. Secaucus, New Jersey: The Citadel Press, 1974.

26a. *The Tibetan Book of the Great Liberation.* Introduction, Annotations, and Editing by W. Y. Evans-Wentz. London: Oxford University Press, 1968.

26b. *Tibetan Yoga and Secret Doctrines.* Arranged and Edited by W. Y. Evans-Wentz. 2d ed. London: Oxford University Press, 1958. Reprinted 1968.

27. *Esoteric Teachings of the Tibetan Tantra, Including Seven Initiation Rituals and the Six Yogas of Naropa in Tsong-Kha-Pa's Commentary.* Translated by Chang Chen Chi. Edited by C. A. Muses. Lausanne: Aurora Press, 1961.

28. *The Hundred Thousand Songs of Milarepa,* Volumes I and II. Translated and annotated by Garma C. C. Chang. New Hyde Park, New York: University Books, 1962.

29. *The Life and Teaching of Naropa.* Translated from the original Tibetan with a Philosophical Commentary based on the Oral Transmission, by Herbert V. Guenther. London: Oxford University Press, 1963. Reprinted 1971.

30a. *Taoist Yoga (Alchemy and Immortality),* by Lu K'uan Yü (Charles Luk). New York: Samuel Weiser, 1972.

30b. *The Secrets of Chinese Meditation,* by Lu K'uan Yü (Charles Luk). New York: Samuel Weiser, 1972.

31. *The Secret of the Golden Flower, a Chinese Book of Life.*

Translated by Richard Wilhelm. New York: Harcourt,
Brace and World, 1962.

32. *Taoism and the Rite of Cosmic Renewal,* by Michael R.
Saso. Pullman, Washington: Washington State University
Press, 1972.

33. *Hara,* by Karlfried Durckheim. New York: Samuel Weiser,
1975.

C. Ashtanga Yoga (the Traditional Raja Yoga system as described by Patanjali and others)

1a. *The Yoga-System of Patanjali.* Translated by James Hough-
ton Woods. Delhi: Motilal Banarsidass, 1972.

1b. *Yoga Philosophy of Patanjali.* Edited by Swami Harihara-
nanda Aranya. Calcutta: University of Calcutta Press,
1973.

1c. *The Science of Yoga,* by I. K. Taimni. Wheaton, Illinois:
The Theosophical Publishing House, 1975.

2a. *Himalya Ka Yogi,* by Swami Yogeshwaranand Saraswati
(formerly Swami Vyas Dev Ji). Rishikesh, India: The Yoga
Niketan Trust, no date.

2b. *Science of Soul (Atma-Vijnana),* by Swami Vyas Dev Ji.
Rishikesh, India: The Yoga Niketan Trust, 1972.

2c. *Science of Divinity,* by Swami Yogeshwaranand Saraswati.
Rishikesh, India: The Yoga Niketan Trust, 1973.

2d. *The Essential Colourlessness of the Absolute, or the Un-
Conditioned Brahma,* by Swami Yogeshwarananda Saraswati. Rishikesh, India: The Yoga Niketan Trust, 1976.

Note: The writings of Swami Yogeshwarand Saraswati are
a unique, first-hand account of the esotericism implicit in
the systems of Hatha Yoga and Ashtanga Yoga. His Way
ultimately transcends the Gross Path of Yogis and explores
the Revelation made by Light, even as the Way of Saints
explores the Revelation most particularly made by Sound.
Although the Realization indicated in his Way is summarized in the Yogic view of Patanjali, his esotericism reveals
much that is hidden in all the usual "secret" texts. He also,
in *Science of Soul,* describes the precise relationship between the heart (as the true seat of the ego-soul) and the
crown (the seat of subtle mind).

II. THE WAY OF SAINTS, OR THE SUBTLE PATH

The books listed in this section are taken mainly from modern sources, which characteristically treat the subtle path (which begins in the brain rather than the lower and vital body) as a religious, dualistic, even theistic system, full of cosmological and super-cosmological visions and auditions. The subtle path is also described in certain texts of the gross path (e.g., *Hatha Yoga Pradipika*), wherever the subject of "nada yoga" appears. In the higher texts of the gross path, nada yoga generally comes at the end, after the lower transformation via pranayama, kundalini yoga, etc. In the texts of modern saints, the yoga of the audible sound current is the absolute principle of the path itself. However, these saints suffer the limitations of the subject-object presumption, in which self (as soul) and Reality (as God) are assigned to an irreducible objective status within a hierarchy of illusions. In the literature of the more ancient Yogi-saints, such as Gorakhnath, hatha yoga, or kundalini yoga, is raised to nada yoga, dissolving the life-principle (or breath) and thought (or mind) into subtle sound, and sound into the Void, the Eternal Unknown. In such a case, the prior, non-dualistic Wisdom of Reality informs and disciplines the yoga itself, providing a more appropriate and balanced view of the course of nada (or shabd) and its purpose. The literature of the more modern saints does provide a more detailed description of the necessarily devotional core of the practice and an elaboration of certain of the conventional contents of mystical experience.

1a. *Radha Swami Teachings,* by L. R. Puri. Amritsar, India: Radha Soami Satsang-Beas, 1972.

1b. *Teachings of the Gurus,* by L. R. Puri. Amritsar, India: Radha Soami Satsang-Beas, 1973.

2. *Sar Updesh Radhasoami (Gist of Radhasoami Teachings),* by Param Purush Puran Dhani Huzur Maharaj. Translated by S. D. Maheshwari. Agra, India: S. D. Maheshwari, 1969.

3a. *Sar Bachan Radhasoami (Poetry) of Param Purush Puran Dhani Soamiji Maharaj,* Parts I and II. Translated by S. D. Maheshwari. Agra, India: S. D. Maheshwari, 1970.

3b. *Sar Bachan Radhasoami (Prose): English Version of the Discourses of Param Purush Puran Dhani Soamiji Maharaj.* Translated by S. D. Maheshwari. 2d ed. Agra, India: Radhasoami Satsang, 1958.

4. *Radhasoami Faith: A Historical Study,* by Agam Prasad Mathur. Delhi: Vikas Publishing House, 1974.

5. *Truth Unvarnished (An Objective Exposition of the Apostatical Beliefs, Teachings and Activities of the Dissentient Groups of the Radhasoami Faith),* Parts I and II, by S. D. Maheshwari. Agra, India: S. D. Maheshwari, 1970.

6. *Truth Eternal: The True Nature of Soamiji's Teachings on Sant Mat and the "Radhasoami Faith,"* by Radha Krishna Khanna. New Delhi: the author, 1961.

Note: The texts entitled *Truth Unvarnished* and *Truth Eternal* represent an interesting and revealing controversy between advocates of two different points of view in the practice of Shabd Yoga.

7. *Elucidation of Japji,* As Dictated by Soamiji Maharaj. Translated by S. D. Maheshwari. Agra, India: Radhasoami Satsang, Soami Bagh, 1975.

8. *Spiritual Gems,* correspondence between Hazur Swami Ji Maharaj and Hazur Maharaj Baba Sawan Singh Ji. Amritsar, India: Radha Soami Satsang-Beas, 1960.

9. *Spiritual Letters, from Baba Jaimal Singh Ji Maharaj 1896-1903.* New Delhi: Radha Soami Satsang-Beas, 1973.

10a. *Naam or Word,* by Kirpal Singh. 4th ed. Delhi: Ruhani Satsang, 1972.

10b. *Surat Shabd Yoga, the Yoga of the Celestial Sound,* by Kirpal Singh. Berkeley: Images Press, 1975.

10c. *The Way of the Saints,* by Kirpal Singh. Sanbornton, New Hampshire: Sant Bani Ashram, 1976.

10d. *The Crown of Life,* by Kirpal Singh. 3d ed. Delhi: Ruhani Satsang, 1973.

10e. *Heart-to-Heart Talks: Volume One, 1969-70; Volume Two, 1971*, by Kirpal Singh. Delhi: Ruhani Satsang, 1975, 1976.

11a. *The Science of Religion*, by Paramahansa Yogananda. Los Angeles: Self-Realization Fellowship, 1974.

11b. *The Holy Science*, by Swami Sri Yukteswar. Los Angeles: Self-Realization Fellowship, 1974.

12. *Mysticism, the Spiritual Path*, Volumes I and II, by L. R. Puri. 3d ed. Beas, India: Radha Soami Satsang-Beas, 1964.

13. *The Science of the Soul*, by Maharaj Sardar Bahadur Jagat Singh Ji. 3d ed. Amritsar, India: Radha Soami Satsang-Beas, 1967.

14. *The Philosophy of the Masters*, Volumes 1-5, by Hazur Maharaj Sawan Singh Ji. 2d ed. Beas, India: Radha Soami Satsang-Beas, 1971-1973.

15. *Radiant Road to Reality*, by Dr. B. S. Thind. Los Angeles: Mrs. B. S. Thind, 1967.

16. *Guru Nanak and the Sikh Religion*, by W. H. McLeod. London: Oxford University Press, 1968.

17. *Guru Nanak and His Times*, by Anil Chandra Banerjee. Patiala, India: Punjabi University, 1971.

18. *Kabir*, Volume I, by Charlotte Vaudeville. (Volume II forthcoming.) London: Oxford University Press, 1974.

19. *Kabir and His Followers*, by the Rev. F. E. Keay. The Religious Life of India. London: Oxford University Press, 1931.

20. *Nadabindu-Upanishad*, in *Thirty Minor Upanishads*, ch. 5, no. 29. Translated by K. Narayanaswami Aiyar. Madras: ?, 1914. (Monistic nada yoga, as per Gorakhnath, et al.)

III. THE WAY OF SAGES (VEDANTIC AND BUDDHIST), OR THE CAUSAL PATH

1a. *Ramana Maharshi and the Path of Self-Knowledge*, by Arthur Osborne. New York: Samuel Weiser, 1974.

1b. *Talks with Sri Ramana Maharshi*, 3 vols. in one. Tiruvannamalai, South India: Sri Ramanasramam, 1972.

1c. *Reflections on the Talks with Sri Ramana Maharshi,* by S. S. Cohen. Tiruvannamalai, South India: Sri Ramanasramam, 1971.

1d. *Sri Ramana Gita, Dialogues of Bhagavan Sri Ramana Maharshi.* 5th ed. rev. Tiruvannamalai, South India: Sri Ramanasramam, 1973.

1e. *The Collected Works of Ramana Maharshi.* Edited by Arthur Osborne. 4th ed. London: Rider, 1974.

1f. *Sat Darshana Bhashya and Talks with Maharshi,* by K. Tiruvannamalai, South India: Sri Ramanasramam, 1968.

1g. *The Teachings of Bhagavan Sri Ramana Maharshi in His Own Words.* Edited by Arthur Osborne. 3d ed. Tiruvannamalai, South India: Sri Ramanasramam, 1971.

1h. *Maha Yoga or the Upanishadic Lore,* by "Who." Tiruvannamalai, South India: Sri Ramanasramam, 1967.

1i. *Guru Ramana,* by S. S. Cohen. Tiruvannamalai, South India: Sri Ramanasramam, 1967.

1j. *Advaitic Sadhana,* by S. S. Cohen. Delhi: Motilal Banarsidass, 1975.

1k. *Ramana Maharshi,* by K. Swaminathan. New Delhi: National Book Trust, 1975.

1l. *The Path of Shri Ramana: An Exposition of the Method of Self-Enquiry Taught by Shri Ramana Maharshi,* by Sadhu Om. Kanpur, India: The City Book House, 1971.

1m. *The Technique of Maha Yoga (Self-Enquiry): Culled from the Talks with Sri Ramana Maharshi and arranged in Order of Sequence for purposes of Practice,* by N. R. Narayana Aiyer. Tiruvannamalai, South India: Sri Ramanasramam, 1962.

1n. *The Heart of the Ribhu Gita.* Edited by Franklin Jones (Bubba Free John). Los Angeles: The Dawn Horse Press, 1973.

2a. *Atmanandopanishat (Atmadarsan and Atmanirvriti),* by Sri Krishna Menon (Atmananda). Tiruvannamalai, South India: Sri Vidya Samiti, 1946.

2b. *Notes on Spiritual Discourses of Sree Atmananda, 1950-1959,* by Nitya Tripta. Trivandrum, India: The Reddiar Press, 1963.

3. *I Am That,* by Sri Nisargadatta Maharaj. Bombay: Chetana Press, 1973.

4. *The Song of the Self Supreme (Astavakra Gita).* Translated by Radhakamal Mukerjee. San Francisco: The Dawn Horse Press, 1977.

5. *Avadhut Gita.* Translated by Hari Prasad Shastri. London: Shanti Sadan, 1968.

6. *Panchadashi: Treatise on Advaita Metaphysics,* by Swami Vidyaranya. Translated by Hari Prasad Shastri. 2d ed. London: Shanti Sadan, 1965.

7a. *Vivekachudamani, of Sri Shankaracharya.* Translated by Swami Madhavananda. 7th ed. Calcutta: Advaita Ashrama, 1966.

7b. *The Quintessence of Vedanta of Acharya Sankara.* Translated by Swami Tattwananda. Calcutta: Sri Ramakrishna Advaita Ashrama, 1970.

7c. *Aparokshanubhuti or Self-Realization of Sri Sankaracharya,* by Swami Vimuktananda. 3d ed. Madras: Ramakrishna Math, 1966.

8. *Kaivalya Navaneeta (The Cream of Emancipation),* by Tandavaraya Swami. Tiruvannamalai, South India: Sri Ramanasramam, 1965.

9. *Advaita Bodha Deepika (Lamp of Non-Dual Knowledge).* Translated by G. N. Venkataram. Tiruvannamalai, South India: Sri Ramanasramam, 1967.

10. *Tripura Rahasya or the Mystery Beyond the Trinity.* Translated by Sri Ramanananda Saraswati. Tiruvannamalai, South India: Sri Ramanasramam, 1971.

11. *Valmiki Maha Ramayana, or Yoga Vasishta.* Translated by S. V. Ganapati. Madras: S. V. Ganapati, 1963.

12. *The Mandukyopanisad.* Translated by Swami Nikhilananda. Mysore, India: Sri Ramakrishna Ashrama, 1968.

13. *The Lankavatara Sutra.* Translated by D. T. Suzuki. Boston: Routledge & Kegan Paul, 1972.

14. *Studies in the Lankavatara Sutra,* by D. T. Suzuki. Boston: Routledge & Kegan Paul, 1972.

15. *Nagarjuna: A Translation of His Mulamadhyamakakarika*

with an Introductory Essay, by Kenneth K. Inada. Tokyo: The Hokuseido Press, 1970.

16. *An Introduction to Madhyamaka Philosophy,* by Jaidev Singh. 2d rev. ed. Delhi: Motilal Banarsidass, 1976.

17. *Nagarjuna's Philosophy: As Presented in the Maha-Prajnaparamita-Sastra,* by K. Venkata Ramanan. Delhi: Motilal Banarsidass, 1975.

18. *Practice and Theory of Tibetan Buddhism,* by Geshe Lhundup Sopa and Jeffrey Hopkins. New York: Grove Press, 1976.

19. *The Surangama Sutra.* Translated by Lu K'uan Yü (Charles Luk). London: Rider, 1973.

20. *Ch'an and Zen Teaching,* First Series (especially "Diamond Cutter of Doubts") and Third Series (especially "The Altar Sutra of the Sixth Patriarch"). Translated by Lu K'uan Yü (Charles Luk). Berkeley: Shambhala Press, 1970, 1973.

21. *The Zen Teaching of Huang Po on the Transmission of Mind.* Translated by John Blofeld. New York: Grove Press, 1958.

22. *The Zen Teaching of Hui Hai.* Rendered into English by John Blofeld. London: Rider & Company, 1969.

23. *Manual of Zen Buddhism,* by Daisetz Teitaro Suzuki. New York: Grove Press, 1960.

IV. PHILOSOPHICAL AND SCHOLARLY WORKS RELATED TO THE TRADITIONAL WAYS

1. *Indian Philosophy,* by S. Radhakrishnan. 2 vols. New York: The Macmillan Company, 1962.

2. *A History of Indian Philosophy,* by Surendranath Dasgupta. 5 vols. Delhi: Motilal Banarsidass, 1975.

3. *The Cultural Heritage of India.* 4 vols. 2d ed. Calcutta: The Ramakrishna Mission Institute of Culture—vol. I, 1958; vol. II, 1962; vol. III, 1953; vol. IV, 1956.

4. *The Essence of Yoga: A Contribution to the Psychohistory of Indian Civilisation,* by G. A. Feuerstein. London: Rider, 1974.

5. *Textbook of Yoga,* by Georg Feuerstein. London: Rider, 1975.

6a. *Sadhana: A Text-Book of the Psychology and Practice of the Techniques to Spiritual Perfection,* by Sri Swami Sivananda. 2d ed. Delhi: Motilal Banarsidass, 1974.

6b. *Concentration and Meditation,* by Sri Swami Sivananda. 4th ed. Sivanandanagar, India: The Divine Life Society, 1969.

6c. *Spiritual Experiences (Amrita Anubhava),* by Sri Swami Sivananda. 2d ed. Sivanandanagar, India: The Yoga-Vedanta Forest Academy, 1960.

7. *The Mysterious Kundalini: The Physical Basis of the "Kundalini (Hatha) Yoga" in Terms of Western Anatomy and Physiology,* by Vasant G. Rele. 11th ed. Bombay: D. B. Taraporevala Sons, 1970.

8. *The Secret of Yoga,* by Gopi Krishna. Religious Perspectives, Volume XXIII. New York: Harper & Row, 1972.

9. *Kundalini—Psychosis or Transcendence?,* by Lee Sannella. San Francisco: published by the author, 1976.

10. *Hindu Yoga: Parapsychology and Modern Thought,* by Vankeepuram Varadachari. Madras: the author, no date.

11a. *Yoga As Philosophy and Religion,* by Surendranath Dasgupta. Delhi: Motilal Banarsidass, 1973.

11b. *Yoga Philosophy (in Relation to Other Systems of Indian Thought),* by S. N. Dasgupta. Delhi: Motilal Banarsidass, 1974.

12. *Obscure Religious Cults,* by Shashibhusan Das Gupta. 3d ed. Calcutta: Firma K. L. Mukhopadhyay, 1969.

13. *History of Sakta Religion,* by Narendra Nath Bhattacharyya. New Delhi: Munshiram Manoharlal, 1974.

14. *Kashmir Saivism,* by L. N. Sharma. Varanasi, India: Bharatiya Vidya Prakashan, 1972.

15. *Kashmir Shaivaism,* by Shri Jagdish Chandra Chatterji. Srinagar, India: Research and Publication Dept., Jammu and Kashmir Govt., 1962.

16. *Kundalini Yoga: A Brief Study of Sir John Woodroffe's "The Serpent Power,"* by M. P. Pandit. 3d ed. Madras: Ganesh & Co. (Madras), 1968.

17. *Sakti and Sakta: Essays and Addresses,* by Sir John Woodroffe. 7th ed. Madras: Ganesh & Co. (Madras), 1969.

18. *Principles of Tantra.* Edited by Sir John Woodroffe (Arthur Avalon). 2 vols. 4th ed. Madras: Ganesh & Co. (Madras)— Part I, 1969; Part II, 1970.

19. *Tantra: The Yoga of Sex,* by Omar V. Garrison. New York: Causeway Books, 1964.

20. *The Principal Upanishads.* Translated by S. Radhakrishnan. London: George Allen & Unwin, 1974.

21. *Minor Upanishads.* Translated by Swami Madhavananda. Calcutta: Advaita Ashrama, 1968.

22. Works by and about Dr. R. D. Ranade:

The literature of Dr. Ranade represents an attempt to summarize the mystical philosophy of the Indian traditions, particularly that of the yogas. The result is a very useful documentation and commentary upon the yogas, especially the whole practice of mystical ascent.

22a. *History of Indian Philosophy: The Creative Period* (Volume 2), by S. K. Belvalkar and R. D. Ranade. 2d ed. New Delhi: Oriental Books Reprint Corporation, 1974.

22b. *A Constructive Survey of Upanishadic Philosophy: Being A Systematic Introduction to Indian Metaphysics,* by R. D. Ranade. An Encyclopaedic History of Indian Philosophy, Volume 2. Poona, India: Oriental Book Agency, 1926.

22c. *Pathway to God in Hindi Literature,* by R. D. Ranade. Bombay: Bharatiya Vidya Bhavan, 1959.

22d. *Pathway to God in Kannada Literature,* by R. D. Ranade. Bhavan's Book University, no. 72. Bombay: Bharatiya Vidya Bhavan, in collaboration with The Karnatak University, Dharwar, 1960.

22e. *Pathway to God in Marathi Literature,* by R. D. Ranade. Bhavan's Book University, no. 89. Bombay: Bharatiya Vidya Bhavan, 1961. [This book was also published in 1933 as *Mysticism in Maharashtra,* History of Indian Philosophy, Volume 7.]

22f. *The Gospel of God-Realisation,* by R. D. Ranade. Compiled by M. S. Deshpande. Bhavan's Book University, no. 15. Bombay: Bharatiya Vidya Bhavan, 1964.

22g. *The Bhagavadgita As a Philosophy of God-Realisation: Being a Clue through the Labyrinth of Modern Interpretations,* by R. D. Ranade. Bhavan's Book University, no. 126 2d ed. Bombay: Bharatiya Vidya Bhavan, 1965.

22h. *Vedanta: The Culmination of Indian Thought,* by R. D. Ranade. Bombay: Bharatiya Vidya Bhavan, 1970.

22i. *Dr. Ranade's Life of Light,* by M. S. Deshpande. Bhavan's Book University, no. 109. Bombay: Bharatiya Vidya Bhavan, 1963.

22j. *Dr. R. D. Ranade's Dhyana Gita.* Elucidated and translated by M. S. Deshpande. Bhavan's Book University, no. 187. Bombay: Bharatiya Vidya Bhavan, 1972.

23. *Methods of Knowledge According to Advaita Vedanta,* by Swami Satprakashananda. Calcutta: Advaita Ashrama, 1974.

24. *The System of Vedanta,* by Paul Deussen. New York: Dover Publications, 1973.

25. *Some Aspects of Vedanta Philosophy,* by Swami Siddheswarananda. Trichur, India: Sri Ramakrishna Ashrama, 1975.

26. *The Concept of Atman in the Principal Upanishads,* by Baldev Raj Sharma. New Delhi: Dinesh Publications, 1972.

27. *The Philosophy of the Upanishads,* by Paul Deussen. New York: Dover Publications, 1966.

28. *Vaisnavism of Samkaradeva and Ramanuja: A Comparative Study,* by H. V. Sreenivasa Murthy. Delhi: Motilal Banarsidass, 1973.

29. *Brahman: A Comparative Study of the Philosophies of Sankara and Ramanuja,* by G. Sundara Ramaiah. Waltair, India: Andhra University Press, 1974.

30a. *Hindu Mysticism,* by S. N. Dasgupta. New York: Frederick Ungar Publishing Company, 1927. Republished, 1959.

30b. *Indian Idealism,* by Surendranath Dasgupta. London: Cambridge University Press, 1933. Reprinted 1962.

31. *Aspects of Indian Religious Thought,* by Shashi Bhusan Dasgupta. Calcutta: A. Mukherjee & Co., 1957.

32. *Philosophy of Hindu Sadhana,* by Nalini Kanta Brahma. London: Kegan Paul, Trench, Trubner, 1932.

33. *Early Buddhism and the Bhagavadgita,* by K. N. Upadhyaya. Delhi: Motilal Banarsidass, 1971.

34. *The Psychological Attitude of Early Buddhist Philosophy,*

by Lama Anagarika Govinda. New York: Samuel Weiser, 1971.

35a. *The Soul Theory of the Buddhists,* by Theodore Stcherbatsky. Varanasi, India: Bharatiya Vidya Prakashan, 1970.

35b. *The Conception of Buddhist Nirvana,* by Theodore Stcherbatsky. 2d rev. and enl. ed. Delhi: Motilal Banarsidass, 1977.

35c. *The Central Conception of Buddhism and the Meaning of the Word "Dharma,"* by Theodore Stcherbatsky. Delhi: Motilal Banarsidass, 1970.

36. *The History of Buddhist Thought,* by Edward J. Thomas. New York: Barnes & Noble, 1971.

37. *The Central Philosophy of Buddhism,* by T. R. V. Murti. London: George Allen & Unwin, 1974.

38. *Buddhism Explained: An Introduction to the Teachings of Lord Buddha,* by Bhikkhu Khantipalo. 4th ed. Bangkok: Mahamkut Rajavidyalaya Press, 1968.

39. *Buddhism: An Outline of Its Teachings and Schools,* by H. Wolfgang Schumann. Translated by Georg Feuerstein. Wheaton, Illinois: The Theosophical Publishing House, 1974.

40. *The Word of the Buddha: An Outline of the Teaching of the Buddha in the Words of the Pali Canon.* Compiled, translated and explained by Nyanatiloka. 15th ed. Kandy, Ceylon: Buddhist Publication Society, 1971.

41. *The Life of the Buddha: As It Appears in the Pali Canon, the Oldest Authentic Record.* Translated by Bhikkhu Nanamoli. Kandy, Ceylon: Buddhist Publication Society, 1972.

42. *The Heart of Buddhist Meditation,* by Nyanaponika Thera. New York: Samuel Weiser, 1969. Reprinted 1971.

43. *Insight Meditation,* by Chao Khun Phra Sobhana Dhammasudhi. 2d and enl. ed. London: The Committee for the Advancement of Buddhism, 1968.

44. *The Way of Mindfulness* (being a translation of the Satipatthana Sutta of the Majjhima Nikaya; its Commentary, the Satipatthana Sutta Vannana of the Papancasudani of Buddhaghosa Thera; and excerpts from the Linatthapakasana Tika, Marginal Notes, of Dhammapala Thera on the

Commentary), by Soma Thera. 3d ed. Kandy, Ceylon: Buddhist Publication Society, 1967.

45. *Mindfulness of Breathing (Anapanasati)*. Translated from the Pali by Bhikkhu Nanamoli. 3d ed. Kandy, Sri Lanka: Buddhist Publication Society, 1973.

46. *The Practice of Zen*, by Garma C. C. Chang. New York: Harper & Row, Perennial Library, 1970.

47a. *Essays in Zen Buddhism, First Series*, by D. T. Suzuki. New York: Grove Press, 1961.

47b. *Essays in Zen Buddhism, Second Series*, by D. T. Suzuki. New York: Samuel Weiser, 1976.

47c. *Essays in Zen Buddhism, Third Series*, by D. T. Suzuki. New York: Samuel Weiser, 1976.

48. *Treasures on the Tibetan Middle Way*, by Herbert V. Guenther. Berkeley: Shambala, 1969. Reprinted 1971. [This book was originally published by E. J. Brill under the title *Tibetan Buddhism without Mystification*.]

49. *The Theory of Eternal Life*, by Rodney Collin. New York: Samuel Weiser, 1974.

Vision Mound Ceremony provides the service of making the books on this reading list available to the public. Please write for a price list of the books that we offer and information as to where the others may be obtained. Write to:

The Dawn Horse Book Depot
P. O. Box 3680
Clearlake Highlands, California 95422

THE BOOKS OF BUBBA FREE JOHN

Truth is not within. The nervous system and the brain are the new "Golden Calf."

—Bubba Free John

Even the most expansive mystic vision is only a reflection in the "sky" of your brain. The Teaching of Bubba Free John cuts through all self-possession and awakens us in the paradoxical happiness of living Truth. The Enlightened Way he teaches is entirely free of concern for internal states and outward experience. To those who respond and prepare themselves through devotional sacrifice, Bubba Free John offers his potent help as a Divinely realized Spiritual Master. Along with *The Paradox of Instruction,* these are the principal source texts of his Teaching: